GREAT CAMPAIGNS

The Appomattox Campaign

GREAT CAMPAIGN SERIES

GREAT CAMPAIGNS

THE APPOMATTOX CAMPAIGN

March 29 - April 9, 1865

Chris M. Calkins

*To Eugene Mavarich —
With best wishes
Hope you enjoy this study
Chris Calkins
January 25, 2002*

COMBINED BOOKS
Pennsylvania

PUBLISHER'S NOTE

Combined Books, Inc., is dedicated to publishing books of distinction in history and military history. We are proud of the quality of writing and the quantity of information found in our books. Our books are manufactured with style and durability and are printed on acid-free paper. We like to think of our books as soldiers: not infantry grunts, but well dressed and well equipped avant garde. Our logo reflects our commitment to the modern and yet historic art of bookmaking.

We call ourselves Combined Books because we view the publishing enterprise as a "combined" effort of authors, publishers and readers. And we promise to bridge the gap between us—a gap which is all too seldom closed in contemporary publishing.

We would like to hear from our readers and invite you to write to us at our offices in Pennsylvania with your reactions, queries, comments, even complaints. All of our correspondence will be answered directly by a member of the Editorial Board or by the author.

We encourage all of our readers to purchase our books from their local booksellers, and we hope that you let us know of booksellers in your area that might be interested in carrying our books. If you are unable to find a book in your area, please write us.

For information, address:
Combined Books, Inc.
1024 Fayette Street
Conshohocken, PA 19428

Library of Congress Cataloging-in-Publication Data available.

ISBN 0-938289-54-3

Printed in the United States of America.
Maps by Paul Dangel.

Contents

Sidebars

Maps

To my father-in-law, W. Berkely Brown (1915-1996), who taught
me the virtues of a true Southern gentleman.

Acknowledgments

My personal friends and fellow National Park Service employees, Ron Wilson, Tracy Chernault and Joe Williams, all of Appomattox Court House National Historical Park, are largely responsible for helping me complete this work. Having them as proof readers and sounding boards has made this narrative come to be.

Both the staffs at Richmond National Battlefield Park and Petersburg National Battlefield were of great assistance to me, those in particular being John R. Davis, Jr., Chief of Interpretation Emeritus, and Historian James H. Blankenship, Jr., both from the latter park. Former Chief Historian of the National Park Service, Mr. Edwin Bearss, also has provided encouragement to me throughout my career.

Cartographer Paul Dangel of Philadelphia should receive all accolades for the fine maps which he produced in this volume. Working with him and his talents was a distinct pleasure.

In 1993 a regional group of city, town and county officials, along with representatives of state and national park systems, met to form what has become known as the "Lee's Retreat" consortium. As an outcome of their efforts, a highly acclaimed historical driving tour following the route of this last campaign was developed. All the while working with these many individuals has been a most pleasurable experience for me. Although space does not allow the mentioning of everyone involved in this project, of special note are Sarah J. Elam (Farmville), William J. Martin (Valentine Museum, Richmond), William W. Martin and John R. Wallace (Amelia), Sherry Swinson (Cumberland), John D. Watt, III (Commonwealth of Virginia), Mark Schuppin, Herbert Doswell, Ann Zahn, Blackburn Booth (Virginia Division of State Parks), Darlene Brown and Suzanne Savory (Petersburg), Wendy Ralph (Dinwiddie), Ronald E. Roark, John Procise and Greg Eanes (Nottoway), Ray Dorsett, Emily Prichard and J. Rodney Lewis among all the others who have given so much of their time and efforts. Of particular notice should be the kind landowners who most graciously allowed their private property to be enjoyed by all.

The efforts of this group can best be summed up by the words of a visitor who took the driving tour. Hailing from North Carolina, she wrote in a letter "we were so very impressed with what you have accomplished! It is so obvious how much work and research and time went into the endeavor, and I just wanted to let you know how very impressive it all is. We... listened to the words and gazed at the area and I must admit that there were times I was weeping. I felt so honored that people cared so much about what my great great grandfather [mortally wounded at Sailor's Creek] and those other brave men went through to pay them such tribute. Thank you..."

Other contributors to this volume are: Bryce Suderow and Noah Andre Trudeau, both of Washington, D.C.; Rusty Hicks, Altavista; Ray Lupold III and Lawrence McLaughlin of Petersburg, Tri-Cities Bureau Chief Wayne Covil, Channel 6 News, Richmond; Harold E. Howard, Appomattox; Dr. Steven Andrus, Fort Lee; Rufus Barringer, Rocky Mount, N.C.; Elva Warren, Amelia; and Lawrence McFall, of Danville.

Without the constant support and encouragement of my wife, Sarah, this work could not have been completed. Having been born and raised in Appomattox, she has inspired me throughout the years to research and write about the history of her native county and chronicle the story of "Where our Nation Reunited."

I also wish to extend a special note of gratitude to artist Keith Rocco for allowing the use of his painting, "Victory or Death, The Last Stand of the Savannah Vol. Guard at the Battle of Sailor's Creek, VA., April 6, 1865." A copy of this fine print can be obtained from the Sayler's Creek Reenactment and Preservation Committee, Inc., 6097 Majors Lane No. 1, Columbia, MD 21045-4109. Sales of this print benefit the Sailor's Creek Battlefield Historical State Park in Amelia County, Virginia.

Map Symbols Key

XXXX : Army　　◪ **: Cavalry**
XXX : Corps　　⊠ **: Infantry**
XX : Division
X : Brigade　　⫿ **: Artillery**
III : Regiment　•••**: Skirmish Lines**

AoJ : Army of the James
AoS : Army of the Shenandoah
AoP : Army of the Potomac
ANV : Army of Northern Virginia

CHAPTER I

The Beginning of the Appomattox Campaign

March 29 - April 1

" . . . *I*t will become a siege and then it will be a mere question of time." Such were the words of General Robert E. Lee in June 1864, as he prophesied about what was to be the final year of conflict in Virginia. After being pinned down for nine and a half months with his army protecting both Richmond and Petersburg, he had only two major supply lines left to fuel continued resistance.

With the coming of spring 1865, the men in the trenches surrounding these two Confederate strongholds knew the final campaign was about to begin. By then, many of the Southern defenders had given up any hope for an independent nation. Their motivation to carry on the struggle was embodied in their revered general, whose life centered around duty and honor to his country. The last grasp at any real chance for these men had faded away more than four months earlier when Abraham Lincoln was re-elected to the presidency and declared, from that point on, it would be a fight to the finish. By March, only the Richmond & Danville Railroad was open to the Confederate capital, and the South Side Railroad, coming from Lynchburg, was all that entered Petersburg. Lee, realizing that the tightening Union noose would soon strangle him, decided he must cut

Lee in 1865.

loose from his defensive position, yet protect these life lines in the process.

As early as February 22, Lee wrote Secretary of War John C. Breckinridge about what was forthcoming. "Grant, I think, is now preparing to draw out his left [flank], with the intent of enveloping me. He may wait till his other columns approach nearer, or he may be preparing to anticipate my withdrawal. I cannot tell yet. I am endeavoring to collect supplies convenient to Burkeville."

On the same day he communicated with Lieutenant General James Longstreet, saying, "With the army concentrated at or near Burkeville, our communications north and south would be by that railroad [the Richmond & Danville] and west by the

South Side Railroad. We might also seize the opportunity of striking at Grant, should he pursue us rapidly, or Sherman, before they could unite.... I desire you also to make every preparation to take the field at a moment's notice, and to accumulate all the supplies you can. General Grant seems to be preparing to move out by his left flank. He is accumulating near Hatcher's Run depots of supplies, and apparently concentrating a strong force in that quarter."

With this in mind, on Saturday, March 25th, Lee allowed his Second Corps commander, Major General John B. Gordon, to take the offensive and attack the Union lines east of Petersburg in the neighborhood of Fort Stedman. Lee's plans, if Gordon was successful, would cause Federal commander Lieutenant General Ulysses S. Grant to shorten or abandon his lines west of the city. If this were to happen, Lee could then shorten his lines in that area and dispatch a portion of his troops to assist the Army of Tennessee in North Carolina.

Although Gordon's assault and penetration of the Union lines was successful that morning for a short period of time, a Federal counter-thrust by Brevet Major General John Hartranft's division of the IX Corps quickly recaptured the position and Lee's gamble was all for naught. Grant's army then took the initiative.

After the roar of battle subsided along the eastern front where Fort Stedman was located, two Union corps, Major General Andrew A. Humphreys' II and Major General Horatio G. Wright's VI, were directed to make an attack against the Confederate picket line and main works defending the Boydton Plank Road. This was in the area north and west of Union Forts Fisher, Welch, Gregg and Sampson and at about 1 p.m. Although both corps eventually captured the entrenched picket line, they found the main line too heavily defended. Wright's corps managed to hold on to a segment of the enemy's picket line in their front and began refacing the numerous picket posts. This placed them closer to the main Confederate works and afforded them a position from which to assemble assaulting columns at a later date. The combined operation brought in 932 prisoners at a loss of 52 killed, 864 wounded, and 207 missing for the Federals.

Grant in 1865—the zenith of his career.

Even before the Battle of Fort Stedman took place, General Grant had formulated plans for his spring offensive. On March 24th the commander issued an order for Major Generals George G. Meade, Edward O.C. Ord, and Philip H. Sheridan to begin operations on the 29th which would effectively start what is commonly referred to as the Appomattox Campaign in the *Official Records of the War of the Rebellion*. Having met with Major General William T. Sherman on the 27th and 28th, Grant was afraid that Lee might retreat from Petersburg before he could prepare to take the initiative. If this were to happen, Lee and General Joseph E. Johnston in North Carolina could combine forces and, as Grant wrote, "a long, tedious, and expensive campaign, consuming most of the summer, might become necessary. By moving out I would put the army in better

Philip H. Sheridan

condition for pursuit, and would at least, by the destruction of the Danville road, retard the concentration of the two armies of Lee and Johnston and cause the enemy to abandon much material that he might otherwise save. I therefore determined not to delay the movement ordered."

By this time the men in blue knew in their minds the war was quickly wrapping itself up. Would it be another summer, months or weeks? Would Lee be successful in evading Grant and reach North Carolina and General Joseph E. Johnston's Army of Tennessee near Raleigh? Would the *Armies of the Potomac* and *James* need to have Sherman's assistance in finishing the job? One thing was certain: even though Lee's army might be in its death throes, it still must be considered dangerous until Lee was brought to submission. After four years of fighting, Grant's men knew their tenacious adversaries well.

The final week of March brought heavy rains to the Petersburg area. Consequently, creeks and rivulets were swollen beyond their banks. The area in which the final operations around Petersburg were conducted was "the forest kind common to Virginia, being well watered by swampy streams. The surface was level and the soil clayey and sandy, and, where these mixed together, like quicksand. The soil after the frosts of winter first leave it is very light and soft, and hoofs and wheels find but little support."

Leading Grant's final offensive were the 50,000 men of Major General Gouverneur K. Warren's *V Corps* (17,000) and Major General Andrew A. Humphreys' *II Corps* (21,000), and the newly arrived Federal cavalry from the Shenandoah Valley. These horsemen were commanded by General Philip H. Sheridan, who led about 9-10,000 of this number. The infantry's first objective was to gain a foothold on the Boydton Plank Road, then use it as a jumping-off point to capture the South Side. Sheridan was to reach the right and rear of the enemy and force it out of its entrenched position if possible.

Major General John G. Parke's *IX Corps* (18,000) was instructed to hold the siege lines east and south of Petersburg (from Fort Cummings to the Appomattox River) while the *VI Corps* (18,000) continued to occupy their position on the left flank of the *IX Corps* (18,000). Ord's *Army of the James* was to move from north of the James River on the night of the 27th to the south side of the Appomattox River. They would then proceed to the left flank of the *Army of the Potomac*. Here the command was to fill the trenches that the *II Corps* had just vacated near Hatcher's Run. Ord would bring with him two divisions of Major General John Gibbon's *XXIV Corps* (16,000) and one division (2,000) of the *XXV Corps* (9,000). One small division of cavalry (2,300), commanded by Brigadier General Ranald S. Mackenzie, also accompanied Ord. Major General Godfrey Weitzel commanded the remainder of the *Army of the James* which held the lines southeast of Richmond.

A general marching order was given by Grant for all troops to have four days' rations (hard bread, coffee, sugar, salt meat and salt) on their persons, plus eight days' subsistence in the wagons. Three days' beef on the hoof was driven in the division herds. The troops carried fifty rounds of ammunition on their persons with sixty rounds per man in the wagon trains. Since the area the army was moving through was densely wooded,

Andrew A. Humphreys, II Corps.

making it somewhat impractical for the use of artillery, each division reduced their guns to either six or eight pieces, that is five four-gun batteries (three smooth bore and two rifled) per corps.

Once the *II* and *V Corps* departed the trenches they were holding, the foot soldiers moved into the countryside of Dinwiddie County. Humphreys held the right flank and moved northward against the Confederate line, keeping Hatcher's Run to his right, Quaker Road on his left. Warren connected with Humphreys' left and then advanced along the Boydton Plank Road, although later Warren was directed to move up the Quaker Road instead.

Sheridan's cavalry was instructed to strike for Dinwiddie Court House, the county seat village, and attempt to outflank the Confederates. If this was not feasible, they could ride away from the area and destroy the two railroads wherever possible. Sheridan could then either join Sherman or return to Grant's army. As Grant later explained about the last part of the order to Sheridan, who was somewhat dismayed by these latter instructions, "I have put [them] in merely as a blind." He explained that, "the nation had already become restless and discouraged at the prolongation of the war, and many believed that it would never terminate except by compromise." The reason he told the cavalry general he could go to North Carolina was that unless this movement proved successful, it would be interpreted as another defeat in the North.

As the Federal expeditionary force began moving into its assigned places on March 29th, Warren was the first to come in contact with enemy forces. With Brevet Major General Charles Griffin's division in the van, they began their move up the Quaker Road around noon. Griffin's lead brigade, commanded by Brigadier General Joshua L. Chamberlain, ran into their first resistance with Confederate pickets at the road crossing over Gravelly Run, a small tributary to Hatcher's Run.

Simultaneously, Sheridan's troopers pushed for Dinwiddie Court House, from which point they could head northward toward the South Side Railroad. Major General George Crook's second cavalry division of the *Army of the Potomac*, led the way, followed by Brigadier General Thomas C. Devin's first division. In the rear was Bvt. Major General George A. Custer's third division which was detached at Malone's Bridge to assist and protect the wagon trains. Both of the latter two divisions were commanded by Bvt. Major General Wesley Merritt and made up the *Army of the Shenandoah*. About 5 p.m. they entered the village and Sheridan posted his men at the various approaches to protect themselves from enemy patrols.

A Union cavalryman wrote later of his surroundings: "In Virginia court-houses mean towns, and the towns are principally court-houses; here, however, there was a hotel thrown in, and a couple of cottages by way of outskirts. Perhaps there were three; there is no intention to be unjust to Dinwiddie.... Yes, there were three. There was the long, low mansion with a leaky piazza, in the hollow on the right; the little house on the hill, where we all took breakfast, for which the man took a dollar a

Wesley Merritt

head; and the brick-house by the temple of justice, which looked like a school-house, but probably was not. We established ourselves at the Dinwiddie Hotel...."

Humphreys'*II Corps* did not get started with their advance until after Warren and Sheridan. His lead division was commanded by Brigadier General William Hays who moved his brigades up to the western bank of Hatcher's Run. Following him was Bvt. Major General Gershom Mott's division which formed on Hay's left flank, then Bvt. Major General Nelson Miles' division which fell in on Mott's left. Miles' left flank rested on Gravelly Run. The men of the *II Corps* then began to erect breastworks north of the Vaughan Road.

* * *

Lee was well aware of Grant's objective, the South Side Railroad, and formed a mobile force of infantry under the command of Major General George E. Pickett, sending them southwestward to protect this supply line. Examining his maps, the commanding general figured the Federals would probably move via Dinwiddie Court House and Five Forks, a march of about fifteen miles or a day and a half under the road conditions. Since his defensive trench lines only extended as far west as the intersection of the Claiborne and White Oak Roads, he had to elongate his army another four miles to cover the Five Forks intersection.

George E. Pickett

At this point in the siege, the Army of Northern Virginia covered an approximately 28-mile front: north of the James River was Lieutenant General James Longstreet's First Corps, supported by Brigadier General Martin Gary's small cavalry brigade. Under Lieutenant General Richard S. Ewell in his Reserve Corps was the Department of Richmond composed of heavy artillery units, Virginia Reserves and Local Defense Troops.

South of the James, and above the Appomattox River, was Major General William Mahone's infantry division guarding the Howlett Line across the Bermuda Hundred peninsula. They replaced the position Pickett's division held for most of the siege before being sent off toward Five Forks.

In the trenches around Petersburg, General Gordon's Second Corps stretched along a four-mile front from the Appomattox River east of town to the point where Lieutenant Run passed through the lines. From that area westward was Lieutenant

Richard S. Ewell

General Ambrose P. Hill's Third Corps extending to the Boydton Plank Road and crossing at Burgess' Mill. Covering the Confederate right flank was Lieutenant General Richard H. Anderson's Fourth Corps, now comprised only of Major General Bushrod R. Johnson's division.

General Pickett later was joined by Southern horsemen under Major General Fitzhugh Lee, the commanding general's nephew. They had to ride from the left flank of Lee's army north of the James along Nine Mile Road. In addition, Major General William Henry Fitzhugh "Rooney" Lee's division came in from their camp at Stony Creek Depot, forty miles to the southeast of Petersburg. Finally, further reinforcements were provided by Major General Thomas L. Rosser's division. They all rendezvoused at Sutherland Station and General Fitzhugh Lee was placed in command of the entire cavalry corps. Colonel Thomas T. Munford took command of Lee's division as the troopers began their ride to combine forces with the infantry commander.

Pickett, the Virginian of Gettysburg fame, had already moved his troops to Five Forks, a starfish-shaped crossroads in Dinwiddie County where only a small blacksmith shop was located. With Pickett were the brigades of Brigadier Generals George H. Steuart, Montgomery D. Corse, and William R. Terry. His other brigade, that of Brigadier General Eppa Hunton, remained behind and did not join the command until later. After taking the train from Petersburg to Sutherland Station, Pickett's men marched down the Claiborne Road to the White Oak Road. Here, two brigades of Anderson's command were attached to his column. They were led by Brigadier Generals William H. Wallace and Matthew W. Ransom. Six guns of Colonel William Pegram's battalion accompanied the force.

On the morning of March 30th, after conferring with General Lee and others, Pickett marched his soldiers four miles west along White Oak Road to Five Forks. By 4:30 p.m. his column had reached its destination and found the cavalry already there. They deployed along the White Oak Road and were entirely in place by 9:45 p.m.

During the night a heavy rain began to fall.

*   *   *

Back along the Quaker Road on the 29th, Chamberlain's brigade, composed of two large regiments of over 1,000 men each, the *185th New York* and *198th Pennsylvania*, had pushed across the flooded Gravelly Run and come in contact with Confederate skirmishers. These proved to be 4,800 troops that had been sent forward from Anderson's command along the White Oak Road trenches. Chamberlain pushed them back and, after his troops waded the waist deep stream, continued the advance until coming into an open area around the Lewis family farmhouse. Here his men found Brigadier General Henry A. Wise's Virginia brigade posted. Waiting for Bvt. Brigadier General Edgar M. Gregory's brigade to arrive for support, Chamberlain formed his men into battleline and forced Wise's brigade to fall back toward the junction of the Boydton Plank and Quaker Roads.

Seeing this retrograde movement of his troops, Anderson then deployed Wallace's South Carolinians to counterattack with Wise. After a fierce fight of about a half hour, Chamberlain's advance was halted as his left flank began to give ground. A battery of artillery (*B, 4th U.S.*) was brought up to the Lewis dwelling and began to pour canister into the attacking Southerners.

Once again Anderson sent more troops in the form of Brigadier General Young Moody's Alabama brigade. They were supported by Matt Ransom's North Carolinians who had been held in reserve. With three Confederate brigades now attacking him, Chamberlain sent a plea for help. General Griffin provided him with four regiments from other brigades in the division.

Anderson then realized that the Federals had been reinforced so he recalled his troops back to the White Oak Road defenses. Griffin's division moved forward and entrenched across the Boydton Plank Road. Bvt. Major General Samuel W. Crawford's third division shifted cross country and connected with Griffin's left to extend the line south along the Plank Road. Bvt. Major General Romeyn B. Ayres' second division remained near the Quaker Road crossing of Gravelly Run in reserve.

The capture of the Boydton Plank Road in this engagement cut one of Lee's intermediate supply routes and gave the Federals a point from which to attack the White Oak Road defenses. Since the use of the Weldon Railroad from North Carolina was curtailed in August 1864, the Plank Road was used by Confederate wagon trains to carry provisions into Petersburg. Supplies were sent as far north up the line as safely possible, then unloaded into wagons. Moving cross-country, they eventually reached the Plank Road and followed it up to Lee's army.

Humphreys' *II Corps* saw little action on this day, although his skirmishers were sent out to probe the area, and eventually captured some rifle pits near Dabney's steam sawmill and the Crow House. General Miles' division made contact with Warren's right flank and began to throw up breastworks. That evening, General Meade sent orders to the *II* and *V Corps* to advance on Five Forks. They were to support Sheridan who was directed to gain possession of the road intersection. The *V Corps* stretched out the left flank of the army and covered all roads leading to Sutherland Station. The *II Corps* remained in contact and supported Warren.

On the 30th, Warren issued three days' rations to his men and cautiously advanced toward the White Oak Road. Humphreys did likewise. In the van of his movement was Ayres' division which took position south and west of the Claiborne Road junction. Crawford followed and covered Ayres' right flank; Griffin was held in reserve on the south side of a branch of Gravelly Run. All of the *V Corps* had now moved west of the Boydton Plank Road.

*   *   *

Finding no enemy at the road forks except some Union cavalry, at about 10 a.m. on the 31st, Pickett began his southern movement to intercept Sheridan coming from Dinwiddie Court House. After marching down Scott's Road, Pickett turned east and sent his infantry and the cavalry across two fords (Danse's and Fitzgerald's) over a swampy creek bottom known as Chamberlain's Bed. Sheridan, then moving his two divisions under Crook and Devin northward against Five Forks, stopped to defend his left flank. Brigadier General Henry E. Davies and Bvt. Brigadier General Charles H. Smith's brigades were sent to cover the two fords. As Pickett's two lead infantry brigades under Generals Corse and Terry (later hurt when a horse fell on him in the battle) pushed back Davies at Danse's ford, two of Devin's brigades arrived in support: those of Colonels Peter Stagg and Charles L. Fitzhugh. They had just been pressed back from the Five Forks area by Southern cavalry under Colonel Tom Munford. Soon they too were forced to retreat toward the Court House with Davies.

Further south at Fitzgerald's ford, W.H.F. "Rooney" Lee's and Tom Rosser's cavalry divisions pushed across the marshy bottomlands. General Smith's Union troopers attempted to hold back the Confederates from forcing a passage, but found themselves outflanked by Pickett's infantry to the north. They also had to fall back to the main road along which Sheridan was moving on his way to Five Forks.

More reinforcements were sent into the fray in the form of Brigadier Generals Alfred Gibbs' and Bvt. Brigadier General J. Irvin Gregg's brigades. At the same time, General Custer was ordered to send two brigades from the wagon trains to assist. By 5:30 p.m. Colonels Alexander C.M. Pennington's and Henry Capehart's brigades arrived at Dinwiddie Court House. They got into position about a half-mile north of the village and built

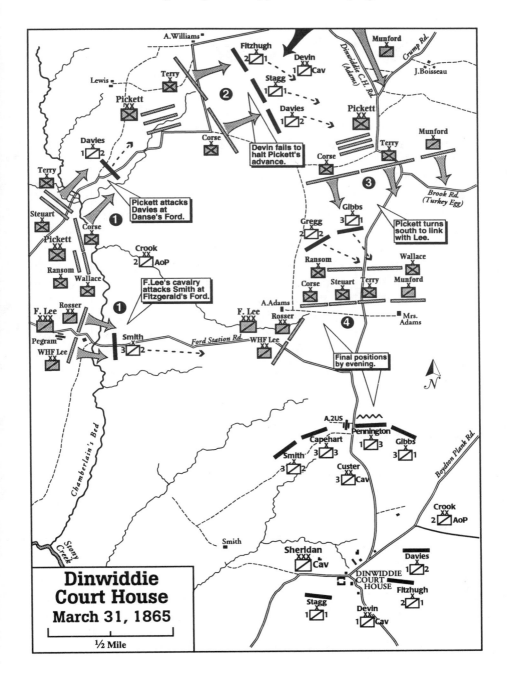

A.Williams

Munford

Cramp Rd.

Fitzhugh
2 X 1

Devin
X
Cav
1

J.Boisseau

Dinwiddie C.H. Rd. (Adams)

Lewis

Terry
X

Stagg
1 X 1

2

Pickett
XX

Davies
1 X 2

Pickett
XX

Munford
X

Davies
1 X 2

Corse
X

Devin fails to halt Pickett's advance.

Terry
X

Terry
X

Corse
X

3

Brook Rd.
(Turkey Egg)

Pickett attacks Davies at Danse's Ford.

1

Steuart
X

Corse
X

Crook
XX
2   AoP

Gibbs
3 X 1

Pickett turns south to link with Lee.

Gregg
2 X 2

Pickett
XX

Wallace
X

Ransom
X

Wallace
X

Ransom
X

Corse
X

Steuart
X

Terry
X

Munford
X

F. Lee's cavalry attacks Smith at Fitzgerald's Ford.

Rosser
XX

A.Adams

1

F. Lee
XXX

Rosser
XX

F. Lee
XXX

4

Mrs.
Adams

Pegram

Smith
3 X 2

F. Lee
XXX

Ford Station Rd.

WHF Lee
XX

WHF Lee
XX

Final positions by evening.

N

A.2US

Pennington
1 X 3

Capehart
3 X 1

Gibbs
3 X 1

Boydton Plank Rd.

Smith
3 X 2

Custer
XX
3   Cav

Crook
XX
2   AoP

Smith

Sheridan
XXX
Cav

Davies
1 X 2

DINWIDDIE
COURT
HOUSE

Stony Creek

Chamberlain's Bed

Fitzhugh
2 X 1

Stagg
1 X 1

Devin
XX
1   Cav

Dinwiddie
Court House
March 31, 1865

½ Mile

small rail breastworks. Four rifled cannon (*A, 2nd U.S.*) were also brought up and put in place.

As "Rooney" Lee and Rosser advanced from Chamberlain's Bed, they attempted to connect with the infantry's right flank so that they could attack Sheridan's position on its left. The Confederate infantry and cavalry made a couple of assaults on the entrenched line but were unable to push Sheridan back into Dinwiddie Court House. Nightfall brought an end to the fighting.

Tactically the Battle of Dinwiddie Court House was a victory for Pickett but strategically he gained nothing. He had stopped Sheridan's movement on Five Forks and, more importantly, the South Side Railroad. On the other hand, Sheridan made this comment: "This force [Pickett's] is in more danger than I am in—if I am cut off from the Army of the Potomac, it is cut off from Lee's army, and not a man in it should ever be allowed to get back to Lee. We at last have drawn the enemy's infantry out of its fortifications, and this is our chance to attack it." He also added in a communication to Grant that Pickett's force "is too strong for us. I will hold on to Dinwiddie Court-House until I am compelled to leave."

To the northeast of the Court House, Warren and his men were not quiet. After Ayres and Crawford followed a small woods road to the White Oak Road just west of the Claiborne Road junction, Warren saw his chance to "block the White Oak Road." This would effectively stop Anderson's division from supporting Pickett near Five Forks via this route.

At the road junction, the main Confederate works, running east and west, bent to the north and were anchored on the southern bank of Hatcher's Run. Visiting with Anderson and Bushrod Johnson this day was General Robert E. Lee himself. Finding the Federals in front of their lines, Lee chose four brigades to attack the Federals before they could take the initiative. Included were Moody (commanded by Colonel Martin L. Stansel as Moody was ill) and Wise of Johnson's division, Brigadier Eppa Hunton, who had remained behind from Pickett's division, and Brigadier General Samuel McGowan of Major General Cadmus M. Wilcox's division. McGowan had been

Charge at Five Forks. (Edwin Forbes)

pulled out of the lines north of Hatcher's Run a few days earlier to support Anderson.

Slipping out of their trenches, the four brigades silently moved up on Ayres' division, which had already sent one brigade forward with orders "to take the White Oak Road and intrench... upon it. But as this brigade approached within ten to fifteen yards of their objective, they heard the order "forward" coming from some woods across the road. Then they saw the Confederates coming. The sudden burst of Southern boldness startled the bluecoats, who quickly began retreating. As the brigades in Ayres' division started to crumble, they fell back on Crawford's column who were soon caught up in this retrograde movement. Eventually, after trying to make scattered stands, both Union divisions fell back across a branch of Gravelly Run and into the supports of Griffin's division.

Four Confederate brigades broke over 5,000 men of the *V Corps*, but their momentum soon ceased as they reached the north bank of the run. General Lee rode forward and met with General Johnson. Both agreed that, without reinforcements, their position was untenable. They ordered the men to fall back toward the White Oak Road and hold the small works that Ayres' men had thrown up earlier that morning. They commenced reversing them for their use.

By 2:30 p.m. both Ayres and Crawford had reformed their commands and Griffin was ready to take the lead in another advance. General Humphreys, whose help was requested, sent two brigades (Bvt. Brigadier Generals Henry J. Madill's and John Ramsey's) of General Miles' division to fall in on Warren's right. Once again General Chamberlain led Griffin's movement. He was supported by Gregory's and Bvt. Major General Joseph J. Bartlett's brigades.

Pressing forward over the same ground lost earlier in the day, Chamberlain ran into stiff Confederate resistance at the old works held by Eppa Hunton's brigade. By 3:40 in the afternoon, the Southerners began withdrawing and, by a roundabout way, returned to their trenches. Chamberlain then successfully swung his troops across the White Oak Road and temporarily cut it off from further use by Anderson.

During the day, Humphreys' corps moved to the left into the trenches formerly occupied by Griffin at the Boydton Plank and Quaker Roads intersection. Miles' division connected with Crawford's right, then Mott fell in next to Miles, and finally Hays anchored his right on Hatcher's Run. Besides Miles' troops, who assisted the *V Corps* in their attack on the White Oak Road, Humphreys sent some of Mott's men to reconnoiter the Confederate position east of the Boydton Plank Road. Mott ordered Brigadier General Byron R. Pierce's and Bvt. Brigadier General Robert McAllister's brigades to "assault the enemy works on their respective fronts." By this action, Mott hoped to keep the Confederate defenders from sending reinforcements to Miles' front.

On Pierce's right was the Confederate Crow House redoubt, anchored on the west bank of Hatcher's Run; in his front, one of two redoubts at Burgess' Mill. Advancing through a deadly crossfire from these two artillery positions, Pierce's brigade was thrown back. McAllister also tried to advance against the Burgess' Mill works but was also stopped.

Hays' division tried a limited attack on the easternmost redoubt at Burgess' Mill, known as Fort Powell, but he too was unsuccessful. Although these *II Corps* movements did not penetrate the main Confederate line on this day, they did accomplish their goal of keeping the defenders from supporting those in Warren's front.

Around 5:00 p.m. Warren received a message from Meade instructing him to secure his position and to send a small force to the southwest to communicate with Sheridan. Bartlett's brigade was assigned this task. Finding a small woods road that eventually led to nearby Crump Road, his men pushed forward until they came to a small branch of Gravelly Run. A few of his advance videttes were captured and interrogated by General Pickett's men encamped in front of Sheridan's cavalry north of Dinwiddie.

After making the Confederate commander aware of the situation, he realized that Federal infantry was now behind him and on his left flank. Early the next morning he was forced to fall back to Five Forks and give up his hard won position.

During the night of the 31st, Sheridan was back in the village busily communicating with Grant. Realizing the predicament he then had Pickett's force in, he needed infantry reinforcements to continue his advance. Initially he asked for Wright's *VI Corps* but was turned down since they were back in the main defenses. The only infantry Grant could offer was Warren's corps. That night at 8:00, Warren received orders to send one division down the Plank Road to join Sheridan. By 10:30 p.m. Ayres' division was on the road but ran into difficulty crossing over the main branch of Gravelly Run which had flooded approaches along the Boydton Plank Road. A forty-foot bridge would have to be constructed before the men could cross. It was not until 2 a.m. that this was accomplished and Ayres' men moved toward Dinwiddie Court House and joined Sheridan after daybreak. Crawford and Griffin moved via the same route Bartlett took earlier to the Crump Road.

At some point during his withdrawal, Pickett received a dispatch from Robert E. Lee which said: "Hold Five Forks at all hazards. Protect road to Ford's Depot and prevent Union forces from striking the Southside Railroad. Regret exceedingly your forced withdrawal, and your inability to hold the advantage you had gained [at Dinwiddie Court House]."

With Fitz Lee's cavalry covering the retrograde movement to Five Forks, by early morning the force was back where it started the day before. By Saturday, April 1, Pickett's men were strengthening their breastworks which ran parallel to the White Oak Road for a mile and three quarters. Stationed at the intersection of the Gravelly Run Church and White Oak Roads was Tom Munford's Virginia cavalry. A short distance beyond the Confederate entrenched left flank, they reconnoitered this area of the country for enemy movements. Dug in along the left (eastern) flank, where the line was refused by a 150 yard "return," was Matthew Ransom's North Carolinians. Behind the northern tip of the "return" were four guns of Captain William M. McGregor's Battery of horse artillery. To the west of Ransom was William Wallace's South Carolinians, with Ransom commanding both brigades. From Wallace's position west were George Steuart's Virginians extending to the Five Forks intersection. Across Ford's Road were three guns of Colonel William Pegram's Battalion (one gun of Ellett's and two of Carpenter's Batteries), then Colonel Joseph Mayo's Virginians (in place of the wounded William R. Terry), followed by three more guns of Pegram's battalion (Ellett's), and Montgomery Corse's Virginia brigade. Finally, and holding the right (western) flank, was William H.F. Lee's two cavalry brigades. They were North Carolinians under Brigadier General Rufus Barringer, and Brigadier General Richard L.T. Beale's Virginians commanded by Captain Samuel H. Burt. Lee's other brigade, also North Carolinians under Brigadier General William P. Roberts, had been strung out along the White Oak Road from Claiborne Road to Munford's position.

Since all seemed quiet in their front, some of the high command (Pickett and Fitzhugh Lee) rode to the rear north of Hatcher's Run and partook of a shad or fish bake with General Thomas Rosser. They failed to tell the other officers in the line where they were going and to place somebody in command of the infantry and cavalry in their absence. As early as 1 p.m., they begin to receive reports from Munford's front that Federal troops were forming there. Still the generals took no action.

Back at the front lines in the heavily timbered area, the men could not see or hear what was actually going on before them

Maj. Gen. Gouverneur Kemble Warren, relieved of command of V Corps after the Battle of Five Forks, April 1.

except close at hand. In reality, Sheridan was placing his troopers in their front, while moving Warren into position to attack their left. As Sheridan anxiously awaited Warren before forming up his men, he received a dispatch from the lieutenant general. "General Grant directs me to say to you, that if in your judgment the Fifth Corps would do better under one of the division commanders, you are authorized to relieve General Warren, and order him to report to General Grant, at headquarters."

The infantry, taking the Gravelly Run Church road off the main road to the Court House, came to a bottomland crossed by an arm of Gravelly Run. On the opposite ridge was a small white edifice known locally as the "Gravelly Run Methodist-Episcopal Church." Here, below the church and on both sides of the road, Warren aligned his commands for the forthcoming assault. On the west side was Ayres' division; on the right and in advance was Crawford. Griffin formed behind and to the right of Crawford. Their orders were to advance up the Gravelly Run Church Road *en echelon*, and at its intersection with the White Oak Road, wheel left and assault the enemy's entrenched left flank.

The problem was, through faulty reconnaissance, a map showed that the Southerners' entrenchments extended eastward to this position. In reality they were three-quarters of a mile to the west. With this false information, Sheridan's plan of attack was thrown off somewhat.

The cavalry general, in overall command, determined the tactics to be used. Since Warren's corps was going to storm the Confederate left, some of Custer's division would make a feint against the cavalry holding the Southerners' right. The rest of his troopers, Devin's division and a portion of Custer's, were to advance along the front of Pickett's line, attacking when the *V Corps* became actively engaged. Crook's division, bloodied the day before at Dinwiddie Court House, would remain behind to guard Sheridan's rear and not be actively engaged.

Earlier in the day, the two small brigades under General Mackenzie, of the *Army of the James*, left Dinwiddie and rode up the Crump Road. As they neared its intersection with the White Oak Road, Colonel Samuel Spear's men saw Robert's cavalry and attacked. The North Carolinians were scattered and the road was secured between Anderson's corps and Pickett. Mackenzie then turned to join Warren in his attack.

Finally about 4:15 p.m., the blue infantry advanced upon the White Oak Road. After brushing away Munford's skirmishers, they wheeled to the left but found no Confederates. Advancing through woods and fields, the two lead divisions, Ayres guided by the road and Crawford to the north, began losing contact with each other. Eventually Crawford swung way north of the Confederate line and actually passed through the woods behind it.

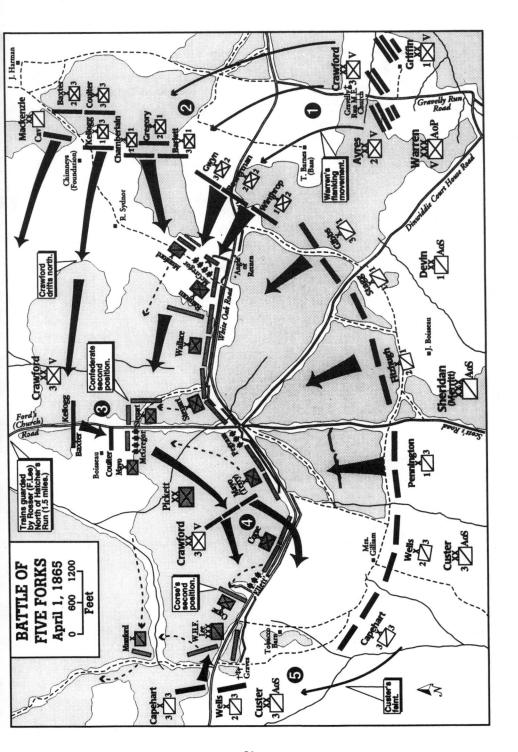

BATTLE OF FIVE FORKS
April 1, 1865

0   600   1200

Feet

J. Harman

Mackenzie
XX
Cav‡

Baxter
2│3

Coulter
3│3

Kellogg
1│3

Chamberlain

Gregory
2│1

Bartlett
3│1

Chimneys
(Foundation)

R. Sydnor

Crawford
drifts north.

Crawford
XX
V
3

Ford's
(Church)
Road

Kellogg

Baxter

Confederate
second
position.

Boisseau
Coulter

Negro

McGregor

Pickett
XX

Crawford
XX
V
3

Corse's
second
position.

Munford
XX

Capehart
3│3

Wells
XX
2│3

Custer
XX
AoS
3

Tobacco
Barn

Graves

W.H.F.
Lee
XX

Custer's
feint.

Crawford
XX
V

Ayres
XX
V
2

Warren
XXX
V
AoP

Gravelly
Run M.E.
Church

Warren's
flanking
movement.

T. Barnes
(Bus)

Gwyn
3│2

Pearson
2│2

Bowerman
1│2

Griffin
XX
1│V

Crawford
XX
V

Gravelly Run
Road

AoP

Dinwiddie Court House Road

Gibbs
3│1

Devin
XX
AoS
1

Stagg
1│1

Fitzhugh
2│1

J. Boisseau

Sheridan
(Merritt)
AoS

Scott's Road

Pennington
1│3

Mrs.
Gilliam

Wells
XX
2│3

Custer
XX
AoS
3

Capehart
3│3

Custer's
feint.

N

Trains guarded
by Rosser (F.Lee)
North of Hatcher's
Run (1.5 miles.)

White Oak Road

Scibert

McGregor

White Oak Road

Wallace
XX

Kellogg

Scibert

31

Sheridan, leading the attack with Ayres' division, headed directly for the "return," feeling it was the key position to the Confederate defenses. Warren himself was forced to leave the main attack force and go after Crawford, trying to bring him back into the fight. Sheridan smashed first into Ransom's North Carolinians, then into Wallace's troops, and in a brief period of time it was all over. Those who did not retreat were either killed, wounded or captured. In all, about a thousand Confederate prisoners were taken. The saddest loss for Ayres' men was the mortal wounding of Bvt. Brigadier General Frederick Winthrop, who died later that evening.

While Ayres was policing up the area he had just taken, Griffin was coming into the battle with supports. Those men of Wallace's and Ransom's commands that did get away fell into Steuart's line. In order to protect his left flank, General Steuart refused it along the edge of a field in which the Sydnor house was located and had his men quickly throw up log breastworks. Griffin, ordered by Warren to advance on Ford's Road, moved to his left and toward the White Oak Road. Finding Steuart's men posted in the edge of the woods, Chamberlain's brigade, supported by other nearby regiments of Bartlett's brigade, attacked. After fierce resistance, Steuart's men began falling back toward Ford's Road and Five Forks.

By this time, Pickett finally recognized the disaster that was occurring along his lines. As he rode down Ford's Road to his troops at the forks, the general was forced to "run the gauntlet" while he passed Crawford's skirmishers who were just coming out of the woods. This Union division had passed around and was now in the rear of the Confederate forces at Five Forks. Crawford and Warren together formed three brigades in a field around the Boisseau house and took advantage of their situation. Pickett, realizing the dilemma he was in, sent regiments from Mayo's brigade to stop Crawford and also to help Steuart. Mayo was supported by McGregor's four guns which managed to escape from the "return" before it was overwhelmed.

Crawford's men pushed through Mayo's stand across Ford's Road and scattered or captured his troops. Continuing along with Warren, they then advanced westward along the White Oak Road until they came in contact with Corse's command. The

"Burnt Quarter," the Gilliam House on the Five Forks battlefield (1953).

Virginian quickly had his men build a "return" perpendicular to the main trench line and also offered resistance. The sun was quickly setting as Warren himself led the attack across the Widow Gilliam's field against Corse. Holding their ground as long as possible, the Southern infantrymen escaped the battlefield by a small woods road in their rear.

All the while that Warren's infantry was at work, Custer's and Devin's cavalry were also busy. Devin's three brigades pushed against the Confederate line as Warren's two divisions rolled up the left flank, eventually joining in the taking of prisoners. Uniting with them was Colonel Pennington's brigade of Custer's command. The flamboyant general sent his other two brigades, the West Virginians under Henry Capehart and Colonel William Wells' troopers, to swing around on the Confederate right and attack "Rooney" Lee's cavalry.

While they were doing this in conjunction with Warren's attack on the other end of the line, one regiment of Wells' brigade, the *15th New York*, was sent on a suicidal mission. They were to make a frontal attack on Corse's infantry and Pegram's three guns as a diversion. After two unsuccessful assaults, they were thrown back with heavy losses.

Maj. Gen. Bushrod R. Johnson commanded the one division making up Anderson's corps.

The rest of Custer's two brigades reached the Confederate right flank and attempted to get around behind Lee. What was to be a "feint" turned into a full fledged attack. Unfortunately for Custer's plans, the Virginians and North Carolinians prevented this from happening and that portion of the Southern line was saved. This proved to be very important as the woods road many Confederates later used to escape the battlefield was located here.

By the time Pickett reached his men at the forks, all was lost. It became every command for itself. There were brief pockets of resistance here and there but nothing could stop Sheridan's momentum. The Southerners escaped through the woods and across Hatcher's Run in small groups or commands only to gather together at the railroad in darkness, 2½ miles away.

One other incident took place before nightfall brought full victory to Sheridan. At some point during the fighting, back at the forks Colonel "Willie" Pegram was directing the fire of his three pieces. He instructed his artillerymen to "fire your canister low." Following this order he was struck in his left arm and side. The 23-year-old Confederate artillerist was mortally wounded and died the next day at nearby Ford's Depot.

Grant waiting for news. (Edwin Forbes)

In the mop-up operation of the battlefield that evening, Mackenzie's cavalry guarded the southern side of Hatcher's Run at the Ford's Road crossing. As Warren was making his attack earlier, this small cavalry division fell in on Crawford's right flank and swung around next to this watercourse. Although not heavily involved in the battle, they did screen that portion of the field since Rosser's entire division was held in reserve on the north side of Hatcher's Run.

Earlier in the evening, at 5:45 p.m., Bushrod Johnson was ordered with three brigades (Wise, Moody and Hunton) to move via the Claiborne Road and South Side Railroad to Church Road crossing. They were to provide assistance to Pickett if they could. Unfortunately it came too late for the Southern general as only Hunton's brigade reached Rosser's command after the battle was over.

The position they vacated in Anderson's former line was filled by the brigades of Brigadier Generals John R. Cooke, William MacRae, Samuel McGowen, and Colonel Joseph H. Hyman (Scales').

By nightfall, with the important crossroads in his clutch, Sheridan had opened the door for the Federal army to capture the South Side Railroad the next day. Word was sent of the victory at Five Forks to General Grant whose headquarters were at nearby Dabney's sawmill. Around 9:00 p.m. the Union

Prisoners captured at Five Forks. (Edwin Forbes)

commander heard the report and then walked into his tent. He emerged shortly afterward and coolly said, "I have ordered a general assault along the lines." Grant later wrote that "some apprehensions filled my mind lest the enemy might desert his lines during the night, and by falling upon General Sheridan before assistance could reach him, drive him from his position and open the way for retreat." To guard against this a bombardment was commenced on the Confederate lines and kept up until 4:00 a.m. when the assault was ordered.

The complete success of the Union forces was somewhat overshadowed that evening, at least for the *V Corps*. For reasons pertaining to his perceived performance before and during the battle, Sheridan relieved Warren of his command and replaced him with Charles Griffin. General Joseph Bartlett took over Griffin's division. General Warren immediately requested a Court of Inquiry, but was not granted one for almost fifteen years. The former *V Corps* commander later returned to Petersburg when it fell, by order of General Grant.

In the fighting at Five Forks, Pickett lost somewhere between 2,000 and 2,400 men as prisoners. Those who escaped met up with the rest of Johnson's command at the Church Road (or Crowder's) Crossing of the South Side Railroad. Both divisions were then put under the command of General Anderson.

In Humphreys' front that evening, his troops occupied the position vacated by Warren on the night of the 31st. Miles' division was ordered to extend across the White Oak Road and thus prevent the enemy from sending reinforcements to Five Forks via this route. This caused Anderson to take the circuitous route in reinforcing Pickett's men.

The Warren Court of Inquiry for the Battle of Five Forks

In the flush of victory, one of the biggest controversies to arise during the final days of the war in Virginia involved Major General Gouverneur K. Warren's removal from command of the *V Corps*. This took place on the evening of April 1, 1865, immediately after the Battle of Five Forks.

With the arrival of darkness that evening and the capture of the strategic country crossroads known as "Five Forks," Grant was ready to cut the South Side Railroad and sever Lee's last supply artery into Petersburg. To most involved in the battle for the road junction, General Warren's conduct there seemed commendable and courageous, particularly since the fight was a success for the Union army.

The Battle of Five Forks was an operation of Union infantry and cavalry, with no artillery on the Federal side. Cavalry general Philip H. Sheridan was the overall commander, with infantry commander Warren reporting directly to him. Sheridan rode with Warren's corps through most of the battle.

The day before at Dinwiddie Court House, Sheridan had requested infantry support from Grant. Asking for Wright's *VI Corps*, he was told that they were too far up the line. Instead, the commanding general sent Warren's corps who were just to the northeast at White Oak Road. Sheridan reluctantly accepted them.

Warren's three divisions finally united with Sheridan in the afternoon due to delays caused by weather-torn roads. While patiently waiting for Warren's arrival, Sheridan had received the following message: "General Grant directs me to say to you, that if in your judgement the Fifth Corps would do better under one of the division commanders, you are authorized to relieve General Warren, and order him to report to General Grant, at headquarters."

At 4:15 the battle opened with Warren attacking the Confederate left flank, while Sheridan's cavalry pressed their front and also charged the right flank. Early in the fighting, Warren became separated from Sheridan as he rode off to bring one of his divisions, General Samuel Crawford's, back into the fighting. He then remained with them until the battle was over.

After a final charge on the Confederate lines, Colonel George A. Forsyth rode across the Widow Gilliam's cotton field and delivered a message to Warren: "Major-General Warren, commanding the Fifth Army Corps, is relieved from duty, and will report at once for orders to Lieutenant-General Grant, commanding Armies of the United States." Confused and dazed, Warren rode to General Sheridan. Asking him to reconsider his decision, the Irishman replied "Reconsider? Hell! I don't reconsider my determination." Warren could do nothing but report to General Grant at his headquarters at Dabney's sawmill.

General Warren immediately requested a Court of Inquiry to address the charges brought against him by Sheridan. Obviously, because of the events of the week following Five Forks, little attention was given to his petition.

In his official report of May 16, Sheridan wrote about Warren's performance and some of what caused his decision. "... I will say that General Warren did not exert himself to get up his corps as rapidly as he might have done, and his manner gave me the impression that he wished the sun to go down before dispositions of the attack could be completed." Later Sheridan said, "During the attack I again became dissatisfied with General Warren. During the engagement portions of his line gave way when not exposed to a heavy fire, and simply from want of confidence on the part of the troops, which General Warren did not exert himself to inspire. I therefore relieved him from the command of the Fifth Corps ...."

It must be remembered that a large part of the responsibility for relieving Warren rests in General Grant's hands. Sheridan was merely his "hatchet man." As the Union commander later wrote, "I was so much dissatisfied with Warren's dilatory movements in the Battle of White Oak Road, and his failure to reach Sheridan in time, that I was very much afraid that in the last moment he would fail Sheridan. He was a man of fine intelligence, great earnestness, quick perception, and could make his dispositions as quickly as any officer, under difficulties where he was forced to act. But I had before discovered a defect which was beyond his control, that was very prejudicial to his useful-

ness in the emergencies like the one before us. He could see every danger at a glance before he had encountered it. He would not only make preparations to meet the danger which might occur, but he would inform his commanding officers what others should do while he was executing his move."

Grant added, "Warren's difficulty was two fold; when he received an order ... it would at once occur to his mind how all the balance of the army should be engaged ... to cooperate with him ... [H]e would forget that the person giving him his orders had thought of others at the same time he had of him. In like manner, when he did get ready to execute an order, after giving most intelligent instructions to division commanders, he would go in with one division holding the others in reserve ... forgetting that division commanders could execute an order without his presence. His difficulty was constitutional and beyond his control."

When one argues the charges made against Warren by Sheridan after Five Forks, on the surface they seem pretty weak. Generally speaking, Sheridan's "accusations or imputations" were:

1. Warren should have moved forward with all three of his divisions against the White Oak Road, instead of just one on March 31. Because he didn't, they, and one other division, were driven back until the third stopped the attack.

2. Warren did not move his corps fast enough for Grant on the night of the 31st, thereby allowing Pickett's army to fall

back from Dinwiddie Court House to Five Forks.

3. General Warren did not encourage his corps to move fast enough on April 1, acting as if he wished the day to end before the enemy could be engaged.

4. When a portion of Warren's attacking column gave way under heavy fire during the battle, it was because of a lack of confidence which the general failed to give.

Five Forks wasn't the first time General Warren disappointed his commanders, particularly Generals Grant and Meade. At Mine Run in November 1863, Warren was in command of nearly half of Meade's army, directing an assault on the Confederate lines. He prophesied, "If I succeed to-day I shall be the greatest man in the army; if I don't, all my sins will be remembered."

At the last minute, Warren called off the attack because the enemy's works had been strengthened overnight and it would take his men eight minutes to reach the Confederate lines. He now felt it would have been suicide for his troops to make an assault.

Upon hearing that Warren suspended the operation, General Meade was reported as "looking as savage as anyone could" over this news.

Near Spotsylvania Court House on May 12, 1864, Warren seemed apprehensive about attacking the enemy lines in his front. General Meade ordered him forward, and if unsuccessful, to move to support Hancock's and Wright's corps, noting "Warren seems reluctant to assault." Grant responded in a note

saying, "If Warren fails to attack promptly, send Humphreys to command his corps and relieve him."

At Cold Harbor, one of General Meade's aides, Colonel Theodore Lyman, remembered an incident with Warren where he could not find him to deliver a message. "This was Warren's great way, to go about, looking thus after details and making ingenious plans; but it kept him from generalities, and made it hard to find him, so that he finally came to trouble as much by this as by anything else."

Finally, after the June 18th assault on Petersburg by Grant's army, Warren once again was in disfavor. General Meade was so angry over his performance, he wrote a letter on June 21 to Brigadier General John A. Rawlins, Grant's Chief of Staff, requesting the relief of the *V Corps* general from his command. He noted, "The defect with General Warren consists in too great reliance on his own judgement and in an apparent impossibility on his part to yield this judgement so as to promptly execute orders, where these orders should happen not to receive his sanction or be in accordance with his views."

In plainer words he added, "I have endeavored to show what I consider a defect in Genl. Warren's character viz: an assumption of responsibility where no discretion is left him by his orders—This defect has been a source of serious embarrassment to me, but my appreciation of Genl. Warren's good qualities, and my strong personal regard for him have been such ... [that I] hoped that Genl. Warren would see himself the necessity of trying to correct it. As however in an interview on the 19th Genl. Warren exhibited so much temper and bad feeling forgetting the respect due to me ...."

Obviously, Meade's wishes were not carried out at this time, but this shows the discontentment of his superior officers with his performance and personality.

Presumably the dislike for General Warren continued throughout the siege. When the time presented itself to relieve him from command, as it did at Five Forks, General Grant used one of his most trusted subordinates to carry out the deed.

It would not be until both Grant and Sheridan were out of political power in the post-war years that General Warren would receive his day in court. In 1879 he was granted the request he made way back in 1865.

Over 1,700 pages of testimony, made both by Union and Confederate officers who served in the battle, along with the owner of the battlefield, Samuel Yates Gilliam, were produced. He validated the newly surveyed battle map used by the court. After examining each of the four imputations made by General Sheridan and hearing statements, the court made the following decisions:

1) Warren was exonerated on the first charge, although it was found that he "should have been with his advanced divisions [at White Oak Road on March 31] and should have started earlier to the front."

2) It was determined to be impracticable for the V corps to reach Sheridan at Dinwiddie Court House by midnight on the 31st.

3) In the march to Five Forks, there was no unnecessary delay by Warren and all efforts were made to keep the corps moving. The court added that "his actions do not appear to have corresponded with such a wish" for the sun to go down and not engage the enemy.

4) During the battle of Five Forks, when Crawford's and Griffin's divisions diverged from the original plan of attack, General Warren did exactly what he was supposed to when he went to bring them back. "This was for him the essential point to be attended to which also exacted his whole efforts to accomplish" noted the court.

On November 21, 1882, these were publicly announced through the press, but nothing further took place. Unfortunately for General Gouverneur K. Warren, this was too late. Three months earlier on August 8, he had died. The stigma of Five Forks followed the "hero of Gettysburg" to the grave. There was no military funeral and the general was buried in civilian attire.

CHAPTER II

Fall of Petersburg

April 2

*A*lthough the early morning assault by the Federal forces was scheduled for 4:00 a.m., the first movement did not actually begin until around 4:30. Astride the Jerusalem Plank Road, which ran north and south out of Petersburg, General John Parke's *IX Corps* prepared for an attack upon the Confederate line centering at Fort Mahone (Battery 29), also known as "Fort Damnation." Their jumping-off point was nearby Fort Sedgwick, or "Fort Hell." One of Parke's divisions, commanded by Bvt. Major General Orlando B. Willcox, was to remain behind in the trenches along the eastern front to provide a diversion to the main assault. His other two divisions, under Bvt. Major Generals Robert B. Potter and John F. Hartranft, were to form up and follow the Plank Road. Hartranft carried the right while Potter, the left. As the infantry pressed forward in their assault, Parke's men found themselves confronted by Major General Bryan Grimes' division of Gordon's Second Corps.

Heavy fighting took place as the Federals scrambled over the many picket and outer lines which made up the Confederate defenses. Men were sent forward with axes to cut through the abatis and chevaux-de-frise which were used to protect even these. Eventually reaching the main entrenchments, Hartranft captured Battery 27 of the old Confederate Dimmock Line. Soon Batteries 25 and 28 followed. By 6:50 a.m. Parke had captured

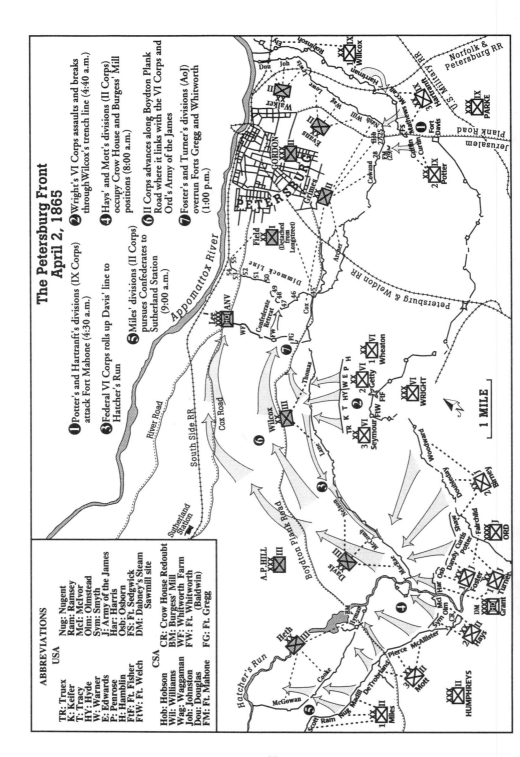

The Petersburg Front
April 2, 1865

❶ Potter's and Hartranft's divisions (IX Corps) attack Fort Mahone (4:30 a.m.)

❷ Wright's VI Corps assaults and breaks through Wilcox's trench line (4:40 a.m.)

❸ Federal VI Corps rolls up Davis' line to Hatcher's Run

❹ Hays' and Mott's divisions (II Corps) occupy Crow House and Burgess' Mill positions (8:00 a.m.)

❺ Miles' divisions (II Corps) pursues Confederates to Sutherland Station (9:00 a.m.)

❻ II Corps advances along Boydton Plank Road where it links with the VI Corps and Ord's Army of the James

❼ Foster's and Turner's divisions (AoJ) overrun Forts Gregg and Whitworth (1:00 p.m.)

ABBREVIATIONS

USA

TR: Truex
K: Keifer
T: Tracy
HY: Hyde
W: Warner
E: Edwards
P: Penrose
H: Hamblin
FsF: Ft. Fisher
FtW: Ft. Welch

Nug: Nugent
Ram: Ramsey
McI: McIvor
Olm: Olmstead
Sym: Smyth
J: Army of the James
Har: Harris
Osb: Osborn
FS: Ft. Sedgwick
DM: Dabney's Steam Sawmill site

CSA

Hob: Hobson
Wil: Williams
Wag: Waggaman
Joh: Johnston
Dou: Douglas
FM: Ft. Mahone

CR: Crow House Redoubt
BM: Burgess' Mill
WF: Whitworth Farm
FW: Ft. Whitworth (Baldwin)
FG: Ft. Gregg

1 MILE

two redans, two forts and twelve guns, but the Confederates tenaciously held onto their inner works.

To the southwest of Petersburg and in front of Forts Fisher and Welch, Wright's *VI Corps* was also preparing their assault on the Confederate lines defending the Boydton Plank Road. Moving out of their trenches, the *VI Corps* assembled behind the former enemy picket line captured on March 25 after the Battle of Fort Stedman. Wright had his three divisions assemble in a "wedge shaped" formation, with Brigadier General Truman Seymour on the left, Bvt. Major General George W. Getty in the middle and in advance, and Bvt. Major General Frank Wheaton holding the right. At 4:40 a.m. a signal gun from Fort Fisher announced the attack, and in the darkness of the early morning the men moved forward. Using axemen to cut through the wooden entanglements, they pushed aside the enemy pickets and reached the main Confederate trenches. After a brief hand to hand combat, they were up and over the works. Some pressed the Confederates to the Boydton Plank Road and even beyond to the South Side Railroad.

Confronting them were North Carolinians of Brigadier General James H. Lane's brigade of Wilcox's division. Following a brief struggle of about twenty minutes, Wright's corps penetrated the Southern defenses and virtually cut in half Lee's army protecting Petersburg. While the Federals regrouped, word of this disaster to their lines came to the nearby headquarters of Generals Lee and A.P. Hill. Hill rode from Indiana, his command post on the western edge of the city, to Edgehill, just a mile and a half further west, to see Lee. The two needed to confer about the situation since Hill has just returned to the army on March 31 after sick leave.

The day before these assaults on the Petersburg defenses, Lee had ordered General Longstreet and Major General Charles W. Field's division to move from north of the James to this front. General Ewell, with Major General Joseph B. Kershaw's division (of Longstreet's Corps), Gary's cavalry, and Major General George Washington Custis Lee's division, remained to take Longstreet's place in those lines defending Richmond. Lee also had ordered General Mahone to send one of his brigades,

Mississippians under Brigadier General Nathaniel Harris, to Petersburg.

As the *VI Corps* regrouped after their breakthrough, they turned southward inside the Confederate lines and began attacking the rest of Hill's troops holding the line on the north bank of Hatcher's Run. While they were doing this, General Hill and an aide rode into the area of the breakthrough just west of the Plank Road. Confronting two Union soldiers on their way back from tearing up the South Side Railroad, Hill called for them to surrender. Instead, the Northerners leveled their muskets and fired. General A.P. Hill was killed on the spot, while his aide escaped and returned to General Lee with the sad news of the Third Corps commander's death.

As Wright's men advanced southward along the entrenchments, they ran into pockets of heavy resistance from Colonel Andrew M. Nelson's (Brigadier General Joseph R. Davis's) Mississippians, followed by Brigadier General William McComb's Maryland-Tennessee brigade and then finally portions of Brigadier General William MacRae's North Carolina brigade. Eventually the Confederate defenders were either overwhelmed and taken prisoners or crossed Hatcher's Run and escaped. By 9:00 a.m. the pursuit was called off as General Wright heard that the *II* and *V Corps* were carrying the line further to the west.

Other *VI Corps* units turned to the north upon reaching the Boydton Plank Road and attacked Brigadier General Edward L. Thomas's Georgians of Wilcox's division, opening the breach in the Confederate lines even wider. Thomas was supported by remnants of Lane's brigade as they fell back toward two Confederate outposts known as Forts Gregg and Whitworth on the western environs of Petersburg.

In Humphreys' front there was also much activity. At 6:00 a.m. he ordered Hays' division to assault the Crow House redoubt located just north of Dabney's sawmill and next to Hatcher's Run. By 8:00 it was captured with three guns and a large part of the garrison. The men then set about reversing the work. Hays and Mott continued their advance, eventually occupying, around 8:30 a.m., the Confederate works running from Burgess's Mill to Claiborne Road. These had been abandoned by

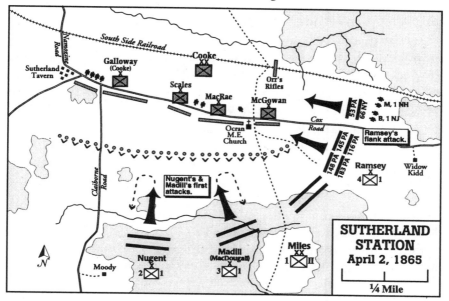

their defenders who fell back upon Sutherland Station at the northern end of Claiborne Road.

Earlier in the morning, between midnight and 1:00 a.m., General Miles was ordered down the White Oak Road to reinforce Sheridan at Five Forks. Finding he was not needed, Miles began returning to his former position near the Claiborne Road junction. Upon reaching the area about 9:00 a.m., he was directed by General Humphreys to enter the enemy works and pursue the Southerners along the Claiborne Road to the station. Hays' second division and Mott's third division were ordered eastward to move up the Boydton Plank Road toward Petersburg and eventually connect with the *VI Corps*.

* * *

As dispatch after dispatch filled with the disastrous news of the day's events came into Lee's headquarters at Edgehill, the commanding general was convinced the time had come to withdraw his army from Richmond and Petersburg. He had to protect Petersburg, however, until darkness fell.

He sent a telegram to Secretary of War John Breckinridge, who received it about 10:40 a.m. "I see no prospect of doing more than holding our position here until night. I am not certain

I can do that. If I can I shall withdraw to-night north of the Appomattox, and, if possible, it will be better to withdraw the whole line to-night from James River. I advise that all preparations be made for leaving Richmond tonight. I will advise you later according to circumstances." This was carried to President Jefferson Davis who received it during a worship service at St. Paul's Episcopal Church in Richmond.

About 10:00 the lead brigade of Miles' first division reached the Cox Road at Sutherland Station. Bvt. Brigadier General Henry J. Madill found the Confederates entrenched parallel to this road, with Sutherland Tavern on the right and Ocran Methodist Church on their left. The South Side Railroad was located directly behind them. In a line approximately a half-mile long, running from the church westward, were the brigades of McGowan, MacRae, Scales and Cooke. One gun was at the church, two in the center of the line, and four near the tavern. Major General Henry Heth placed the units in position then returned to the main lines at Petersburg, about eight miles east. He gave the command over to General Cooke.

Sometime around 11:00 a.m. Madill made the first assault on the Confederate breastworks. The Federals were thrown back with heavy casualties, including General Madill who was severely wounded. Bvt. Brigadier General Clinton MacDougall took his command.

Miles's next brigade then arrived on the scene led by Colonel Robert Nugent. Between 12:30 and 1:00 p.m. another frontal assault took place with both of MacDougall's and Nugent's brigades present. This too was repulsed and MacDougall was wounded. General Miles decided to bring up General John Ramsey's brigade for use in a flank attack. By 2:45 p.m. all three brigades were in place and prepared for a third assault. The flank attack fell upon McGowan's men who broke, allowing the Federals to scatter the rest of the commands. Those not taken prisoner retreated up the Namozine Road toward the Appomattox River.

Besides destroying this pocket of Confederate resistance, the importance of the Battle of Sutherland Station was symbolic. For here on the afternoon of the 2nd, Sheridan's efforts at Five Forks were brought to completion. Officially the South Side Railroad

Retreat from Petersburg: Halt at a well. (William L. Sheppard)

was severed as the final supply route for Lee's army at Petersburg.

Back in the main Union siege lines vacated by Humphreys' *II Corps* a few days earlier, Ord's *Army of the James* was playing its role in the final assault. Connecting with Hays' division of the *II Corps* on their left, the rest of Ord's troops were spread along the lines with Bvt. Major General John W. Turner's *Independent Division* next, then Brigadier General Robert S. Foster's first division (both *XXIV Corps*), and finally Brigadier General William Birney's second division, *XXV Corps*. Once the *VI Corps* cleared the Confederate lines down to Hatcher's Run, Brigadier General Thomas M. Harris' brigade of Turner's division moved in to occupy the abandoned trenches. As part of John Gibbon's corps, they eventually passed through Wright's command and proceeded up the Boydton Plank Road toward Petersburg. Running into resistance about noon, they pushed the Confederates back into Forts Gregg and Whitworth. A short distance east of these outposts, and across Rohoic (or Old Town) Creek, was the Confederate inner defensive Dimmock Line running from

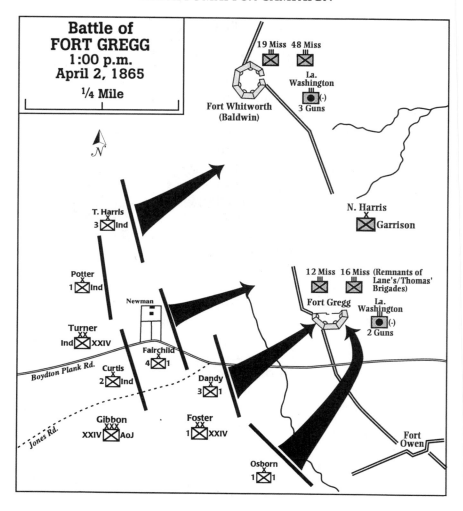

Battle of
FORT GREGG
1:00 p.m.
April 2, 1865
¼ Mile

Batteries 45 to 55. Filing into these positions were remnants of Lane's and Thomas's brigades, supported by Charles Field's division, arriving from Richmond.

Moving into Forts Gregg and Whitworth (both named for the farms they were built on) were approximately 270 Mississippians of Harris's brigade and 25 men of the Louisiana Washington Artillery. Fort Whitworth was a fully enclosed work located a few hundred yards north of Fort Gregg. Three sided and restricted by a palisade across the back, Fort Gregg faced to the south and the Boydton Plank Road which headed east into the city.

At 1:00 p.m. Gibbon formed his nearly 5,000 troops for an assault upon these two positions. Turner's division held the left flank, while Foster's division held the right. As the forward movement began, Gibbon's commands were raked by fire from the forts. Centering the attack on Fort Gregg, the Federals reached the moat surrounding the redan. Trapped for a length of time in their attempt to scramble over the parapet, the Northerners finally got over and into the fort. Fierce hand to hand combat took place until finally the brave defenders surrendered about 2:30 p.m. Some 57 Southerners were killed, 129 wounded and 30 taken prisoner. Federal casualties amounted to 714 men. This "Homeric" defense of Fort Gregg allowed the rest of Lee's army to reinforce the old Dimmock Line west of the city in case the attack continued.

With the capture of Fort Gregg, Fort Whitworth was outflanked and its garrison commander gave orders to fall back. It too was taken by Gibbon's men, but with little loss of life. Birney's division of the *XXV Corps* then arrived on the battlefield and went on picket duty facing Lee's newly fortified line. With the swampy grounds of Rohoic Creek in their front, and the Confederate line being placed along the high ground on the opposite side, apparently Ord decided not to press the attack any further.

Parke was not having as much success with his assault as the others on this final day of the siege. Even though he was able to capture some Confederate positions near the Jerusalem Plank Road, his adversary, General Gordon, continued to counterattack. Around 11:00 a.m. Grimes' division began a push to retake some of the lost batteries, which degenerated into a series of small struggles in the numerous trench systems. Federal supports stopped this effort. About 12:30 Parke wired Meade's headquarters that he desperately needed further reinforcements.

Another Confederate offensive started after 1:00 p.m. during which General Potter was wounded. His command fell to Brigadier General Simon G. Griffin. Finally around 3:00 p.m. the last of Gordon's counterattacks took place.

Union troops assault Fort Mahone, as sketched by Alfred Waud.

The Federals around Fort Mahone were beginning to fall back to their lines, when suddenly more Union troops arrived on the scene in the form of Bvt. Brigadier General Charles H.T. Collis's *Independent Brigade*. They had been sent from the City Point defenses. Their attack ended the fighting on Parke's front which had failed to break through the main Confederate defenses and saved Petersburg in this sector of the lines. Gordon soon received the order to begin withdrawing his men from the trenches and head into the city.

Once the *VI Corps* finished mopping up the Confederate lines down to Hatcher's Run, they turned northward and started to march up the Boydton Plank Road. Where this major turnpike veered to the east toward Petersburg, they followed Long Ordinary Road and eventually came in sight of Lee's headquarters at "Edgehill" on Cox Road. Defending the Confederate commander's post were guns from Lieutenant Colonel William T. Poague's Battalion. The closest infantry around were those holding the Dimmock Line just to the east. As General Lee rode to safety within these lines, one of Poague's batteries fired canister at the advancing Federals. They came so close that they could actually see Lee ride away. Eventually the guns were silenced and two divisions of the *VI Corps* formed in line of battle.

These troops proved to be Wheaton's and Getty's as Seymour was sent to assist Parke's *IX Corps* on their front. They arrived but were not put into action. Because there was a gap between the left of the *XXIV Corps* and Getty's right, newly arriving *II Corps* troops of Mott's division filled the space on the Whitworth farm. The Federals began erecting a line a breastworks but they did not attack Field's position in the old Confederate line. The men of Wright's corps had been under arms for eighteen hours and were too exhausted for another assault.

At the far western sector of this huge battlefield around Petersburg, Sheridan's cavalry and Griffin's infantry had spent a somewhat quiet day. Around daybreak on the 2nd, the *V Corps* marched east down the White Oak Road to the vicinity of the Claiborne Road junction before halting. At 11:00 a.m., after seeing that Miles's division had the situation under hand, the corps returned to Five Forks and headed north up the Ford's Road and across Hatcher's Run and the South Side Railroad. Upon reaching the Cox Road and forcing aside some Confederate cavalry posted there, Chamberlain's men heard musket fire to the east, so the brigade led the corps in that direction. What they were hearing was the fight at Sutherland Station, but upon approaching that area, they saw that Miles had already completed his task. The *V Corps* then moved to the intersection of the Namozine and River Roads and went into bivouac on the Williamson farm.

Sheridan, after having Miles' division report to him in the morning, had the *II Corps* general return to Claiborne Road where he pursued the enemy north to Sutherland Station. Following him up this road as far as the crossing of Hatcher's Run, the cavalry commander then returned to Five Forks by way of the White Oak Road. Heading north from there to Cox Road after passing over the South Side Railroad, his troopers turned to follow the main route of the Confederate retreat.

The night before the remnants of Pickett's, Johnson's and Fitz Lee's commands had assembled at Church Road Crossing on the South Side Railroad about 2½ miles north of Five Forks. During

Retreat from Petersburg: Grinding corn. (William L. Sheppard)

the day they moved toward the Appomattox River by way of Brown's Road to the Namozine Road. They hoped to eventually cross the river at nearby Exeter Mills.

Bringing up the rear of this column was Fitz Lee's cavalry which informed the infantry around 3:00 p.m. that the Federal cavalry would soon be arriving. Johnson had his men erect barricades along the Namozine Road at what was locally known as Scott's Cross Roads. At 5:00 the Union troopers appeared to the south of the intersection.

Pickett had already continued along to Exeter Mills but found the Appomattox River too deep to ford and could only use the ferry to get across. While many of Ransom's men did cross on

The rebel army retreating from Richmond. (Edwin Forbes)

the ferry boat, Pickett thought it would take too much time so he moved further up river in search of a bridge.

General Devin's division of cavalry were the first to come upon the Confederate's fortified position at the cross roads. General Griffin sent Crawford's division to support them. At 6:30 p.m. the horsemen assaulted the barricades but were thrown back by artillery and infantry fire. They tried unsuccessfully two more times, the last at 8:00 p.m. Darkness brought an end to the attacks. Most of the cavalry went into camp as the other two divisions eventually came up.

After General Robert E. Lee was forced from his headquarters at "Edgehill," he moved eastward toward the city and set up in the McIlwaine house. His adjutant general, Lieutenant Colonel Walter Taylor, was away in Richmond getting married, so he had to act as his own adjutant. Lee's last words to the war department were: "It is absolutely necessary that we abandon our position tonight, or run the risk of being cut off in the morning...."

THE APPOMATTOX CAMPAIGN

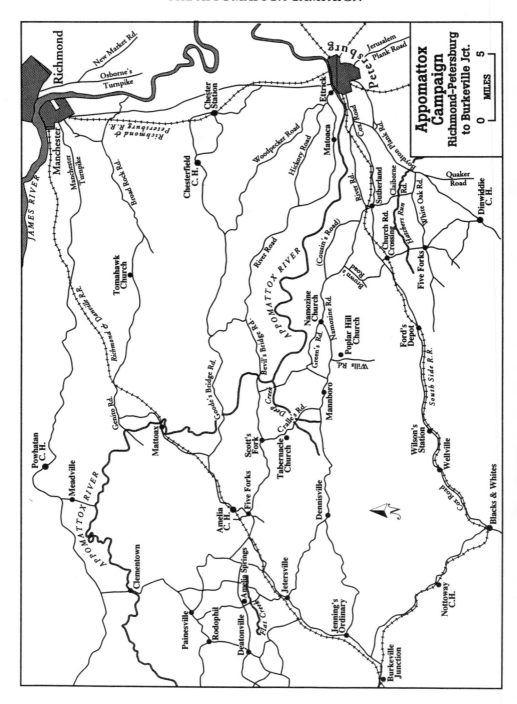

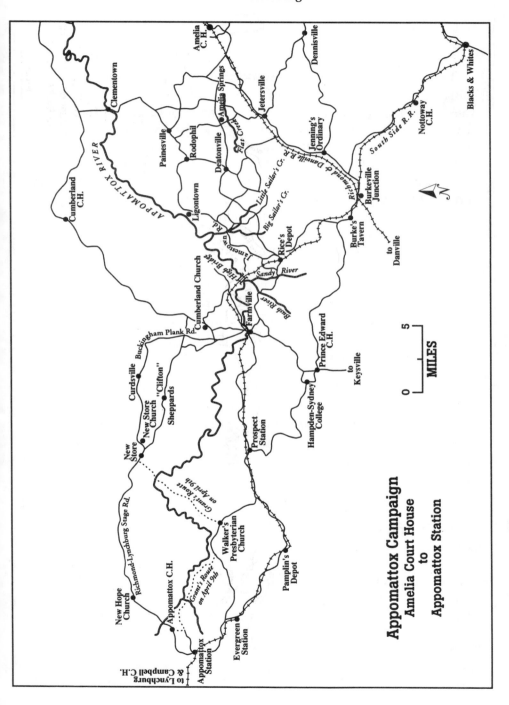

Appomattox Campaign
Amelia Court House
to
Appomattox Station

MILES

At 8:00 p.m., under the cover of darkness, his troops began to quietly evacuate the city. Those troops elsewhere along the lines followed.

Prior to vacating the Richmond and Petersburg fronts, Colonel Thomas M.R. Talcott, commander of the Confederate engineer troops, laid out various routes for a withdrawal. The immediate destination was Amelia Court House on the Richmond Danville Railroad, located thirty-nine miles southwest of Richmond and thirty-six miles northwest of Petersburg.

Those troops at Petersburg, except for Anderson's infantry and Fitz Lee's cavalry, would cross to the north side of the Appomattox River and begin their march. They used four bridges to pass over the river. In the lower area of town some of Gordon's corps and the remaining pickets from the lines crossed on the Pocahontas and Richmond & Petersburg Railroad bridges. To the west, others used Campbell's bridge which lead into the cotton mill village of Ettrick. Finally, those troops holding the western front (some remnants of Field's, Heth's and Wilcox's divisions) used a pontoon bridge laid at the Battersea Cotton Mill which also lead into Ettrick. Lee probably also used this avenue. After his army passed over the river, the commander ordered Pocahontas, the railroad and Campbell's bridges burned. Tobacco warehouses were also set aflame.

General Mahone's division (minus Harris's brigade), holding the Chesterfield front at Bermuda Hundred, fell back on Chester Station and then to Chesterfield Court House. From that point they followed the road to Old Colville and then Goodes' Bridge. Along the way they eventually joined up with Longstreet and Gordon.

In Richmond, Ewell's Reserve Corps was instructed to cross the James into Manchester and then "take the road to Chesterfield below Richmond, taking the road to Branch Church, via Gregory's to Genito Road, via Genito Bridge, to Amelia Court House." Custis Lee's division used a pontoon bridge (Wilton's) from Chaffin's to Drewry's bluff, while Gary's cavalry and Kershaw's division crossed on Mayo's bridge in the city, all others having been destroyed. The provost marshal ordered warehouses filled with tobacco and cotton to be set aflame as the troops began to leave.

George Washington Custis Lee, eldest son of Robert E. Lee.

By 11:00 p.m Confederate President Jefferson Davis and his cabinet left the Richmond & Danville Railroad depot on their journey south. Their immediate destination was Danville, just north of the North Carolina border. Here the president could stay in contact with both Lee's and Johnston's armies.

Accompanying Lee on this movement were about two hundred pieces of artillery and over one thousand wagons. The wagons alone would have occupied thirty miles of road if they had lined up one behind the other on the same route. Lee left behind all heavy artillery but disabled this ordnance before departing. All light artillery, except ten pieces, and some small mortars were taken with the army.

In the evening Generals Meade and Grant set up temporary headquarters at Bank's house along the Boydton Plank Road, just north of the earlier *VI Corps* breakthrough. By dawn they were back in the saddle.

The Death of Confederate General Ambrose P. Hill, April 2, 1865

On March 31, Third Corps commander Ambrose Powell Hill returned to duty at the Petersburg front from sick furlough. Although his military headquarters were located on the western edge of the city at the Widow Knight's residence, "Indiana," he decided to stay in another dwelling with his wife, Dolly, and his two children. This was located across Cox Road from "Indiana" in a cottage on the estate of James M. Venable.

While spending the night of April 1 with his family, in the early morning hours of the 2nd between 2-3 a.m., he heard the sound of heavy artillery fire along the front. From his headquarters, Colonel William H. Palmer, Hill's Chief of Staff, sent out Major William N. Starke, acting adjutant general, to find the cause of the barrage. By daylight he returned with the report "that the enemy had part of our line near Rives' Salient [on the Jerusalem Plank Road], and that matters looked critical on the lines in front of the city."

Before sunrise, General Hill had reported and asked Palmer for reports from Wilcox's and Heth's divisions. Colonel Palmer replied that he had heard nothing except what was reported by Starke. After having his horse saddled, General Hill obtained the services of couriers, Sergeant George W. Tucker, William H. Jenkins, and a soldier by the name of Kirkpatrick. He then rode off to the west for General Lee's headquarters at "Edgehill," the Wil-

liam Turnbull house also along Cox Road.

Upon arriving, Hill instructed Kirkpatrick to ride back to "Indiana" and tell Colonel Palmer to "follow him to the right, and the others of the staff, and couriers, must rally the men on the right." The general then entered the house and reported to General Lee in his room. Colonel Charles S. Venable soon came in and reported wagons were retreating towards town along the Cox Road. General Lee instructed Colonel Venable to reconnoiter the situation while Hill, Tucker, and Jenkins rode along with him.

*   *   *

A mile directly south of "Edgehill," General Horatio Wright's *VI Corps* was preparing to assault the Confederate lines in their front. Formed in echelon, from left to right were: Seymour's 3rd division (two brigades), Getty's 2nd division (three brigades), and Wheaton's 1st division (three brigades). It was 4:40 a.m. when General Wright ordered the attack to begin.

By 5:00 the Federal infantry were over the Confederate entrenchments, through their encampments, and capturing the Boydton Plank Road. Their breakthrough was complete.

As Hill's group left "Edgehill," they crossed to the south of Cox Road and entered the plantation of Thomas Whitworth, passing his residence, "Mayfield," which had earlier been the site of General

Nathaniel Harris's Mississippi brigade's (of Mahone's division) winter encampment. After crossing Cattail Run, which flowed eastward into Old Town or Rohoic Creek, they stopped to water their horses. Soon they came across two Federal infantrymen in the area and captured them. Jenkins took them back to Lee's headquarters.

Seeing Confederate artillery moving along Cox Road to the west, Hill requested Venable to go and put them into position. These turned out to be Lieutenant Colonel William T. Poague's Battalion. Colonel Venable leaped over the branch and left the group, crossing over Long Ordinary Road, a connecting avenue between the Cox and Boydton Plank Roads.

General Hill and Sergeant Tucker soon crossed Long Ordinary Road as they continued on their journey. They next rode through the remainder of General Mahone's division's winter campsite, abandoned on March 15, when Mahone was ordered to the Bermuda Hundred front. The two were now heading for General Heth's headquarters at the Z.W. Pickerall house on Boydton Plank Road. At the edge of the encampment they found a military road which ran from the Cox to the Plank Road. Following it, after crossing a small declivity, they entered the corner of a field, opposite Heth's headquarters. Here they sighted six to eight Federals, two in advance of the others.

Most of the VI Corps began reassembling itself after the breakthrough, while others looted the Confederate winter huts or cut the telegraph wire along the Boydton Plank Road. Some were even more adventuresome. They continued along in small squads across the Plank Road and headed for the South Side Railroad.

Two members of *Company F, 138th Pennsylvania Infantry*, Corporal John W. Mauk and Private Daniel Wolford, were among those advance skirmishers. They soon found Lee's last supply line near a sawmill, after passing to the right of a swamp. The soldiers tore up two rails, fired upon a wagon train, then moved back in the direction of the swamp, located about ½ to ¾ mile from the sawmill.

As they entered the swamp, they saw two men on horseback, Hill and Tucker, coming from the direction of Petersburg. The Confederate horsemen, upon seeing another group of Federal soldiers, turned and rode toward Mauk and Wolford.

Within ten yards of the corporal and private, Hill and Tucker called for them to surrender. Instead, the Union infantrymen fired at the mounted Confederates. General A.P. Hill was hit first in the left thumb, but the bullet then passed through his body over the heart.

Sergeant George Tucker managed to escape, using Hill's horse, and rode toward General Lee's headquarters. On his way he met Colonel Palmer near the Harmon house, along with General Longstreet, his staff, and other members of General Hill's staff, including Major R.J. Wingate, his Assistant Adjutant General. All rode off to advise General Lee of the dreadful news. They found him at the Cox Road in front of Turnbull's residence. The Confederate commander's remark was, "He is at rest, and we who are left are the ones to suffer." Palmer and Tucker were then instructed to go to Venable's cottage and tell Mrs. Hill what had transpired.

The Fifth Alabama Battalion, Provost Guard to General Hill, found the general's body while skirmishing and took it to Venables. From there it was sent to Richmond. Here, while the city was being evacuated, a casket was found for the general. Although the family wanted Hill buried in Hollywood Cemetery, under the circumstance it was impossible. His casket was taken back across the James River into Chesterfield County, and up river to the Hill homestead. Here General Hill was buried in the nearby Winston family cemetery, located close to present day Bon Air. In 1867 he was moved from there and reinterred in Hollywood Cemetery. Again in 1891 his remains were relocated, this time under a monument to him at Laburnum Avenue and Hermitage Roads in Richmond. With this honoring gesture, General Hill was finally put to rest.

CHAPTER III

Rendezvous at Amelia Court House

April 3- 4

As the contingents of the Confederate army reached Amelia Court House, the men were to receive food and supplies to allow them to continue toward their objective. This was still to follow the Richmond & Danville Railroad into North Carolina and then join up with Johnston and the Army of Tennessee. Lee had about 55-58,000 effectives, in total, on this, his final campaign.

Making an all night march on the 2nd-3rd, Lee's troops successfully evacuated the Richmond-Petersburg fronts. Gordon, after getting across the Appomattox River, proceeded along Hickory Road while his wagon train followed the parallel Woodpecker Road to the north. Longstreet, with whom Lee rode, took the River Road which passed through the cotton mill village of Matoaca.

Lee's army was generally able to move unmolested this day as elements of Grant's army occupied the former Southern strongholds. This provided an advantage to Lee's columns since the Federals would not pursue them directly along these routes of their retreat.

Early in the morning of the 3rd, Union troops began entering the two cities. Into Richmond marched Bvt. Major General August Kautz's division of Major General Godfrey Weitzel's

Union troops entering Richmond. (Edwin Forbes)

XXV Corps and Brigadier General Charles Devens' division of the *XXIV Corps*. What they found was a general conflagration and mob rule.

It seemed that as Ewell's troops were departing the Confederate capital under darkness, fires set in the riverfront warehouses began spreading to other buildings in the district. The area on fire centered along the streets south of the capitol building and north of the James. Large groups of unruly citizens were breaking into businesses and warehouses, adding to the havoc. While some of Kershaw's and Gary's troops tried to quell the rabble, they were generally unsuccessful. Eventually the Confederate troops withdrew across the river to Manchester and left the fate of the city to the incoming Federal army. Mayo's bridge was set to the torch as the last of Gary's troopers passed over to the south side.

Around 5:30 a.m. General Weitzel, who commanded the *Army of the James* facing Richmond in Ord's absence, sent an envoy to receive the surrender of the city. A flag of truce carried by a small group along Osborne Turnpike was delivered by Mayor Joseph Mayo and others to one of Weitzel's staff officers and provost guard Major Atherson H. Stevens. The party then continued into Richmond where Stevens placed two guidons of the *4th Massachusetts Cavalry* on top of the former Confederate capitol building.

Back in the main Union lines southeast of the city, the Federal troops prepared to move in. Devens' division followed the New Market Road while Kautz's *United States Colored Troops* took the Osborne Turnpike. At 8:15 a.m. General Weitzel reached the capitol square and ordered his troops into action. Devens ordered his men to extinguish the fires. Kautz moved his troops into the forts nearest the city and across the river into Manchester. Weitzel noted in his report to Grant that "The people received us with enthusiastic expressions of joy."

To the south, Major General George L. Hartsuff's command from the Defenses of Bermuda Hundred advanced on the Howlett line, only to find it evacuated. The next day they were ordered by Grant to assume control of Petersburg, City Point, and the surrounding area.

East of Petersburg, the command of Bvt. Colonel Ralph Ely of Willcox's *IX Corps* division began to pass through the deserted Confederate lines in their sector about 3:10 a.m. Seeing the famous clock tower of the city's courthouse in the distance, two of his regiments, the *1st Michigan Sharp Shooters* and the *2nd Michigan Infantry*, rushed into the town. The sharp shooters reached the courthouse first and a member of the unit climbed up into the clock tower. Opening one of the glass faces, he thrust out the regimental United States colors, the first raised over Petersburg in four years. It was 4:28 a.m. A half block away, the *2nd Michigan* raised its colors from the roof of the Customs House.

South of Petersburg, some of General Hartranft's troops reached the city limits at 4:15 a.m. and proceeded forward, the *200th Pennsylvania* claiming to be the first to enter the city. They were also joined by Bvt. Brigadier General Joseph E. Hamblin's brigade of the *VI Corps*. Hartranft eventually ran into Colonel Ely who informed him the city had already been surrendered. The *IX Corps* division commander then withdrew his troops to the outskirts.

Petersburg's mayor, William W. Townes, along with a member of the Common Council, headed for the western outskirts of Petersburg, where they ran into Federal soldiers advancing from their lines west of Rohoic Creek. Eventually they were led to Colonel Oliver Edwards, a brigade commander of the *VI Corps*, and "officially" surrendered the town to him. The note handed to him read: "The city of Petersburg having been evacuated by the Confederate troops, we, a committee authorized by the Common Council, do hereby surrender the city to U.S. forces, with a request for the protection of the persons and property of its inhabitants."

A little after 8:00 a.m. General Meade rode into the city. After looking around, he found General Grant at the home of Thomas Wallace on Market Street. They tried to determine Lee's possible strategy. Grant decided that Lee would retreat along the Richmond & Danville Railroad. Therefore, to stop the Army of Northern Virginia from reaching North Carolina, the Union commander should not follow him but rather cut him off from that avenue of escape.

Meade soon left the Wallace house although later President Lincoln and his staff found Grant still there. After greeting each other, Lincoln said "Do you know, general, I had a sort of sneaking idea all along that you intended to do something like this; but I thought some time ago that you would so manoeuver as to have Sherman come up and be near enough to cooperate with you." Grant replied, "Yes, I thought at one time that Sherman's army might advance far enough to be in supporting distance of the Eastern armies when the spring campaign against Lee opened; but I had a feeling that it would be better to let Lee's old antagonists give his army the final blow, and finish the job. If the Western troops were even to put in an appearance against Lee's army, it might give some of our politicians a chance to stir up sectional feeling in claiming everything for the troops from their own section of the country. The Western armies have been successful in their campaigns, and it is due to the Eastern armies to let them vanquish their old enemy single-handed."

In their discussion of events at Wallace's dwelling, Lincoln brought up his plans for reconstruction and that he intended to pursue a lenient policy toward the South. Shortly thereafter,

Lincoln left to tour the city while Grant headed westward after his army.

The most logical place for Grant to cut off Lee's path of retreat was Burkeville Junction where the South Side and Richmond & Danville Railroads crossed. From Petersburg via Amelia to Burkeville, which would be Lee's eventual route, was fifty-five miles. Grant's intended course by way of Sutherland Station and the Namozine Road, was thirty-six miles. Grant had a nineteen mile advantage if all went as planned.

*　　　*　　　*

The first problem that confronted the Southern troops on the march was that all, except for Anderson and Fitz Lee's commands, would have to recross the Appomattox River in order to get to Amelia Court House. Previous plans had been made for three bridge crossings: one at Genito, one at Goodes and the other at Bevil's. Unfortunately, the spring flooding made the approaches to Bevil's impassable and failure to get a pontoon bridge to Genito caused complications there.

Joining Mahone's division on his march were Confederate marines and sailors from the Drewry's Bluff garrison, commanded by Commodore John Randolph Tucker. Their admiral, Raphael Semmes, had taken some of the seamen to Manchester where they caught the last train out of the city to Danville. Before leaving their post, the seamen were armed as infantry and ordered to destroy their vessels. The men set fire to their four ironclads. With a tremendous series of explosions, the ironclads *Virginia*, *Torpedo*, *Richmond* and *Fredericksburg* were blown up, and the wooden ships *Raleigh*, *Hampton* and *Nansemond* of the James River Squadron ceased to exist.

As General Lee and Longstreet rode along the Bevil's Bridge Road (which River Road leads into), they came to the terminus of the Clover Hill Railroad, part of a local coal mining operation. Just off the road was Clover Hill, home of Judge James H. Cox. This gentleman extended an invitation to the generals and their staffs to dine with him. Mint julips were offered but Lee declined. He had ice water instead.

Judge Cox's young daughter, Kate, noticed General Longstreet was having difficulty eating because of the wounded right

Commodore John Randolph Tucker commanded sailors and marines with Ewell's corps.

arm he had received at the Wilderness. His plate was being brought to her so that she might cut up the food, when her father told her to go sit next to Longstreet. General Lee kindly remarked, "No, don't leave me."

After dinner Kate prepared coffee for the generals. They had to ask for cream since they had not had full strength coffee for quite some time. The brief respite was one of the last they received in the forthcoming week.

Shortly thereafter, Lee learned from the advance elements of his army that Bevil's Bridge was impassable. This posed a serious problem as the route was the most direct into Amelia Court House. Longstreet and Gordon were to have used this crossing, while Mahone, along with his and Gordon's wagons, were to cross at Goode's. Ewell still planned to utilize the pontoon bridge at Genito Crossing. Now, the only thing Lee could do was send Longstreet and Gordon further north to cross at Goode's with the others. The column then turned in that direction and headed for the Goode's Bridge Road.

Custis Lee and Kershaw united their forces outside Manchester and then Ewells' command moved out toward Amelia Court House. Once they reached the Genito Road and turned north on it, they proceeded to Tomahawk Baptist Church, where the men went into camp.

Custis Lee's wagon train took a different route than his division. It left via the Manchester Turnpike, followed the Buckingham Road through Coalfield Station, and then eventually passed Powhatan Court House and Meadville. Near the latter place it was to cross the Appomattox River and rejoin its command.

By evening of the 3rd, most of Longstreet's men were in camp west of Goode's Bridge after crossing the river, with Gordon's east of it. It had been a time consuming process to get all his troops across this one passage, although Lee did have the help of some adjoining pontoon bridges. The commanding general camped somewhere near Hebron Church, a short distance east of the bridge.

Behind him, and west of Chesterfield Court House on Captain Flournoy's place, Mahone and his troops stopped for the night. Generally speaking, the Southern army had marched twenty-one miles on their first day away from the trenches of Richmond and Petersburg.

*   *   *

While Lee and those troops with him did not have to deal with the enemy on this day, the same could not be said for Anderson and Fitz Lee. The night before, after skirmishing with the Federal cavalry at Scott's Cross Roads, Bushrod Johnson moved his troops westward along the Namozine Road across nearby Namozine Creek. By 2:00 a.m. the Confederates were safely over the fifty-foot wide stream.

On the morning of the 3rd, Sheridan put Custer's division in the van since Devin covered that post the day before. His troopers moved past their comrades and pushed for the Namozine Road, turning to follow the Confederate column. Colonel William Wells' brigade led the column.

Earlier, at 1:00 a.m., Johnson received a dispatch from General Anderson at his Namozine Presbyterian Church headquarters. It contained instructions for the movements of his division into Amelia Court House. General Robert's North Carolina cavalry brigade, along with some infantry, were to act as the rearguard

Cavalry pursuing General Lee's army. (Edwin Forbes)

and erect a defensive position on the west bank of Namozine Creek.

In the early morning Custer appeared on the opposite bank to face Roberts. Firing canister from *Lord's Battery (A, 2nd U.S.)* to keep the Southern rearguard occupied, the *1st Vermont Cavalry* crossed the creek further down and hit Roberts' position on their flank, causing them to retreat. Sheridan's men then forded Namozine Creek without further resistance.

About five miles further down the road at Namozine Church, "Rooney" Lee's cavalry made another stand. This time they were under the command of General Rufus Barringer who had relieved Roberts from his rearguard post. The general placed his three Tarheel regiments at the church to stop the forthcoming Union cavalry. At the church itself was the 5th North Carolina, while the 2nd and 1st regiments covered the adjacent intersection of Green's, Cousin's and Namozine Roads to the north. One gun of McGregor's Battery also assisted this battle line of about 800 men. The 3rd North Carolina was guarding the wagon train and so was not present.

The first of Custer's units to come upon Barringer's stand was the *8th New York Cavalry*. After briefly probing the enemy position and falling back, they were joined by the *1st Vermont*. This time both regiments attacked, the *8th* swinging around on

Brig. Gen. Rufus Barringer was captured near Namozine Church on April 3.

the left flank of the North Carolinians' line. The Confederate general, seeing this, ordered the 2nd North Carolina to counter-attack. This effort proved futile as his 1st regiment was out-flanked and breaking. Orders were given to the 5th North Carolina at the church to fall back and regain their horses, but keep up the skirmish in their retreat.

Custer's two regiments were joined by a third, the *15th New York.* As they entered the action, Barringer's men broke and either fell back or surrendered. Captured were 350 men and 100 horses, including McGregor's one gun. The battleflag of the 2nd North Carolina was taken by Tom Custer, the general's brother, for which he later received the Medal of Honor.

As the remaining Tarheels retired down Green's Road, which eventually led to the Bevil's Bridge Road, Barringer and some of his staff became separated from the 5th regiment and rode about six miles down Cousin's Road. Encountering what appeared to be friendly cavalry pickets, Barringer rode up to them to find either General Fitzhugh or "Rooney" Lee. The others were some of Sheridan's scouts dressed in Confederate uniforms under the command of Major Henry Young. Before they realized what was happening, General Barringer and his men were taken prisoners. The next day, after spending the night in Sheridan's head-quarters at Mrs. Cousins', they started the forty-five mile trek

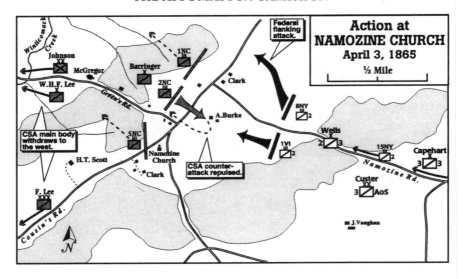

Action at
NAMOZINE CHURCH
April 3, 1865
½ Mile

back to Petersburg. Eventually, the men were sent to City Point and then off to prison.

In front of Barringer's and Robert's rearguard were marching or riding the rest of Anderson's and Fitz Lee's forces. Johnson's division and "Rooney" Lee's brigade had followed Green's Road, turning onto it at Namozine Church. The rest of the cavalry, Fitz Lee's old division (now Munford's) and Rosser's division continued along Cousin's Road. This by-way through Amelia County was merely an extension of Namozine Road. At its junction with Cralle's (or Crawley's) Road, the troops turned northward to the bridge over Deep Creek.

As Custer marshaled his division around the church, he dispatched Well's brigade after Fitz Lee and Capehart's brigade following "Rooney" Lee. Pennington was to hold some of his regiments in reserve at the cross roads, while the rest went to support the other brigades. By 1:00 p.m. those pursuing the Confederates up Green's Road reached the crossing of Deep Creek, after having carried on a running skirmish all the way.

After marching up Green's Road a distance, Johnson's division was ordered by Anderson to take the next road left and return to Namozine (or Cousin's) Road. The reason for this was that the bridge over Deep Creek at Green's Road crossing was found to be impassable. Upon reaching the Namozine Road and

Union cavalry in the Appomattox campaign, as sketched by Edwin Forbes.

pushing aside some Federal cavalry, Johnson joined up with Fitz Lee's command and followed it. Near the small settlement of Mannboro, Custer's cavalry came in contact again with the Confederate column. This time the Southern infantry made a stand. Johnson placed Moody's, Wallace's and Wise's brigades in line to stop them. After another running fight, which ended at Sweathouse Creek, the Federals stopped their advance. The Southerners moved on and crossed Deep Creek at Brown's Bridge along Cralle's Road, passed Tabernacle Methodist Church, then went into camp in the vicinity of the Bevil's Bridge Road intersection. Here the remnants of General Pickett's division rejoined the army.

Those of Pickett's command which did not cross the river earlier at Exeter Mills continued up the south (or western) bank of the Appomattox River to Bevil's Bridge Road. They then followed it in the direction of Amelia to its intersection with Cralle's Road. In the evening, Eppa Hunton's brigade rejoined Pickett's division.

On the Federal side, Custer went into bivouac along Sweathouse Creek. General Wesley Merritt, who followed the others up Green's Road, informed Sheridan of the situation in his front just south of Deep Creek. From his headquarters at Dr. Taylors', he said that it appeared the Confederates might be heading east toward Bevil's Bridge to cross the Appomattox. He suggested the next day the cavalry move upon Amelia Court House. He did not know that the Deep Creek Bridge was impassable.

At 4:10 p.m. General Sheridan, now at Namozine Church, reported "up to this hour we have taken about 1,200 prisoners, mostly of A.P. Hill's corps, and all accounts report the woods filled with deserters and stragglers, principally of this corps." What he was probably referring to were the remnants of Heth's and Wilcox's commands which escaped from Sutherland Church the day before.

Back along the Namozine Road and behind the Union cavalry, marched Griffin's *V Corps*, still under the command of Sheridan. They would push as far as the crossing of Deep Creek over this torn up and muddied roadway before going into camp. Behind them on the same route was Humphreys' *II Corps* and then Wright's *VI Corps*. The majority of the *II Corps* set up their encampment on the Coleman Farm near Winticomack Creek, with Hays' division, three miles in the rear, near Namozine Church. Wright bivouaced around Mount Pleasant Church along Namozine Road, just west of where River Road entered.

Further south, and along the Cox Road which generally paralleled the South Side Railroad, moved Ord's *Army of the James* with Turner's division in advance. They completed the day, stopping about three miles west of Sutherland Station. Coming out of Petersburg behind them was Parke's *IX Corps*. Leaving Willcox's division to garrison the city, the other two divisions (Griffin's and Hartranft's) followed behind the *VI Corps* on the River Road and went into camp in the vicinity of Sutherland's. Nearby were the command posts of both Generals Grant and Meade who would be sending about 76,000 effectives after Lee's army.

Earlier in the day, before leaving Petersburg, Grant sent a message to General Sheridan with instructions that "The first object of present movement will be to intercept Lee's army, and the second to secure Burkeville." That night, upon reaching Sutherland Station, the commanding general communicated with General Sherman in North Carolina: "The troops from Petersburg, as well as those from Richmond, retreated between the two rivers, and there is every indication that they will endeavor to secure Burkeville and Danville. ... It is also my intention to take Burkeville and hold it until it is seen whether it is a part of Lee's plan to hold Lynchburg and Danville. ... Should Lee go to Lynchburg with his whole force and I get Burkeville there will be no special use in you going any farther into the interior of North Carolina."

As darkness fell over the troops which stayed south of the Appomattox on the 3rd, Namozine Church and local homes served as hospitals for the wounded of that day's actions. Most were eventually transported to a major Federal hospital center set up later at Burkeville Junction.

*   *   *

At dawn on Tuesday the 4th, Longstreet's troops finished crossing at Goode's Bridge and marched toward Amelia Court House, eight and a half miles to the west. Early in the morning, General Lee, after not hearing from his Richmond column, sent a messenger to find General Ewell. He was to tell him to cross the Appomattox River wherever he could and head for Amelia Court House. Should he too have to use the Goode's Bridge crossing, the commanding general ordered Mahone to remain at the site until he learned that Ewell was safely across. General Lee then rode off to join Longstreet's column.

As the Confederate soldiers began to fill the streets of the county seat, they found a relatively small settlement. Twenty years earlier a visitor to the court house said it consisted of "county buildings, several dwelling houses, one tavern, and several mechanics. The population was 40." Lee and his officers soon arrived and headed for the railroad station on the Richmond & Danville Railroad. Here they opened the waiting boxcars only to find large amounts of ordnance stores but no subsistence. There had been a reserve of 350,000 rations in Richmond which were supposed to have been sent here but somehow they had not arrived. It seems there were a series of mix-ups in transmitting orders back and forth to the capital on April 2nd. Now Lee's men would have to rely on what was in their own wagon trains. Knowing his men could not go on without extra food for their long march to North Carolina, the commanding general issued a proclamation to the local citizens for help.

> Amelia C.H., April 4, 1865

> To the Citizens of Amelia County, Va.

> The Army of Northern Virginia arrived here today, expecting to find plenty of provisions, which had been ordered to be placed here by the railroad several days since, but to my surprise and regret I find not a pound of subsistence for man or horse. I must therefore appeal to your generosity and charity to supply as far as each one is able the wants of the brave soldiers who have battled for your liberty for four years. We require meat, beef, cattle, sheep, hogs, flour, meal, corn, and provender in any quantity that can be spared. The quartermaster of the army will visit you and make arrangements to pay for what he receives or give the proper vouchers or certificates. I feel assured that all will give to the extent of their means.

> R.E. Lee, General

At the same time he ordered 200,000 rations to be sent up the railroad from Danville to sustain the troops while waiting for a response from surrounding farmers.

During the day, Brigadier General William Nelson Pendleton, commander of the Confederate artillery, was ordered to pare down the number of guns that followed the army. Colonel James Lawrence Corley, Lee's chief quartermaster, did likewise with his wagon train. The surplus cannon and wagons were to follow a more northeasterly route than the army to Danville.

South of Amelia Court House, those who escaped the debacles at Five Forks and Sutherland Station started to arrive in the area. By 4:00 p.m. some elements of Heth's and Wilcox's divisions began to wander into the village. Behind them came Anderson and Fitz Lee who were still skirmishing with enemy cavalry.

After crossing Deep Creek at Brown's Bridge in the morning, General Merritt, with Devin's division, moved forward to reconnoiter. Running into the enemy near Tabernacle Church, the Federal cavalry continued to press them past Drummond's Mill and then across Beaverpond Creek. Still pushing the

Confederate rearguard, they found them eventually covering the main road to Amelia Court House. Stagg's and Fitzhugh's brigades skirmished with the Southerners, who proved to be portions of Heth's, Pickett's and Johnson's infantry. This lasted until around 10:00 p.m. when Devin's men withdrew, but only after burning the nearby mill.

That night Anderson and Fitz Lee remained where they were—near Washington Academy at the junction of Bevil's Bridge and Tabernacle Church Roads.

By this time it was becoming apparent to the Federal commanders that Lee was indeed concentrating his army at Amelia Court House. Merritt rejoined the rest of the cavalry who were riding westward along the Namozine Road.

The day before, Ranald Mackenzie's small cavalry division spent most of the day picking up prisoners near Leonard's Mill. That evening they rode near Deep Creek along the Namozine Road and into camp. On the 4th they crossed the creek and reached the Five Forks of Amelia County, located about a mile south of the Court House. Here the *1st Maryland Cavalry* (U.S.) skirmished with the 14th Virginia Cavalry, which Lee had sent to scout the Avery Church Road (one of the branches of Five Forks). Finding the Federals so close, they fell back to the village. Mackenzie went into bivouac at the forks.

In Amelia Court House, General Lee camped in the yard of Mrs. Francis L. Smith, a refugee from Alexandria. While here he received a report on Ewell's column. His men had reached the Genito Bridge crossing over the Appomattox River but the pontoons had not been laid as expected. Consequently, they moved in a southerly direction until they reached the Richmond & Danville Railroad. Using its bridge across the river at Mattoax Station, the men placed planks on top of the rails. Before they could cross over, however, they had to wait until a large artillery train crossed. Upon reaching the western bank the command went into camp about a mile beyond near a plantation called "The Oaks."

Gordon's Corps waited for Ewell's column five miles east of Amelia Court House at Scott's Shop while Mahone was ordered to go ahead and cross at Goode's bridge. He then proceeded to the village after he was informed of the Richmond contingent's passage over the river.

On the morning of the 4th, Sheridan ordered General Crook's division to ride for the Richmond & Danville Railroad where he was to strike at Jennings' Ordinary, located halfway between Burkeville Junction and Jetersville Station. Crook was to then move up to the latter place. At the same time, the rest of the cavalry, followed closely by the *V Corps*, passed through Dennisville and then turned north toward Jetersville. Arriving there about 5:00 p.m., Sheridan had the infantry begin entrenching across the railroad. The cavalry commander was now sure that Lee and his army were at Amelia Court House and would have to pass through Jetersville to get to Danville. While here, Sheridan intercepted the message sent by Lee to Danville for the 200,000 rations.

The *II* and *VI Corps* moved along the same route this day as Sheridan's troopers. In fact, from 11:00 a.m. to 7:00 p.m., Humphreys' corps was held up from making much progress along the road by the cavalry's movements. Consequently, they only marched as far as W.W. Jones' farm on Namozine Road where it crossed Deep Creek. Here they received orders to proceed to Jetersville early the next morning. The *VI Corps* moved only a short distance on this day, camping near Mr. Featherston's, two miles beyond Winticomack Creek.

Following along Cox Road and the South Side Railroad, Ord's command continued their march. They reached Wilson's Station after a fifteen-mile trek.

Having followed the *VI Corps* until 3:30 p.m. along the Namozine Road, Parke's men were ordered to the Cox Road to fall in behind Ord's troops. Their purpose was to guard wagon trains and picket the railroad to the rear of the army, near Ford's Depot. Apparently, at least some of this corps was given the assignment to realign the rail gauge on the South Side. As the army headed westward, Grant would need to send his U.S. Military Railroad rolling stock behind the army to deliver supplies and to evacuate his casualties. The South Side Railroad was 5-foot gauge, whereas the Federal army's trains required a narrower one. The rails had to be lifted and reset to accommodate Grant's machinery, a task probably given to the *IX Corps* soldiers. Consequently, Parke's men were not actively engaged in the Appomattox campaign. Eventually they were spread out from Sutherland Station to Farmville on picket duty.

In the evening, from his headquarters at Wilson's Station on the South Side, General Grant sent a dispatch to Secretary of War Edwin M. Stanton. "All of the enemy that retain anything like organization have gone north of the Appomattox, and are apparently heading for Lynchburg."

Still not cognizant of Lee's exact plans, the commanding general communicated with Sheridan after interrogating a captured engineer from the South Side Railroad. Among the things he reported was that two trainloads of supplies were sent up the road from Burkeville to Farmville. Grant added, "It was understood that Lee was accompanying his troops and that he was bound for Danville by way of Farmville. Unless you have information more positive of the movements of the enemy push on with all dispatch to Farmville and try to intercept the enemy there."

The Geography of Southside Virginia

Southside Virginia, is that portion of the state which lies below the James River and extends to the North Carolina border. It is made up of two physiographic (natural) regions: the eastern Coastal Plain, better known as Tidewater, and the mid-section, called the Piedmont. The former extends from the coast to the fall zone while the latter extends westward to the Ridge and Valley Province which is Southside's western boundary. The fall zone elevation ranges from 100 to 300 feet above sea level near Petersburg, and in the Piedmont elevations reach between 700 and 800 feet at Appomattox. Willis Mountain, in Buckingham County, is the highest prominence with an elevation of 1,159 feet. Southside is comprised of the James River Basin, which includes the Appomattox River, and the Chowan River Basin, embracing the Nottoway, Blackwater, and Meherrin Rivers.

The average temperature in the region ranges around 39 degrees in January, to 79 degrees in July. Precipitation averages about 45 inches per year.

In 1860, the twenty-four counties which made up the Tidewater/Piedmont regions had a total population of 373,174. Broken down by race, this figure includes 162,738 Whites (44%), and 210,436 Blacks (56%).

The soils found in the area are generally clay and sandy loam, with the Appling, Atlee, Cecil, Duplin, Durham, Madison and Norfolk varieties prevailing. Minerals found include Granite and Kyanite, while coal was mined in Chesterfield County during the 19th Century.

Loblolly, Short Leaf, and Virginia Pine are in abundance, along with numerous species of hardwoods, making timbering a major livelihood for many.

Southside was and still is largely agricultural in nature, with dark leaf tobacco, hogs, wheat, and corn being the major crops during the ante-bellum period. Cotton and peanuts became more abundant during the post-war years, particularly in the counties south of Petersburg.

In 1860 the City of Petersburg was the second largest in Virginia, the eleventh largest in the South, and 50th in the United States, with a population of 18,266 residents. 47% of the total population were African-Americans; 53% White. Of the 47% Black population, 16% (or 3,164) of those were free Blacks, thus making Petersburg the city with the largest concentration of free Blacks in the South. Many of the freedmen prospered as barbers, blacksmiths, boatmen, draymen, livery stable keepers, and caterers. In the communities of Blandford and Pocahontas, located within the city limits, lived free Blacks wealthy enough to own considerable property.

During the war years, in manufacturing wealth Petersburg was 49th in the country. Some of the industries included tobacco factories, along with numerous cotton and flour mills. Most of the cotton mills were located on the Appomattox River in the nearby villages of Ettrick and Matoaca. Because the city was the main commercial and railroad center for Southside, there were locomotive shops and iron works located here.

Since Petersburg was located at the head of navigation on the fall line of the Appomattox River, this waterway was passible up to the city. With a 12 foot channel, and river about 80 feet wide, a port and customs house were established in the city.

In the thirty years prior to the war, Petersburg's population exploded and the city could boast many modern conveniences of that time. The streets and homes were illuminated with gas lighting, and there was a gravity fed municipal water system, complete with fire hydrants, and a volunteer fire department to man them. Many of the streets were paved with cobblestones, and the sidewalks were bricked. A well run city government also presided over the daily operations of Petersburg.

To help with the Confederate war effort, Petersburg provided many hospitals throughout the four years of conflict. Other war related industries included a Lead Works, a Copper and Zinc Works, a wagon repair shop, and Niter Beds for the production of gun powder, along with a Confederate Navy Powder Works and Navy Rope Works.

Upon departing the Richmond - Petersburg front on April 3rd, the two armies would pass through the following Southside counties during the final campaign: Chesterfield,

Dinwiddie, Amelia, Nottoway, Powhatan, Prince Edward, Cumberland, Buckingham, and Appomattox. All but Nottoway have a common boundary with the Appomattox River.

Since the soldiers had not advanced through this region before, many commented on its beauty. "The country was enchanting; the peach orchards were blossoming in the southern spring, the fields had been peacefully ploughed for the coming crops, the buds were beginning to swell, and a touch of verdue was perceptible on the hills and along the hillsides. The atmosphere was balmy and odorous, the hamlets were unburnt, the farmhouses inhabited, the farms all tilled."

Once the surrender took place, the area was occupied by the Union soldiers who acted as provost guards. One particular soldier, stationed at Nottoway Court House, remembered, "Fruit trees are all in bloom. I presume there is an abundance of peaches. Tobacco is raised in great quantities, some farms have four, five and six tobacco houses on them. A man could do worse than to come here and live....any quantity of fine pine land on the Nottoway [River] could be had for a low price."

Fortunately today, the beautiful rural setting of this area still remains much as it did in those tumultuous days in the spring of 1865.

The Capture of General Rufus Barringer near Namozine Church

After his rearguard stand was broken by Custer's cavalry at Namozine Church on April 3, Confederate General Rufus Barringer managed to escape with about 110 of his men, many of whom were dismounted after losing their horses. Riding cross country for about six miles with his staff and Captain Tidwell, Barringer continued to look for the rest of the brigade and his commander, General W.H.F. Lee. Suddenly, he came upon members of the 1st North Carolina in conversation with a group of other Southern cavalrymen who said they were from the 9th Virginia. As close as can be determined, this was on the road from Boydton to Blacks & Whites, known locally as Wills Road and near Poplar Hill Church.

It was late in the evening when these "Virginians" let it be known who they really were. They were actually Union spies of Major Henry Young's command dressed as Southern soldiers. One tar heel remembered what happened next: "we all looked down cocked pistols drawn from their cavalry boots, and were ordered to surrender." General Barringer tried to wheel his horse and ride away when Young dropped his hand on the bridle rein of the generals' horse with the remark, "General, we do not want to kill you." The real Confederates around their commander began to work the actions of their weapons. Major Young then remarked, "If you can kill us and not your own men, fire away."

He then ordered the North Carolinians to "ride like hell."

The general was taken, along with Lieutenant Frederick C. Foard, Sergeant Major William R. Webb, Sergeant Stephen O. Terry and L.F. Brown, by Major Young and Sergeant J.E. McCable to General Sheridan's headquarters. This was at Mrs. Cousin's house on the Namozine Road. Reaching there about 10:00 p.m., all were temporarily paroled and allowed to rest after having dinner with the Federal cavalry commander, his staff and Mrs. Cousin.

Others captured in the area were also brought in, including Major R.E. Foote of Bushrod Johnson's staff, and adjutant-general Major James Dugue Ferguson of Fitzhugh Lee's staff. The next morning, most of the Confederate officers were invited to a breakfast of biscuits and coffee with Sheridan.

Sergeant McCable remembered that when Barringer was captured he was riding a horse which had been taken earlier from Union General George Crook, and so presented it to Sheridan. Evidently the cavalry commander declined the offer, since Barringer rode his horse back to Petersburg.

As the captured officers began their trip back to City Point, they were riding and walking against the procession of Union infantry, artillery and wagons which were moving on the same road. One member of their party, Major Foote, saw General Meade ride past and yelled to him, "General Meade, I saw General [Henry] Wise yesterday and he is very well" (the Union commander and Wise had married sisters). Foote then introduced Barringer to him. General Meade offered the North Carolinian some greenbacks to take with him to prison, but the general refused. He did ask for one favor though. This was to be allowed to communicate with friends who could supply his wants while a prisoner.

Meade noticed that Sheridan had placed only a corporal over the Confederate officers and immediately ordered a general officer to take his place, instructing him to tell the provost marshal in City Point that Barringer could reach anybody he wanted. The men continued on the forty-five mile journey to Petersburg, and from there another nine miles to City Point. Rufus Barringer was the first captured general to be taken to City Point. Barringer noted of his ride: "Passed through nearly the whole of Grants army fine looking men magnificently equipped—sufficient transportation. Treated respectfully except by the 9t Corps—a little noisy. Introduced to Gens Meade, Wright & Sheridan."

On April 5 General Barringer met with the post commander of City Point, Major General Charles H.T. Collis, along with President Abraham Lincoln. The president talked of his days in congress when he served with the general's brother, Daniel Moreau, before the war. He also asked Barringer, "Do you think I could be of any service to you?" In turn, he wrote a card introducing the Confederate general and said his brother was a very good friend of his. He requested that his prison stay be made as "comfortable as possible under the circumstances."

Barringer himself noted in his diary of the occasion: "Dined with Brig. Gen. Collins [sic] Called to see Mr. Lincoln at Gen. Grant's H. Qtrs—Pleased with him. His leadership & manners have been misrepresented [by the] South. Gave me a card to Mr. Staunton [Secretary of War Edwin Stanton]."

The general was first sent to the Capital Prison in Washington, then to Fort Delaware on Pea Patch Island in the Delaware River. He was released from prison on July the 25th and arrived home August 8.

CHAPTER IV

A Roadblock at Jetersville Causes a Change in Plans

April 5

As the forage wagons began returning to the village of the Court House on the rainy Wednesday morning of the 5th, Lee saw that little subsistence had come in from the area residents. Not only had he failed to feed his army, but more importantly he had lost his day's lead on Grant's forces. He later lamented, "This delay was fatal and could not be retrieved." At 1:00 p.m. his commanders set about putting the army in motion, heading down the railroad toward Danville and its next station, Jetersville.

Earlier, at 11:00 a.m., his Reserve Artillery and wagon train under the command of Brigadier General Rueben Lindsay Walker began its northwesterly journey toward the Clementown bridge crossing of the Appomattox. Before leaving, Chief of Artillery General William N. Pendleton ordered ninety-five caissons, mostly loaded, to be taken to the southern outskirts of the village and destroyed; the explosion of this ordnance sent to Amelia Court House earlier in the winter was heard for miles.

On the 5th, General Custis Lee's wagon train, having been separated from Ewell's column since leaving Richmond, attempted to reunite with the army. The day before, after failing to find a crossing of the Appomattox near Meadville, it proceeded to Clementown, using the bridge there and going into

Brig. Gen. Henry E. Davies captured the Confederate wagon train at Painesville, April 5.

park. In the morning the train continued its journey to Amelia, passing near the small settlement of Painesville, sometimes called Paines Cross Roads. It was soon within four miles of its destination.

*   *   *

With Sheridan's troopers now at Jetersville, and the *V Corps* strengthening their breastworks perpendicular to the Richmond & Danville Railroad, the cavalry commander informed Generals Meade and Grant about the state of affairs. Later in the day the lieutenant general received this communication: "We can capture the Army of Northern Virginia if force enough can be thrown to this point, and then advance upon it [at Amelia C.H.]."

As the cavalry looked over their surroundings, one horse soldier described Jetersville as "A small village on the railroad of scarcely a dozen buildings, a store or two, Blacksmith shop, Post Office, and small Railroad Depot where were found a few cars, ... The little place wore an air of comfort and respectability." Another soldier, not so impressed, wrote: "[Jetersville] was an insignificant station on the railroad, comprising a half-dozen buildings all told, with nothing to boast of but an old

Union cavalry, including some skirmishing dismounted, capture Confederate artillery and wagons, Painesville, April 5, 1865.

Revolutionary Church, built in some remote period in the history of the state."

In the morning Sheridan also directed General Crook to send General Davies' brigade of cavalry to reconnoiter his left flank and front. Davies rode from Jetersville by way of Amelia Springs, passing through Painesville and encountering Custis Lee's wagon train at a point about four miles beyond. The caravan was guarded by a contingent of white troops and newly recruited black soldiers from Richmond. Apparently the train not only had 20,000 good rations, but also some artillery pieces. Seeing that the Southerners were placing a cannon to fire upon his column, Davies' cavalry charged through a deep swamp and captured the gun, scattering about 400 men of the train guard. He then sent the *1st Pennsylvania* and *24th New York Cavalry* to ride along the length of the train, capturing animals and prisoners while destroying the wagons. Davies then turned back to Jetersville with his spoils, including 11 flags, 320 white and 310 black prisoners (he refers to the latter as "teamsters"), and over 400 animals. He left behind 200 blazing ammunition and baggage wagons, along with accompanying caissons and ambulances.

Maj. Gen. George Gordon Meade, the commander of the Army of the Potomac, *rode in an ambulance sick during most of the campaign.*

On the return ride near Flat Creek, they encountered a small contingent of Confederate artillery from Lieutenant Colonel John Haskell's Battalion. They too were captured along with eight or ten 24 pdr. iron coehorn mortars and five English Whitworth rifled guns of Ramsay's North Carolina Battery (one of these mortars is now on display at Amelia Court House).

When word filtered back to General Lee at Amelia Court House about this attack upon Custis Lee's wagon train, he dispatched Fitz Lee's cavalry (minus W.H.F. Lee's command) after Davies. Finding the burned wagons, Lee pressed on toward Painesville, where he encountered General Martin Gary's small brigade, sent from near Amelia, which had already made contact with Davies' rearguard. Reinforcing the South Carolinian's troopers, they carried on a running fight all the way to Amelia Springs and the crossing of Flat Creek, a distance of about three miles.

As they reached the area of the springs, Rosser's division, supported by Munford, attacked the Federal column. In this deadly encounter of mounted cavalry, about 30 Union troopers were killed, "principally with the sabre," and 150 wounded and captured. The Confederates' loss, although not as heavy, included the mortal wounding of Captain Hugh McGuire, 11th

Virginia Cavalry, and Captain James Rutherford, assistant in-spector-general of Brigadier General James Dearing's staff.

Pursuing Davies to within a mile of Jetersville, the Southern cavalry found the Federals were now supported by Gregg's and Smith's cavalry brigades. Calling off the chase, they fell back toward Amelia Springs and went into camp on the north side of Flat Creek.

Between 2:30 and 3:00 p.m., Humphreys' corps began to arrive at Jetersville. General Meade was with Sheridan at this time but was not feeling well. He requested the cavalry com-mander to place the infantry in battleline. The *II Corps* moved around to the left of the *V Corps* and started building entrench-ments. A few hours later, at 6:00, the head of the *VI Corps* appeared and they were put in line on the right. The three corps now firmly dug in at Jetersville covered a four-mile front facing northeast, with Custer's cavalry eventually guarding the right flank. Devin's division, after a long and tedious night ride, arrived around noon and was first placed on Custer's left. Later after being relieved by the *II Corps*, they rode to the rear of the army and went into bivouac. That night, General Griffin, who until then had been under Sheridan's immediate command, was ordered to report back to General Meade.

In the afternoon Ranald Mackenzie's small cavalry division, with Colonel Andrew Evan's (formerly Spear's) brigade in the lead, continued to skirmish with the Confederates just outside Amelia and beyond Five Forks. Seeing Southern infantry mov-ing three miles west of the village along the Danville Railroad, the Federal troopers made a brief demonstration, causing the enemy to attack. At this point Mackenzie withdrew from the field.

South of this contingent of the Union army and following the South Side Railroad was General Ord's column. Grant was still riding with the *Army of the James* commander when the two stopped to rest at Nottoway Court House. Ord had left Birney's *United States Colored Troops* to guard the railroad behind them at Blacks & Whites (present day Blackstone), while Gibbon's *XXIV Corps* pressed on to Burkeville Junction, which they reached late in the evening, having marched fifty-two miles since leaving Petersburg. Twenty-eight of these miles were on this day.

The Nottoway County seat where the two generals conferred was described by an army newspaper reporter: "The village of Nottoway Court House as it is usually called, is an old, dilapidated looking concern, composed of a few dozens of old unpainted frame houses, and two or three brick ones. The courthouse and surrounding offices are substantial brick edifices, and stand in a pleasantly shaded square, about two hundred yards to the left of the main road going westward. Streets or street Nottoway has not. The road through it is rather more sinuous and cut up by gullies than elsewhere in the neighborhood. A few empty box cars were captured and a few dollars of saddlery trimmings. Nearly all else of value had been removed. ..."

With the South Side Railroad passing through the village, a way station was located here. While Grant and Ord were talking on the porch of an old tavern, "a young staff officer rode up to Ord in a state of considerable excitement, and said: 'Is this a way-station?' The grim old soldier, who was always fond of a quiet joke, replied with great deliberation: 'This is NOTT-A-WAY station.'"

Shortly thereafter the commanding general continued his ride with Ord's column until he reached a point some four miles west of Nottoway and halfway between the county seat and Burkeville. Here the headquarter's escort was approached by a courier.

*   *   *

Leading the army out of Amelia Court House in a southwest direction was Longstreet's corps, with the cavalry in advance. Mahone's division followed, then Anderson with Pickett and Johnson. Back at the Court House, Ewell was just arriving with Kershaw's and Custis Lee's divisions. Tucker's Naval Battalion and Major Francis W. Smith's Battalion of Reserve Artillery from the Howlett Line were added to Custis Lee's division. They did not follow Anderson until later in the day.

Mahone initially lost contact with Longstreet's rear after taking the wrong road out of Amelia Court House. Coming onto General Lee, who informed him of the mistake, he returned to Longstreet's route only to find Federal cavalry had intervened.

These were probably members of Mackenzie's division. Driving them away, Mahone soon regained his position with the main column.

General Lee eventually joined the van of the column after hearing skirmish fire in that front. A mounted cavalry officer riding toward the commander proved to be his son, General "Rooney" Lee. Generals Lee and Longstreet rode into the woods near Jetersville with the cavalry officer to reconnoiter. There appeared to be trouble up ahead that might possibly change their plans to go directly to North Carolina via Burkeville. "Rooney" reported dismounted Federal cavalry across the road and infantry sure to follow (actually the *V Corps* was already there). Should Lee attack and clear the road, or try another alternative? Some of his generals thought he should assail the enemy position since the spirit of the men was still relatively high and not all of Grant's army had yet arrived. Because of the lateness of the day and the fact that Lee's column was so spread out, the general decided to change his original plans. He would make another night march passing north of the Federal left flank, and then head west for Farmville, twenty-three miles away on the South Side Railroad. There he could obtain supplies for his army, then head south and reach the Danville railroad at Keysville. To be successful, once again he would have to outdistance Grant's army. The orders were given and the commanders set their men in motion. Longstreet had to retrace his steps up the railroad before coming to the road the army would then travel upon.

As the Confederates groped through the night, they had to first cross Flat Creek before proceeding through the famous country resort of Amelia (Sulphur) Springs. When the head of the column reached the bridge, they found it collapsed, so time was lost as the engineers of the pioneer corps repaired it for passage of wagons and artillery. The creek itself was fordable so some of the infantry waded across, although it appears that Mahone's division waited until the bridge was repaired.

Nearby General Lee had supper at Richard Anderson's home, "Selma," before riding off to Amelia Springs, two miles away. Here he found Commissary General Isaac St. John waiting. From St. John he learned that 80,000 rations were waiting at Farmville.

These were the trains originally sent to Burkeville but returned after the Federal army advanced on the junction. Lee instructed St. John to proceed to Farmville and prepare for the issuance of rations to his army.

At some point during the night, General Lee received a message intercepted from two of Henry Young's Federal spies dressed in Confederate uniforms. The dispatch was from General Grant to General Ord and across the top was written: "Jetersville, April 5, 1865 - 10:10 P.M." It directed the *Army of the James* commander to take a position where he could watch the roads between Burkeville and Farmville. Lee then knew that Grant was at Jetersville, Ord at Burkeville, and the relative position of both armies.

At some point during the night march from Amelia Court House to Amelia Springs, as Custis Lee's division was moving, there was a tragic accident. A horse tied to a fence rail broke away, causing havoc among the soldiers. Many of Lee's inexperienced men believed that enemy cavalry were attacking and began firing into each other. Before the shooting stopped, Major Frank Smith was mortally wounded and several others seriously injured.

*   *   *

Departing along the road to Burkeville around 6:30 p.m., General Grant's little entourage broke into the woods only to find a courier in Confederate uniform. It was one of Sheridan's scouts who carried a message sent at 3:00 p.m. from the cavalry commander at Jetersville. He related Davies' success earlier in the day and sent a captured letter from a Southern soldier telling of the distress some members of Lee's army were exhibiting:

AMELIA COURT-HOUSE, April 5, 1865

Dear Mamma:

Our army is ruined, I fear. We are all safe as yet. Shyron left us sick. John Taylor is well; saw him yesterday. We are in line of battle this evening. General Robert Lee is in the field near us. My trust is still in the justice of our cause and that of God. General Hill is killed. I saw Murray a few moment since. Bernard Terry [he] said was taken prisoner, but may get out. I send this by a negro I see passing up railroad to Mecklenburg. Love to all.

Your devoted son,
WM. B. TAYLOR
Colonel

Sheridan had ended his own note with: "I wish you were here yourself. I feel confident of capturing the Army of Northern Virginia if we exert ourselves. I see no escape for Lee."

Changing horses from "Jeff Davis" to a fresh mount, "Cincinnati," Grant decided to ride to Sheridan and left the road with the scout, his staff, and a mounted escort of fourteen men. In the moonlight, the commander and his men rode nearly twenty miles cross-country to Jetersville. Arriving about half-past ten, they finally ran into the Federal picket line.

At Sheridan's headquarters on the Childress farm near midnight, the group was served a meal and then Grant with Sheridan sought out General Meade who was still suffering from his cold. Discussing the next days' movements, the lieutenant general directed Meade to advance early in the morning on Amelia Court House. He also emphasized that "it was not the aim only to follow the enemy, but to get ahead of him." In fact, Grant remarked, "He had no doubt Lee was moving right then."

Grant's orders to Meade for operations on the 6th contradicted those given earlier by the *Army of the Potomac* commander. Meade felt that Lee's movements would be by the right flank but Sheridan was convinced he would not remain to be attacked. The events of the 5th clearly showed that Lee would probably operate by way of the left flank. Consequently, the men were given coffee at 4:00 a.m. with a directive to be ready to move at daylight.

The *V Corps* moved toward Amelia along the Danville railroad, with the *II Corps* on the left about a half mile west of it, and the *VI Corps* on the right or eastern side. At the same time Sheridan dispatched his cavalry in the direction of Deatonville, five miles west of the railroad, while Ord was ordered to cut the railroad bridge (High Bridge) over the Appomattox River near Farmville. Mackenzie was returned to Ord's column.

The Almost Battle of Jetersville

The Confederate delay at Amelia Court House not only allowed Grant to gain on the one day lead which Lee still held, but might have cost the Southern general his one chance for a successful movement into North Carolina. It must be remembered that Lee lingered a day in Amelia for his foraging parties to return, and for Ewell's column to arrive and join up with the army.

The delay allowed Sheridan's cavalry, and later Meade's infantry, to deploy across Lee's path of retreat at Jetersville on the evening of April 4. The question is: Should Lee have made an attempt to break through the Federal roadblock and follow the direct line of the Richmond & Danville Railroad into North Carolina?

The answer may be in the arrival times of the armies at Jetersville. Sheridan and the *V Corps* came on the scene and began entrenching about 5 p.m. on the night of April 4. The other Union infantry support did not arrive until the 5th. The head of the *II Corps* reached the area between 2:30-3:00 p.m.; the van of the *VI Corps* not until 6 p.m.

Lee's army did not withdraw from Amelia until the morning of the 5th, and it was not until 1:00 p.m. that Lee himself rode forward the seven miles towards Jetersville to reconnoiter in response to skirmishing he heard up ahead. Lee knew Federal cavalry were across his path and he intended to attack them. According to a witness, General E.P. Alexander, "I never saw General Lee seem so anxious to bring on a battle in my life as he

seemed this afternoon; but a conference with General W.H.F. Lee in command of the cavalry in our front seemed to disappoint him." His son, "Rooney" Lee, reported Sheridan had been reinforced by two infantry corps who were now entrenching.

In retrospect, General Sheridan wrote in May 1865 about the night of April 4: "It seems to me that this was the only chance the Army of Northern Virginia had to save itself, which might have been done had General Lee promptly attacked and driven back the comparatively small force opposed to him and pursued his march to Burkeville Junction."

The *V Corps* artillery commander, Bvt. Brigadier General Charles S. Wainwright, the next day also observed: "In the same position [Jetersville], and Lee said to be still at Amelia, yet no fight. It seems to me queer for Lee must have known that there was only one corps of infantry here, until quite late in the afternoon. I cannot understand it; for it was a grand chance for him, if he has any large force with him. Now we are much too strong for him to break through..."

General William Mahone remembered the situation in Lee's army on the 5th. "Genl Longstreet had now run up against the Federal Calvalry [sic] at Jeters Station [Jetersville]— Genl Lee sent for me to come up to him. I found [him] near Genl Longstreets line of battle on the porch of a farm House. He got out his map and wanted to know what I thought of pressing the fight. It was near sun down, quite sun down in fact. I argued that it was too late in the evening to effect results and that his army was not sufficiently compact to deliver a heavy blow—that he should diverge to the right and as soon as could be done, get his army as compactly [together] as could be and then turn upon the enemy and give him a stunning blow and hasten on his march. To this [he] agreed and directed me to take the diverging road to the North, leading by Amelia Springs...."

In later years, Lee's biographer, Douglas Southall Freeman, had this analogy of the situation. Referring to Lee's decision, he said, "Should he stake everything on one last assault, throw all his men forward, like the 'Old Guard' at Waterloo, and either win a crushing victory or die where the flags went down?" Freeman went on to say, in his opinion, "He [Lee] would have been driving himself into a sack, the neck of which could easily have been closed behind him. The least that could have happened to him would have been the complete loss of his wagon train and the almost certain envelopment of his left flank."

On a topographic map of the Jetersville area, it can be seen that the Federal right flank (*VI Corps*) rested about a mile north of South Buckskin Creek. On the left flank (*II Corps*) of the entrenched line, Flat Creek was located two and a quarter miles to the north; Vaughan's

Creek, a tributary of Flat Creek, ran parallel and just to the rear of the Union line.

Had Mahone's plan been carried out on the morning of the 6th, Lee's flank attack would have fallen in the area between Flat Creek and Meade's left. The only obstacle in that area for Lee's army would have been another tributary of Flat Creek known as Beaverpond Creek. Of all the watercourses in the immediate area, Flat Creek was the widest, but was possible for infantry to ford. Also to be considered are the times at which the last two Union infantry corps arrived on the 5th, and about how long it would have taken them to get into position and build field breastworks.

Possibly W.H.F. Lee's intelligence of the situation in their front was not as complete and accurate as it should have been, which eventually led the Confederate commander to change his plans that evening. Obviously he did not follow Mahone's plan but chose to change his course and head directly to Farmville instead. A night march allowed him to cross Flat Creek, move through Amelia Springs, and pretty much leave Grant's army behind at Jetersville. Meade moved his army the next morning toward Amelia Court House, only to find that Lee had slipped away. The almost "Battle of Jetersville" failed to materialize.

CHAPTER V

The Race for Farmville: High Bridge and Sailor's Creek

April 6

As the morning of the 6th broke with showers, the Southern troops had nearly bypassed the unsuspecting Federals, while back in Jetersville Meade's army pressed forward in a nearly opposite direction. About 9:00 a.m. the first and third divisions of Humphreys' *II Corps* observed the rear of Lee's column moving westward along the opposite ridge across Flat Creek. They immediately changed direction and set out in pursuit. This was the beginning of what is later referred to as "Black Thursday" for Lee's army.

The route the Confederates followed was through a couple of hamlets on the way to Farmville, which was nineteen miles from Amelia Springs. The first was merely a crossroads with a few buildings called Deatonville. Here the Jamestown Road, along which the army marched, crossed the Genito Road. From this point it went through bottomlands traversed by tributaries of the Appomattox River: Sandy Creek, then Little and Big Sailor's Creeks. The terrain was gentlly rolling as the muddy roadway continued westward to the South Side Railroad at Rice's Depot. From there the road ran directly into Farmville after crossing the Sandy and Bush Rivers. To the north the only crossings of the

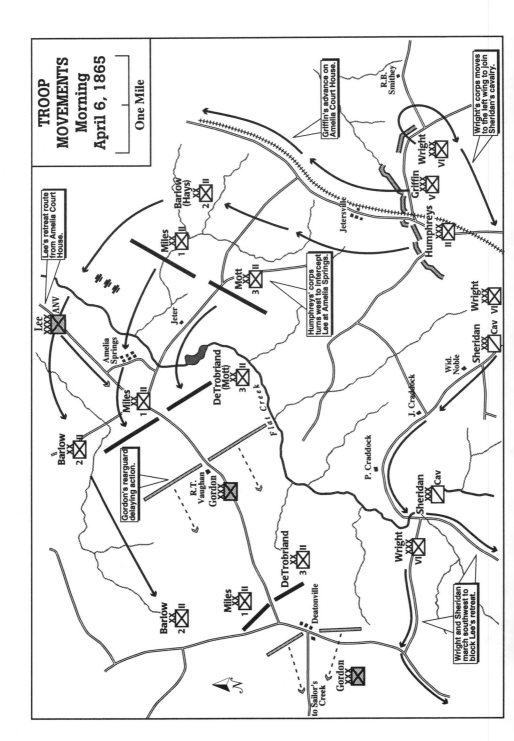

TROOP MOVEMENTS
Morning April 6, 1865

One Mile

Lee's retreat route from Amelia Court House.

Griffin's advance on Amelia Court House.

Wright's corps moves to the left wing to join Sheridan's cavalry.

R.B. Smithey

Wright
XXX
VI

Griffin
V

Humphreys
II

Jetersville

Barlow (Hays)
XX
2 II

Miles
XX
1 II

Mott
XX
3 II

Humphreys' corps turns west to intercept Lee at Amelia Springs.

Jeter

Lee
XXX
ANV

Amelia Springs

Wright
XXX
VI

Sheridan
XXX
Cav

Wid. Noble

J. Craddock

Miles
XX
1 II

DeTrobriand (Mott)
XX
3 II

Flat Creek

Barlow
XX
2 II

P. Craddock

Gordon's rearguard delaying action.

R.T. Vaughan

Gordon
XXX

Sheridan
XX
Cav

DeTrobriand
XX
3 II

Wright
XXX
VI

Miles
XX
1 II

Barlow
XX
2 II

Deatonville

Wright and Sheridan march southwest to block Lee's retreat.

to Sailor's Creek

Gordon
XXX

N

98

Appomattox River were at Farmville and three miles northeast at High Bridge, the South Side Railroad trestle.

In the van of Lee's column was General James Longstreet's combined First and Third Corps, followed by Richard Anderson's two-division corps, then General Richard S. Ewell's Reserve Corps (Richmond garrison troops), the army's main wagon train, and finally John Gordon's Second Corps which acted as the rearguard.

When Humphreys' men observed the enemy wagon train and infantry column passing near Amelia Springs, skirmishers were sent out after it. General Gershom Mott advanced his division toward Flat Creek while Federal artillery was brought up to fire upon the Confederates. General Nelson Miles also carried his division up hoping to fall in on Mott's left, which he later did. While Mott's skirmishers began wading across the creek, the general moved forward to reconnoiter with the skirmish line. After he was shot through the leg he was taken to the rear. Control of his third division was then given to first brigade commander Brigadier General Philip Regis de Trobriand.

That same morning, second division commander Brigadier General William Hays was reassigned to the *Artillery Reserve*. General Humphreys noted to his Chief of Staff, Bvt. Major General A.S. Webb, that: "At 6:30 o'clock this morning I proceeded to the Second Division to see how its movement was being conducted. The division was not in motion. At General Hays' headquarters I found everyone asleep. ... I have relieved General Hays from the command of the Second Division and assigned General Smythe to it." Brigadier General Thomas A. Smyth assumed control for a short period of time when the command was turned over to Bvt. Major General Francis Barlow who had just reported for duty.

Sheridan, upon leaving Jetersville, instructed his three divisions to follow a road parallel to and more southerly than the one the Confederates were on and attempt to intercept Lee's line of march. Since the area was cut up by small farm roads and creek bottoms, this would be relatively easy. Near Deatonville, Crook's cavalry began a series of hit and run tactics on the Confederate wagon train and its supporting infantry column.

High Bridge of South Side R.R. across the Appomattox River at Farmville, VA, April, 1865. (T.H. O'Sullivan)

As they continued the strikes, Custer's and Devin's divisions rode up in support.

At 6:00 a.m. the *VI Corps* had gotten underway and headed toward Amelia Court House. Moving cross-country on a three-mile march, they received information that Lee was actually heading in a westerly direction. Wright was ordered to return to Jetersville by way of the road running parallel to the railroad. About two miles southwest of the station, the corps turned to the north and followed behind the cavalry.

Griffin's *V Corps* had moved from their position in the center of the entrenched line also at 6:00. With Ayres' division in the lead, they reached a point known as Smith's Shop, three miles northeast of Jetersville. Here orders were received for the corps to turn north on the Pridesville Road, then move around to the right of the Union army. This order essentially took Griffin's men out of any fighting that day although they did manage to capture about 300 prisoners and some wagons along the way. The column continued its movement by way of Painesville and Rodophil, then on to the vicinity of Ligontown Ferry. Just south of Ligontown, after a thirty-two mile march, the men went into camp on the Shepard farm.

Since it appeared to the Union high command that Lee was heading for either Danville or Lynchburg, General Ord was directed to destroy any bridges the Confederates might be able to use. He was also ordered to wait at Burkeville with the bulk of his forces. The only structure in the vicinity of obvious military importance was High Bridge. Built in 1852, this man-made wonder had a span of over 2,400 feet and was 125 feet high. Resting on twenty-one brick piers, it, and a smaller wagon bridge below, crossed the seventy-five foot wide river. A contemporary writer said of the bridge: "There have been higher bridges not so long and longer bridges not so high, but taking the height and length together, this is, perhaps, the largest bridge in the world."

At 4:00 a.m. Ord sent two infantry regiments, the *54th Pennsylvania* and *123rd Ohio*, along with three companies (*I, L & M*) of the *4th Massachusetts Cavalry*, to make a reconnaissance of the area and, if not too well guarded, attempt to burn the bridge. Colonel Francis Washburn of the Massachusetts cavalry led this expedition with his eighty troopers. Lieutenant Colonel Horace Kellogg of the *123rd Ohio* commanded the eight hundred infantry.

Ord, apprehensive that Confederate cavalry might have been sent to hold the bridge, ordered his chief of staff (assistant adjutant general), Bvt. Brigadier General Theodore Read, to take command of the raiding column in case there was a threat. Read soon overtook the bridge-burning party and continued on with them. Later, between 9 and 10 a.m., Ord received a dispatch from Sheridan warning him that Lee's army might be heading his way. Ord then sent another staff officer to caution Read that the Confederates were probably in his rear. He was told to return to Burkeville by way of Prince Edward Court House. Unfortunately for Read, this staff officer never reached the group because he was cut off by the Southern cavalry.

After Read arrived in the vicinity and took command, he sent the cavalry to scout the bridge a mile away while he remained behind with the infantry at Major Watson's farm. When Washburn's men crossed Sandy River and approached the bridge they found it guarded by strong earthen redoubts. Skirmishing with its defenders (3rd Virginia Reserves), the troopers at-

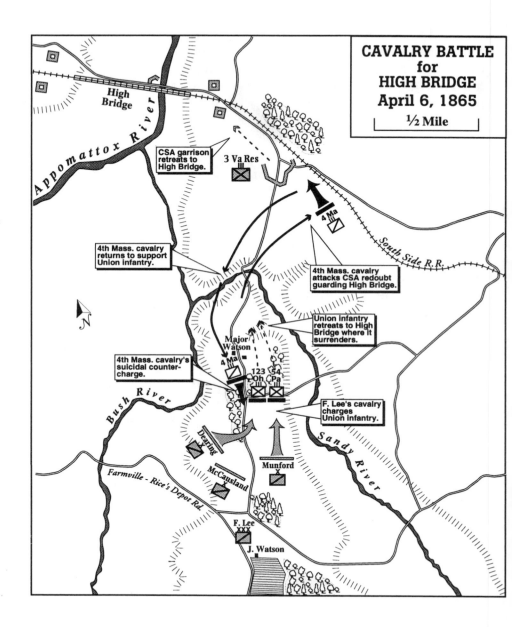

CAVALRY BATTLE for HIGH BRIDGE
April 6, 1865
½ Mile

High Bridge

Appomattox River

CSA garrison retreats to High Bridge.

3 Va Res

4 Ma

South Side R.R.

4th Mass. cavalry returns to support Union infantry.

4th Mass. cavalry attacks CSA redoubt guarding High Bridge.

Union infantry retreats to High Bridge where it surrenders.

Major Watson

4 Ma

123 Oh Pa

4th Mass. cavalry's suicidal counter-charge.

F. Lee's cavalry charges Union infantry.

Bush River

Dearing

Munford

Sandy River

Farmville - Rice's Depot Rd.

McCausland

F. Lee

J. Watson

N

Colonel Francis Washburn in action at High Bridge.

tempted to outflank the garrison, which soon retreated toward Farmville. Washburn then heard firing back at Read's position.

Between 12 and 1 p.m., lead elements of Rosser's and Munford's cavalry attacked the Federal infantry at Watson's. Earlier that morning General Longstreet had received news of this enemy column passing in his front toward High Bridge. He had dispatched the cavalry to locate and try to stop them. When they found Read, posted with his infantry along the edge of a woods, Munford began to dismount his troopers. The men made a frontal attack on Read, while McCausland's and Dearing's brigades of Rosser's division struck them on their right flank.

Just as the Confederates began their advance on Read, Washburn arrived with his troopers. Seeing that the infantry was beginning to fall back, the Massachusetts cavalryman rode around the foot soldiers with his eighty horsemen and charged into the three lines of advancing Southern troops. As the two forces clashed the fighting degenerated into hand-to-hand sabering and personal combats. Washburn was shot in the mouth and slashed across the skull with a saber as he lay on the ground. General Dearing fell while discharging his pistol at General Read, who possibly was killed by the shot. Major John Locher Knott, commanding the 12th Virginia Cavalry, was also killed in this charge, shot through the head.

By this time, the *4th Massachusetts* troop had literally ceased to exist as the two infantry regiments continued their retrograde movement toward High Bridge. Payne's Brigade, commanded by Colonel Reuben B. Boston of the 5th Virginia, continued the pursuit. The enemy infantry then took a position to stop the Confederate advance.

General McCausland ordered Captain Frank M. Myers, of White's 35th Virginia Battalion Cavalry, to take the 6th Virginia and attack this force. Colonel Boston joined in the charge and was shot through the brain while Major James W. Thomson, Stuart Horse Artillery, was killed by a bullet through the vertebra of his neck. In haste the Federals retreated once again, this time to High Bridge itself. At that point they threw down their weapons and surrendered.

The spoils for Rosser and Munford proved to be most of the Union infantry as prisoners (about 780 men), six flags, an ambulance, and even a large brass band. More importantly they had saved High Bridge for further use by Lee's retreating army.

The cost of this victory was dear for the Southern cavalry. General James Dearing was mortally wounded although he lingered until April 23rd to become the last general to die from wounds in the Confederacy. The services of Knott, Boston, and Thomson were also lost, while General Rosser received a slight wound to the arm.

After the fight, Captain Henry Lee, brother of Fitz Lee, was sent by Munford to make a verbal report of the action. When he returned he informed Munford that he would receive a promotion for his efforts. That night, General Lee sent a courier to Thomas Munford with a corps promotion to brigadier general, although the commission was never received because the war ended.

Not only had Ord's bridge-burning party been dispersed, but General Read was killed and his body left on the field. Washburn, who was still alive, was retrieved and sent home to recuperate. General Grant brevetted him as a Brigadier General. Unfortunately, he died on April 22nd.

*   *   *

That forenoon, while Longstreet and Lee were arriving at Rice's Depot, the rear of their column, under General Mahone, became separated from the head of Anderson's Corps. The reason for what became a two-mile gap was that Anderson was being attacked by George Crook's cavalry at Holt's (sometimes referred to as Hott's on period maps and in reports) Corner. At 11:00 a.m., when Crook discoverd Lee's army moving along the Rice-Deatonville Road through Holt's Corner, he sent Smith's brigade to assault their line of march. Consequently, Anderson halted Pickett and Johnson and had them throw up some slight breastworks. After a brief encounter at this point, Crook withdrew his troopers and rejoined the rest of the cavalry.

Custer, after passing Pride's Church, crossed Little Sailor's Creek at Gill's Mill where he became aware of the opening between Mahone and Anderson near Marshall's Crossroads. It was then about 2:00 p.m. After seeing Frank Huger's Battalion of First Corps artillery try to pass through this break in the line, Union cavalry swept down upon it, capturing most of the guns. Soon, some of Pickett's men arrived on the scene and Custer withdrew his men until the other two divisions came up. General Merritt was placed in immediate command of Federal cavalry operations, as Sheridan rode with Wright and the *VI Corps*.

With Crook's threat at Holt's Corner eliminated, Anderson continued ahead, crossed Little Sailor's Creek, and arrived at Marshall's Crossroads about a mile away. Here he found the Federals in his line of retreat to Rice's Depot. General Fitz Lee then informed Ewell of the situation in Anderson's front. General Ewell decided he must send the wagon trains which followed him onto another route, so he instructed them to go via the Jamestown Road. They took a turn in a northerly direction at Holt's Corner. General Gordon brought up the rear behind the trains.

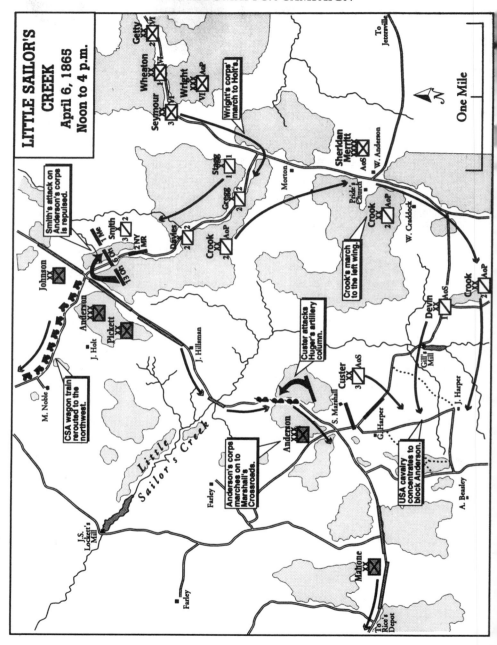

LITTLE SAILOR'S
CREEK
April 6, 1865
Noon to 4 p.m.

One Mile

To
Jetersville

Wright's corps'
march to Holt's.

Getty
XX
2 VI

Wheaton
XX
1 VI

Wright
XX
VI AoP

Seymour
XX
3 VI

Sheridan
Merritt
XX
AoS
W. Anderson

Stagg
1

Pride's
Church

Crook
XX
2 AoP

Gregg
2

Crook
XX
2 AoP
W. Craddock

Smith's attack on
Anderson's corps
is repulsed.

Devin
2

Smith
2

Morton

Crook
XX
2 AoP

Crook
XX
2 AoP

2 NY MR

Crook's march
to the left wing.

Crook
XX
2 AoP

Johnson
XX

Devin
XX
1 AoS

Anderson
XX

Pickett
XX

Custer attacks
Huger's artillery
column.

Gill's
Mill

J. Holt

J. Hillman

J. Harper

M. Noble

Custer
XX
3 AoS

S. Marshall

G. Harper

CSA wagon train
rerouted to the
northwest.

Anderson
XX

USA cavalry
concentrates to
block Anderson.

Little
Sailor's
Creek

Anderson's corps
marches on to
Marshall's
Crossroads.

Farley

Farley

A. Beasley

J.S. Lockett's
Mill

Mahone
XX

Farley

To
Rice's
Depot

Little Sailor's Creek battlefield at the Hillsman House. The heaviest fighting between Wright's and Ewell's men took place in the open ground at the far right in the distance.

As the wagons were departing the main column, Ewell moved his force to the high ground on the opposite side of Little Sailor's Creek. He left behind a group of Colonel William H. Fitzgerald's Mississippians and dismounted cavalry under Colonel Theophilus Barham (24th Virginia) at the James Moses Hillsman house to act as his rearguard. Once across the creek he formed his main force into a line of battle along the ridge, facing northeast, and overlooking the Hillsman farm. Ewell then rode to confer with Anderson over the impending situation. They could either unite their two forces and try to breach the cavalry roadblock, or head through the woods for the road to Farmville. Before the two could decide, Wright's *VI Corps* appeared in Ewell's rear, setting the stage for what is known as the Battles of Sailor's Creek.

Leading Wright's column was General Truman Seymour's third division, followed closely by Frank Wheaton's first. George Getty's second division brought up the rear. After leaving the Jetersville area, the corps followed the cavalry for a distance, crossed Flat Creek, then turned on a more northerly route just south of Deatonville. Eventually they came in behind Crook at Holt's Corner and headed cross-country to the ridge where the Hillsman house was located. Here, General Sheridan took command of the operations and ordered Seymour to clear the road ahead. Apparently it was his troops who came in contact with Fitzgerald's rearguard and forced them to retreat.

While waiting for Wheaton to arrive, General Wright was directed to emplace his twenty pieces of artillery in front of the house. It was then about quarter past five in the evening as Bvt. Major Andrew Cowan's artillery brigade opened up on Ewell's line across the creek.

Although only two divisions of the *VI Corps* were on the field, Sheridan decided not to wait for Getty and placed Wheaton in line of battle on the left, with Seymour on the right. Wheaton had only two of his three brigades with him, Bvt. Brigadier General Joseph E. Hamblin's and Colonel Oliver Edward's, since Bvt. Brigadier General William H. Penrose's brigade was guarding the wagon train. Seymour placed Colonel William S. Truex and Bvt. Brigadier General J. Warren Keifer in his line, although three regiments under Bvt. Colonel Otho H. Binkley of Keifer's brigade were detached at Holt's Corner to pursue the enemy wagon train.

Simultaneously, Sheridan's subordinate, General Wesley Merritt, was preparing his three cavalry divisions for an assault on Anderson's two divisions. They were building breastworks out of fence rails as they dug in along the road to Rice's Depot. Ewell's and Anderson's forces were literally back to back, with Federal cavalry in front and infantry in their rear.

When Ewell put his divisions into position, Custis Lee held the left of the line, with Tucker's Naval Battalion behind Lee's right, and Kershaw occupying the right of the road. The ordnance had left with the wagon train so no artillery was available to reply to Cowan's guns. The creek was approximately 300 yards in the front with brush pines along it, then a cleared field led up to the Hillsman house about 800 yards away.

After a half hour bombardment on the Confederate position, at 6:00 p.m. Wright's nearly 7,000 men advanced in battleline to the creek where they ran into enemy skirmishers. Because of the spring rains, Little Sailor's Creek was out of its banks and

Little Sailor's Creek battlefield looking from Wheaton's Federal position at Kershaw's Confederate position on ridge.

running from two to four feet deep. The Federals crossed with great difficulty, reformed their line, and began an assault on the Confederate position. As they came into range, Ewell's men rose and fired a volley into Wheaton's division, causing a portion of Edward's brigade (the *2nd Rhode Island* and *49th Pennsylvania*) to break and fall back to the creek. Caught up in the spirit of the moment, a group of Southerners, led by Colonel Stapleton Crutchfield, made a counterattack. They were units from Custis Lee's division—the 18th Georgia Battalion, the Chaffin's Bluff Battalion, and the 10th and 19th Virginia Battalion Heavy Artillery (acting as infantry).

As the Confederates chased the Federals down to and across the creek, deadly hand to hand fighting took place during which Crutchfield was killed by a bullet through the head. Major Robert Stiles, of the Chaffin's Bluff Battalion, then took over his command. Guns from Cowan's artillery were sent forward to resolve the dilemma of Wheaton's men. Their canister fire on the Confederate troops caused them to retreat to their lines. Seymour was now completely across the creek with his troops since he had to cover a larger expanse of ground in getting there.

The Federals regrouped and once more charged Ewell's line. This time their sheer numbers overwhelmed the flanks but not without more brutal combat. Again the two armies became

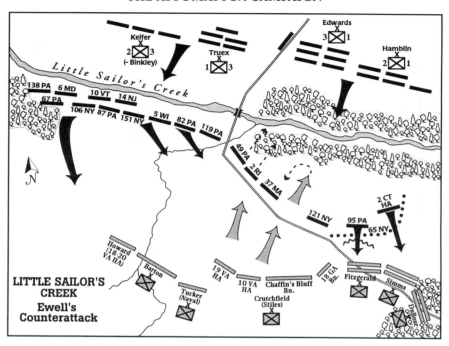

LITTLE SAILOR'S CREEK
Ewell's Counterattack

Sailor's Creek where the Federal VI Corps crossed (1936). The creek was about two to four feet deep.

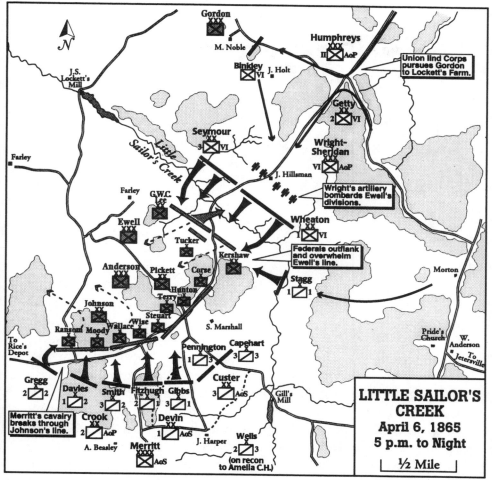

Little Sailor's Creek

Union IInd Corps pursues Gordon to Lockett's Farm.

Wright's artillery bombards Ewell's divisions.

Federals outflank and overwhelm Ewell's line.

Merritt's cavalry breaks through Johnson's line.

LITTLE SAILOR'S CREEK
April 6, 1865
5 p.m. to Night

½ Mile

locked in hand to hand fighting before the Southerners started surrendering. Close to 3,400 of the Reserve Corps laid down their arms this day along with six generals: Ewell, Custis Lee, Seth Barton, Joseph Kershaw, Dudley DuBose, and James Simms. Some 1,450 escaped the field and surrendered a few days later at Appomattox.

A mile to the south of the Hillsman house was the crossroads at which were located the Marshall and two Harper farms. Here Anderson deployed Pickett on the left and Bushrod Johnson on the right along the Rice-Deatonville Road. In their front and to the south was an open field with a long stretch of woods beyond. At the far edge of the field, and about 800 yards away, Merritt formed his three divisions in preparation for their

Joseph B. Kershaw

assault. Custer held the right, Devin the center, with Crook on the left facing Johnson and covering the road to Rice's Depot.

Attacking concurrently with Wright's corps, Crook was to move upon the Confederate right flank, while the others stormed their front. Gregg's dismounted brigade of Crook's division attacked Johnson's flank which was forced to fall back upon their wagons. Custer attempted to ride through Pickett's line but was driven back several times before he was successful. Finally the mounted troopers shattered Anderson's infantry, as many men broke for the woods and headed for the main body of Lee's army up ahead. Some 300 wagons were captured including 15 pieces of artillery, along with about 800 mules and horses. There were 2,600 men who surrendered as did two more generals, Eppa Hunton and Montgomery Corse.

* * *

After the morning crossing of Flat Creek, General Regis De Trobriand's third division led the *II Corps* as they pressed Gordon's rearguard. At every piece of high ground along the way the Confederates made a stand in an attempt to hold back the Federal column. The first of these was in the vicinity of Truly Vaughan's small farmhouse, later used as a hospital by Humphreys' men. The next major point of resistance was at Deatonville, described as "a cluster of half-a-dozen brick farmhouses."

Lockett House near Sailor's Creek, the scene of the fight between the Federal II Corps and Gordon's Corps.

Here Gordon's men, supported by "Rooney" Lee's cavalry, threw up breastworks to oppose the van of the *II Corps*. Six Union regiments formed in battleline and attacked this force. Some 400 prisoners were taken as well as several battle flags, and Deatonville was occupied.

By this time Nelson Miles' first division had come up and fallen in on the third's right. Barlow did not follow the same road as the others this day, but was assigned to guard Miles' right flank. Consequently, his division was not actively engaged with the enemy during the day.

The Federals kept pressing the Southern column until another stand was made at Sandy Creek, just west of Deatonville. A few miles beyond this, at Holt's Corner about 4:30 p.m., Humphreys turned on to the Jamestown Road and continued his pursuit of Gordon and the wagon train. As his men were changing their course, they ran into members of the *VI Corps* and some cavalry who were heading for Hillsman's.

The Federal *II Corps* commander noted of this running fight on the 6th that: "The country was broken, and consisted of open fields alternating with forest with dense undergrowth, and swamps, over and through which the lines of battle followed closely on the skirmish line with a rapidity and nearness of connection that I believe to be unexampled, and which I confess astonished me. Nothing could have been finer than the spirit of the officers and men."

Two miles to the northwest, Gordon was making his passage over the double bridges which crossed at the confluence of Little and Big Sailor's Creeks near James S. Lockett's farm. Before reaching Lockett's, another road branched off to the north and crossed Sailor's Creek further up at Perkinson's Sawmill. The Confederate wagon train became bogged down at the bridges and Gordon's infantry had to rally in support. It was near sunset when Humphreys' forces appeared on the high ground overlooking the valley of Sailor's Creek.

At 5:00 p.m. De Trobriand's division formed into battleline around the Lockett farm, while Miles did likewise and moved down the road to the mill. Skirmishing heavily with the Confederate wagon guard, the two divisions continued into the bottomlands of Sailor's Creek. After seeing Miles' column coming in on their left flank, Gordon's men fell back to the opposite bank and up the high ground where they had artillery posted. While darkness eventually brought a halt to the Union advance, some of the men pressed the Southerners beyond the creek. The day ended with 1,700 prisoners taken by the *II Corps*, along with thirteen flags, three pieces of artillery, more than three hundred wagons and seventy ambulances. The Federals went into camp on the battlefield, while the nearby Lockett house served as a hospital for the days' casualties.

What is referred to in history as the Battle of Sailor's Creek was in actuality three separate engagements: the fight at the Hillsman farm between Wright and Ewell, Merritt vs. Anderson at Marshall's Crossroads, and between Gordon and Humphreys at Lockett's farm. The leadership of eight Confederate generals was lost to Lee, with close to 7,700 men taken prisoner. This placed almost a fifth of Lee's army *hors-de-combat*.

Back near Marshall's Crossroads, as Anderson's refugees fled the battlefield and headed west toward Rice's Depot, they eventually had to scramble across the valley of Big Sailor's Creek. General Lee, wondering about the status of his column and wagon train, rode back from the station with Mahone's division to a knoll overlooking the creek and saw this disorganized mob. Mortified he exclaimed: "My God! Has the army been dissolved?"

Earlier in the day, when Lee and Longstreet arrived at Rice's Depot along the South Side, they learned of Ord's location at Burkeville. The first corps commander directed his divisions to take up line of battle covering the roads to Rice's and perpendicular with the railroad. Wilcox, supported by Heth, dug in south of the tracks, while Field and Mahone were north of them. From this position Mahone returned with Lee to the Sailor's Creek battlefield later in the evening.

At 11:00 a.m. General Gibbon's *XXIV Corps* departed the junction and advanced upon Rice's Depot. After a march of eight to ten miles they found the entrenched Confederates. Preparations were made for an attack with Osborn's brigade of Foster's division on the left (or south of the Farmville Road) and Fairchild's on the right. Dandy, who arrived later in the evening was placed in reserve. Turner's division, upon reaching the field, fell in on Foster's left. A heavy line of skirmishers was sent forward, but darkness brought an end to all major fighting on this front.

General Grant apparently stayed at Jetersville for a better part of the day because at 4:20 p.m. he sent a dispatch from there to Ord with his most recent intelligence: "The enemy is evidently making for Ligontown and Stony Point bridges." The commanding general then rode to Burkeville where he spent the evening. Before he rested, he communicated with Colonel T.S. Bowers at City Point. "The finest spirits prevail among the men, and I believe that in three days more Lee will not have an army of 5,000 men to take out of Virginia, and no train or supplies." General Meade and his staff, following Humphreys' column, went into camp two miles west of Deatonville near Holt's Corner.

Grant also received a message from Sheridan, who with the *VI Corps* and the cavalry, bivouaced near the Sailor's Creek battlefield. "The enemy made a stand .... I attacked them with two divisions of the Sixth Army Corps and routed them handsomely, making a connection with the cavalry. ... If the thing is pressed I think that Lee will surrender." This report was passed on to

President Lincoln at City Point. Grant received his response at 11:00 a.m. the next day, "Let the *thing* be pressed."

*　　　*　　　*

After viewing the disaster of his army at the Big Sailor's Creek overlook, General Lee returned to Rice's Depot. Before he did however, he placed Mahone in charge of Anderson's fugitives. The instructions were to take the men and cross the Appomattox River at High Bridge under the cover of darkness. If Gordon could escape, he too was to cross over the railroad structure. The plan was for these two segments of the army to cross the river and then burn a span of the High Bridge, along with the adjoining wagon bridge below. This had to be done before the Federals arrived. Since the river was generally unfordable in this area, Grant's men would have to await the arrival of a pontoon bridge to provide them passage.

After midnight at his headquarters in an open field north of Rice's Station, Lee received a courier from President Jefferson Davis, who was then at Danville. When Lee was asked if there was an objective point for the army, he remarked, "No; I shall have to be governed by each day's developments. ... A few more Sailor's Creeks and it will all be over—ended—just as I have expected it would end from the first."

Realizing he must still feed his army and outdistance Grant's forces once again, Lee decided to make another night march. This time his immediate objective was Farmville where St. John's subsistence was awaiting the arrival of the army. Longstreet was ordered to resume the march with Field's division leading, followed by Heth and Wilcox, while the cavalry covered the rear. If Lee could reach Farmville unmolested and successfully issue the rations, his men could then cross to the north side of the river as Mahone and Gordon were passing over High Bridge. Lee would then have all the bridges in the area destroyed behind him and thwart the Federals.

As Longstreet's van reached Farmville in the early hours of the 7th, they found the supply trains sent earlier from Burkeville waiting for them. Commissary General St. John ordered the cars to be opened and some 40,000 rations of bread and 80,000 of meal were distributed. The men also reveled in such delicacies as French soup packaged in tin foil along with whole hams. The difficulty facing the army was getting these distributed to everybody as soon as possible before the Federal army arrived on the scene.

The problem Lee had had all during his retreat was not the lack of food for his men, but being able to procure and issue it. St. John had 300,000 rations of bread and meat in Richmond when the armies left, which, of course, never made it to Amelia. At Danville there were 1,500,000 rations of meat along with 500,000 of bread, and at Lynchburg 180,000 rations of bread and meat. Now at Farmville the question was merely one of time.

Lee himself arrived in the village at early dawn and rode to the home of Patrick Jackson on Beech Street where he got some needed rest. He also took time to have a conference here with Secretary of War John Breckinridge, Quartermaster General Alexander R. Lawton and Commissary General St. John. After their discussion, Lee crossed the street to pay his respects to Mrs. John T. Thornton. Her late husband, colonel of the 3rd Virginia Cavalry, had been killed a few years earlier at Sharpsburg. Lee then rode off to the north bank of the river.

Sayler's, Saylor's, Sailor's, or Sailer's Creek: The Correct Spelling

Assuming that this eight-mile water-course, a tributary to the Appomattox River, was named for a local family, records of early settlers in the area were researched. The creek runs through Prince Edward, Amelia, and Nottoway counties. The only land-owner with the name was found in Prince Edward.

In 1795 a Marte[i]n Saylor was named in connection with a proposal to clear, improve and extend navigation of the Appomattox River for batteaus to carry hogsheads of tobacco. Prior to 1809, Marten Saylor and George King were partners in a Prince Edward County tannery.

In 1842, a J.D. Sayler expressed opposition to a change of court day. Exactly where either of these men lived or whether they had any influence on the name of the stream is unknown.

One of the earliest maps to show the branch was *A Map of the most inhabited part of Virginia, all of the province of Maryland, part of Pennsilvania, New Jersey and North Carolina*. It was distributed by Peter Jefferson and Joshua Fry. Produced in 1751, it

shows Sailor's Creek emptying into the Appomattox.

On the 1867 *Michler Survey Map* of the region, completed by the military after the war, the creek was further defined as Sailor's Creek, and was fed by two branches, Big and Little Sailor's Creek. Most of the April 6, 1865, battle was fought along Little Sailor's Creek, the Civil War period spelling.

No substantiation of the Sailer's Creek spelling is found anywhere except in post-war writings.

In 1879, *Jacob's Official Map of Prince Edward County* was produced, and names the creek, Sayler's. No homestead with that last name is shown along the creek on the map.

Finally, in 1960, the *United States Board of Geographic Names* made a determination about what would be used on current Virginia maps. Their decision was Sayler's Creek.

Consequently, in examining the documentation provided, those wishing to correctly refer to the Civil War engagement should use the Battle of Little Sailor's Creek.

Lieutenant George Peck, 2nd Rhode Island Infantry, and His Experiences at Little Sailor's Creek

On December 14, 1864, George B. Peck was mustered into service with a newly recruited company, *G, 2nd Rhode Island*, and joined his unit at the Petersburg front. He was assigned the rank of Second Lieutenant. Because his company was on special detail, he did not participate in the April 2, 1865, *VI Corps* assault and following breakthrough. Consequently, the first and only time he "saw the elephant" was in the Battle of Little Sailor's Creek on April 6th. His reminiscences of details, particularly since it was his only engagement, are very descriptive. Peck's story, taken from *A Recruit Before Petersburg* (1880), depicts the action of Wright's corps at the Hillsman house.

We were on the crest of a hill, where we halted for some minutes. A second glance towards the left revealed a farmhouse [Hillsman's] in the distance. I noted its bearings, feeling sure a field hospital would speedily be established there, and ere long I might need to visit it. I also noted a group of horsemen on a projecting knoll, gazing at the opposite height. They soon turned and rode up the rear of the first line toward the right, affording me my first glimpse of General Sheridan and General Wheaton. ... These and other accompanying dignitaries appeared decidedly rough, the former especially. I was now satisfied that I was about to engage in my first battle.

... The colonel's clear voice sounded "ATTENTION!" ... Descending the hill, "Prepare to cross a marsh!" was passed along the line. I trod gingerly and on the hummocks, for I did not care to loose my whangs, broad, flat, low-heeled shoes of the pattern issued the enlisted men, the very best for continued heavy tramps. Three or four minutes later we found ourselves confronted by a hedge so high and so dense, it was impossible to see what was beyond. There was an involuntary pause—but only for an instant. Glancing around to find some available opening, I discovered the colors, some twenty paces on the left, had advanced about a yard and a half beyond the obstruction, and that every one in their neighborhood had clustered around the breach thus made. My own men were scattering to the right and left. The colonel stormed, and the officers shouted, "Go ahead," but no perceptible progress was made. Thinking I could clear a passage for my own men, I thrust my hands into and through the hedge, spread them apart, and found a stream of muddy water a dozen feet wide [Little Sailor's Creek]. Visions of New England brooks at once rose before me. I was slightly held by numerous withes, and moreover was unwilling to injure my hands with briars, so with the exclamation "Company G, this way," I boldly jumped for the middle of the stream expecting to land knee-deep in water. I went through the hedge and struck where I expected, but immersed above the sword-belt, and with feet firmly imbedded it was impossible to stir them in the least. Thoroughly startled at the idea that perchance I had jumped into a Virginia quicksand, I seized hold of the farther bank and held on tightly.

Finding I did not sink, I began working my feet gently to the right and left, soon extricated them from the mud, and then clambered out. ...

As the brigade [Colonel Oliver Edward's] came into position, it was found some of the advanced regiments occupied more space in column than was requisite; they accordingly closed up to the right immediately on crossing the creek, so that we found ourselves, on gaining the farther bank, separated from the remainder of the line by a very considerable interval. Due regard to our own well-being forbade this, of course, so we faced to the right, without doubling, and marched until the distance was reduced to little more than fifty yards. As we started, a regular battery on the hill we so recently occupied, opened fire and dropped a ball in the morass some thirty feet short of us. It was amusing to see the men, naturally disturbed and irritated, shake their fists and hurl maledictions at the blunderers. A second shot just cleared our heads, but the third

struck half way up the hill on our front, and the fourth reached the enemy's lines. At the same time the bullets began to fall as hailstones around us, and twigs from the hedge just passed covered the ground like snow-flakes. Under this double fire the men became slightly, but only slightly, nervous, and diminished the distance from breast to knapsack, so that when we faced again to the front the files were a trifle crowded. I endeavored to impart mathematical precision to my company, but speedily relinquished the impossible venture, with the consoling reflection. "There'll be enough elbow room soon!" The men were now directed to crouch, as the bullets fell thicker and faster around us. ... Having, as a file-closer, no particular responsibility, I busied myself with observing the situation. We were at the foot of a moderately steep, turf-covered declivity over whose summit the foliage of dense trees was visible. Some twenty rods to our left this growth, sufficiently dark and threatening, extended down the hillside to the creek. Fine place for a flanking party, thought I. ...

Next I studied the line. I was always very curious as to the deportment of men under fire, so with rare eagerness turned from right to left and left to right, watching the movements of each individual. Every imaginable position was assumed, from the half erect to an apparent attempt to tunnel the hillside. ... Suddenly, "Whit!" sped a ball by my right ear; involuntarily I imitated those I had been ridiculing, and thereafter stooped about two inches lower. All this time, while the leaden missiles were as thick as mosquitoes in early autumn, I saw not a grayback, nor yet a rifle flash.

"At length the order to charge was given. The tactical combination ensuing, I will not describe. How the regiment made a charge, virtually unsupported; how it received a murderous fire at short range, from three sides, and indeed from the left rear also; how it was driven to the foot of the hill, and, after re-forming, again charged in time to participate in the bagging of eight thousand men and seven [eight] generals will be told by the commanding officer. ... At the word "FORWARD!" the men sprang to their feet, fired into the woods, and with a cheer dashed forward on the run. Gaining a few rods, they fell, loaded (officers meanwhile simply stooping), rose again, fired, and made a second dash. ...

With the third dash came the words: "Now close on them—Go for them!" I always had a horror of stepping on the wounded, especially my own; besides this was my first charge, and that over anything but smooth ground; so naturally I devoted considerable attention to seeing where I was going. At length I imagined I had about reached the summit, and must be ready to close on the hostiles, so I looked up; but lo! no one was before me. Surprised and perplexed, I turned to the left and no one was there. The colors were already half way down the hill and

moving deliberately to the rear; the soldiers on the extreme left had already reached the creek. Glancing now to the right, I found the nearest man, eight or ten feet away, was wheeling about. As I did not care to present any Confederate with either sword, watch or revolver, and could offer but slight resistance when single-handed, I concluded to retrace my steps also, and accordingly commenced a march in common time to the rear.

In taking my rapid survey, I noticed thirty or forty "secesh" on a projecting knoll, enjoying a comfortable little target practice. I thought if any expert chap should take a fancy to send a ball after me, I preferred the bullet should pass through by the most direct route, reducing thereby all damage to the minimum; hence I made a half face to my left, and quietly travelled down the hill. Just before effecting this change of direction, I saw one man run— the only one in the entire regiment. ... I had reached the foot of the hill, and was about thirty feet from the edge of the creek, when I felt a dull blow in the neighborhood of my left hip. I realized I was shot, and was at once curious as to the amount of damage. I looked down and saw the hole was too far to one side to implicate the groin; forgetting a possibly severed artery, I threw my weight on my left leg, and finding no bones broken, began to laugh as the ludicrousness of the whole affair flashed upon me. "You're never hit till you run," was my first reflection. ...

On reaching the border of the creek, I hesitated for a moment. I did not relish the idea of having that muddy water run through my side, moreover I was fearful it might hurt; yet no alternative presented, so I lowered myself gently, crossed, and looked for that farmhouse heretofore mentioned. Failing to discover it, I started for my former position on the crest of the hill. After trudging on a spell, using my sword meanwhile for a cane, I discovered myself directly in front of Captain [Crawford] Allen's battery [H, 1st Rhode Island Lt. Art.]. A cannoneer was beckoning to a fellow obstructing the range of one of the pieces, who at once ran toward the gun, delaying its fire so many seconds longer. The artilleryman's gesture indicated that I too was bothering them, so I made a square face to my left, and had stepped not half a dozen paces when a shell shrieked by, taking my benedictions to friends across the flood.

Passing to the rear of the battery, I occasionally met fellows whom I asked concerning the location of a hospital, but could elicit no information. Attaining the crest, I spied the little [Hillsman] farmhouse on the extreme left of the original line of battle, and with glad heart thitherward directed my weary steps. ... When within a hundred feet of the house, I was laid upon the grass, and one [member of the ambulance corps] went for a surgeon. ... He took my silk handkerchief, rinsed it thoroughly in cold water, and laid it on the double wound. That was all the dressing it received in three days. ...

An hour later it began to rain, so Private [William A.] Lincoln went to the house to secure, if possible, my removal thither, for every other officer had been quartered there as soon as he was brought in. He returned with a litter on which I was taken to the house. I was then placed on the floor of a room in which there were two beds, each occupied by two severely wounded officers, while in the third corner, on the floor, were at least a half dozen more. The only place found for me was in front of one of these beds; my head close beside the hall doorway, where stood the operating table, with surgeons working the entire night, my body forming the bound of a passage-way to the kitchen door in the fourth corner, whence people continually passed and repassed. Yet when my wet cloths had been removed ... and myself wrapped in a couple of army blankets, I slept quietly, happily, until daylight.

By noon of the 7th, Peck was loaded on an ambulance and after a six-hour ride reached the hospital set up at Burkeville Junction. After receiving further care here, by the 12th he was back at City Point and placed in the Depot Field Hospital. He was absent from his regiment through June, and on the 30th, resigned his position.

CHAPTER VI

A Fatal Mistake: High Bridge and Cumberland Church

April 7

*F*armville was a tobacco town of some 1,500 inhabitants in 1865 and served the Confederacy in numerous ways during the war years. A wagon and ambulance works were located there as well as a major hospital with 1,200 beds. Built mainly for chronic cases and convalescents rather than battle casualties, with fighting in the area for the first time in the war, it was soon to be used by both armies.

The South Side Railroad, entering Farmville from the east, followed a roundabout path. From Rice's Station, about six miles distant, the line crossed to the north side of the Appomattox River over High Bridge, then ran parallel to the river, before it crossed back to the south bank and went into town. From that point westward, it stayed south of the river. The reason for this route was that Farmville was in a valley of low hills surrounded by a high ridge, particularly to the east. Locomotives leaving the town in that direction needed the gradual grade which was provided by this circuitous route.

Consequently, there were two railroad bridges over the Appomattox in the vicinity of Farmville, one north of town, the other,

High Bridge.

High Bridge, four miles to the northeast. There was also a wagon bridge located next to each railroad bridge.

The majority of Longstreet's column began to arrive in Farmville around 9:00 a.m., and the rations were quickly issued. Upon receiving them, the men were ordered to the north side of the river where they started their meal preparation. At the same time, Gordon's corps, having crossed over High Bridge on its pedestrian walkways, followed the South Side Railroad into Farmville.

Meanwhile, Longstreet's rear on the march to Farmville was being pressed by Crook's division of Federal cavalry. At each bridge crossing, like those over the Sandy and Bush Rivers, the assisting Confederate cavalry made a stand. Directly behind Crook marched Ord's column providing infantry support to the troopers. Although the Southerners attempted to burn the bridges, the fires were quickly extinguished by the pursuing Union troops. Later, after crossing Bush River, Longstreet relieved the cavalry of its post and replaced it with Scale's Brigade (Hyman's) of Wilcox's division as the rearguard into Farmville.

*   *   *

Back at Lockett's farm on the Sailor's Creek battlefield, Humphreys put his corps in motion at 5:30 a.m. Following behind them were Griffin's *V Corps* which began their march from near Ligontown at 5:00. General Wright did likewise and set out toward Rice's Depot. Crook's cavalry operated separately from the other two divisions, while Sheridan moved with Custer and Devin around to the south of Farmville, heading for Prince Edward Court House.

Leading the *II Corps* line of march on their cross-country journey to High Bridge was Barlow's second division. Arriving at this location around 7:00 a.m., they found that the Confederates had failed to destroy the structure as planned. It seems that through a delay in the passage of troops and receiving orders, a company of engineers, under Captain William R. Johnson, were just firing the western spans.

Later it was learned why it took so long for the Confederate army to pass over the two bridges during the night march. It seems that General Anderson, riding ahead of General Mahone, had placed sentinels at each bridge with orders not to let anybody cross. With men and wagons ready to move on, Mahone rode for General Anderson whom he found conferring with General Gordon. When Anderson was asked to relieve his sentinels, he replied that General Lee ordered him to collect all stragglers. General Mahone reminded him that he should assemble them on the opposite (west) side of the river since the enemy was surely approaching. After receiving the appropriate orders from Anderson, the guards allowed Mahone's troops to cross over High Bridge, and the wagons down below.

As his men crossed and fell out to rest, Mahone again rode to Anderson and Gordon. He brought up the possibility of the army surrendering, as all seemed to feel the end was near. They designated General Anderson to carry their sentiments to General Longstreet. Whether he did so is unknown. Mahone also mentioned the fact that Colonel Thomas M. Talcott's Engineers needed orders to burn the bridges. The authority for this was

125

The burning bridge. (Edwin Forbes)

given to General Gordon who was supposed to dispatch a staff
officer to carry it out.

After scouting the roads during the night, General Mahone
returned to his men at daylight, only to find the bridges had not
been burned. Shortly afterwards, he did see smoke rise from
that direction, but it was too late. The Federal skirmishers were
now pressing forward so Mahone sent back a brigade to cover
his rear.

As the Federals advanced, the last Confederates to cross the
river blew up one of the two redoubts guarding the southeast
approaches. Barlow's first unit to arrive at the bridges was the
19th Maine Infantry commanded by Colonel Isaac W. Starbird.
His men rushed upon the lower wagon bridge just as flames
were beginning to spring from it. With some acting as skirmishers to keep the enemy away, others used their canteens, boxes
and tents and put out the fires out. It took little time for the men
to cross over with the rest of the brigade soon following. Colonel
Starbird was left behind though, seriously wounded along with
four others.

Above this active scene, Barlow's division pioneers were
desperately trying to extinguish the fire on High Bridge. Flames
had already consumed the first three spans of the structure and

were fast weakening the fourth. Resting on the twenty-one brick piers was a tarred wooden superstructure. It had a truss from ten to twelve feet high and was covered with tin.

The pioneers, working 125 feet above the valley floor, tore through the tin and floor boards while cutting away at the main timbers.

The fourth span was beyond saving and fire was spreading to the fifth, when the latter fell off and the rest of the bridge was saved.

Mahone's skirmishers, supported by a line of battle, then attempted to retake the wagon bridge, where they ran into Colonel William A. Olmsted's first brigade. The colonel advanced the *7th Michigan* and *59th New York* on the left of the railroad as skirmishers and flankers. Then General Thomas Smyth's third brigade joined the fray. They were pressing the Confederates at about 9:00 a.m when Nelson Miles' division crossed over and fell in behind the second division as it was being driven back. Miles deployed a heavy skirmish line and ordered Captain A. Judson Clark's *1st New York Lt. Arty.* (*Battery B*) and Captain Dakin's *1st New Hampshire* (*Battery M*) to shell the enemy line. They were supported by Captain J. Webb Adams' *10th Battery Massachusetts Lt. Arty.* and Lieutenant William B. Westcott's *1st Rhode Island Lt. Arty.* (*Battery B*). The *39th* and *52nd New York* were spread out along the river bank as further protection for the bridge crossing.

The combined forces eventually pushed back Mahone's men who rejoined the rest of the column marching westward along the Jamestown Road. While the remaining *II Corps* passed over the charred wagon bridge, the Federals counted their spoils. From the two forts on the southeast side of the river, they extricated eight pieces of artillery, along with ten more from the two forts on the northwest side. Five hundred Enfield rifles were also found. The weapons had been used by the forces which had served these defensive positions at various times throughout the war. These were the three hundred thirteen men of Colonel Richard A. Booker's 3rd Virginia Reserves and the forty-three of Major Victor Maurin's Donaldsonville (Richardson's Battalion) Artillery. The ordnance left behind was an assemblage of different guns: a rare 3-inch Clay (sometimes referred to as an Armstrong) rifled piece, 12 pdr. iron and bronze howitizers, 10 and 20 pdr. rifled Parrotts, a 12 pdr.(3.5 inch) rifled Blakely, along with 3-inch rifled and 6 pdr. iron guns.

As Mahone's troops continued marching toward the Farmville-Lynchburg (and Cumberland Court House) Road, Gordon's column headed down the railroad to Farmville itself. Barlow's division went after them, while Miles and De Trobriand took the Jamestown Road behind Mahone. In the van of Barlow's second division was Smyth's brigade, supported by McIvor's second and Olmsted's first. Just before noon, General Smyth was seen riding with his skirmish line within fifty yards of Gordon's rearguard.

Suddenly the general fell off the right side of his horse. He had been hit by a sharpshooter's bullet on the left side of his face, about an inch above the mouth. Cutting away a tooth, the ball traveled into his neck, fracturing a cervical vertebra and driving a piece of bone against the spinal cord. Smyth was entirely paralyzed.

Colonel Daniel Woodall of the *1st Delaware* then assumed command of the brigade. Barlow continued to advance his men but not before members of the 1st North Carolina Battalion Sharpshooters, of General James Walker's division, made a stand. Finding a group of Federals in a railroad cut, they captured the whole lot of them, 103 men of the *7th Michigan* and *59th New York* sent ahead earlier by Colonel Olmsted.

Once Barlow reached the northern outskirts of Farmville, he called off the chase, but not before Lee's men burned 135 wagons along the Farmville-Lynchburg Road.

*   *   *

As the commotion of the fight between Gordon and Barlow could be heard on the north side of the river, General St. John realized he must dispatch the ration trains in order to save them. He sent them westward down the South Side to Pamplin's Depot. The crack of carbine fire could also be heard to the east of town as Crook's cavalry was beginning to arrive on the scene. It proved to be General Charles Smith's brigade which had ridden into Farmville, led by the *1st Maine Cavalry*. As the troopers penetrated the streets of the town, many had become separated and had to be recalled to the command. Henry Davies' brigade arrived and took charge while Smith had his men reform.

On the northern edge of town near the railroad station, General E.P. Alexander started to burn the covered wagon and adjacent railroad bridges before the Federals could reach them. He was successful in destroying the structures but it was before all the Confederates were able to cross. Rosser's and Munford's cavalry had to ford the river further up, along with Brigadier General John Bratton's South Carolinians.

Once the Southerners were across the river from Farmville, they moved to the high ground, known as Cumberland Heights, overlooking the town, and went into battle line. Artillery was set into position and fired on the Federal columns as they filled the main street. Shortly thereafter, the Confederates were withdrawn and ordered into position three miles further north around Cumberland Church.

Prior to the Union threats to his army, Lee had crossed over the river and once again conferred with Secretary of War Breckinridge near the home of Elizabeth Rosa Thackston. At some point he also discussed the current situation with General Alexander. The First Corps artillery commander informed the commanding general that they should have stayed south of the river and followed the road which generally paralleled the South Side Railroad. Since their next destination was to be Appomattox Station, it would have been a much shorter march, about 30 miles, along this route. The route the army intended to take via New Store and Appomattox Court House, three miles from the station, was almost 38 miles. Lee questioned this intelligence and asked Alexander to check his maps with area residents. They confirmed the mileage.

About this time, General Lee heard that the enemy had crossed at High Bridge and were now on the same side of the river as he was. Hopes of breaking contact with Grant's advance forces now ended. After venting his rage at having burned the bridges, he soon regained his self control. Thinking the rear was still safe, he prepared to ride ahead toward the threat surfacing from Humphreys' corps.

Before he did, however, he responded to General Alexander about his concern: "Well there is time enough to think about that. Go and attend to these matters." The artillery officer later observed, "Indeed, no man who looked at our situation on a map, or who understood the geography of the country, could fail to see that General Grant had us completely in a trap. ... We were now in a sort of jug shaped peninsula between the James River and Appomattox and there was but one outlet, the neck of the jug at Appomattox Court House, and to that Grant had the shortest road!"

By 1:30 p.m. Farmville was in Federal hands. Once Crook's cavalry had all arrived, they moved to the river and found a spot to ford just northwest of the town limits. They soon reached the Buckingham (or Maysville) Plank Road and rode up it.

Coming directly behind Crook into Farmville was Ord's *Army of the James*, followed shortly by Wright's *VI Corps* from Rice's Depot. One of the infantrymen noticed that "stores were shut up, houses closed, frightened women peeped through dilapidated doorways, [and] sullen men lolled about the porches." Grant and his staff rode in shortly from Burkeville and made his headquarters in the Randolph House (Prince Edward Hotel) on the corner of Second and Main streets.

Other Northerners who viewed the town had this to say about it: "Before the war it must have been quite an enterprising place. There are some large tobacco warehouses in the place which are stored with tobacco sent here from Richmond for safe keeping little dreaming Grant would soon pounce upon it. We have captured tobacco enough in this place to pay off the whole army. All the citizens are left in the town and there is also a female seminary filled with young ladies from Richmond, Petersburg and Danville."

Another wrote: "Farmville, a quiet country village, contained about fifteen hundred inhabitants, three or four churches, and a number of fine residences. ... Our course through the town was quite circuitous, and took us by a rebel hospital, around which paced sentries clad in blue. It was crowded with patients who came to the neat rustic fence enclosing it to watch us pass. Pleasant and sociable, they remarked freely that they had done their last fighting. They seemed particularly anxious to secure souvenir bargains, offering in exchange Confederate money and tobacco with which they were abundantly supplied. The article most eagerly sought was the pocketknife, which had long been in great demand among them."

*   *   *

Earlier in the day, General Lindsay Walker's reserve artillery and wagon train returned to the army by way of Cumberland Court House. Having camped the night before on Mrs. Ben Harrison's farm, they rejoined the column and continued along to Appomattox Court House by way of Curdsville and New Store. It was this contingent, and later the rest of Lee's wagon train, that Mahone and the others would be forced to protect.

Cumberland Presbyterian Church was located about five miles northwest of High Bridge and was described as a "rural Virginia church, painted, but without a steeple and rudely finished." When Mahone's 3,500 man force reached the high ground around the church by way of the Jamestown Road, they began digging a line of slight breastworks that eventually resembled a giant fish hook, facing north and east. The church was in the center, behind the trenches and men.

About 1:00 p.m., lead elements of the *II Corps* appeared in front of the Confederate position. It had taken three hours for Miles to march from High Bridge. Colonel Scott's brigade arrived first and skirmishers from the *26th Michigan* and *140th Pennsylvania* advanced upon the Southern line where it crossed the Jamestown Road. Lieutenant Colonel William T. Poague's battalion was holding Mahone's right at this point and Captain Arthur B. Williams' North Carolina Battery was temporarily captured by the Federals. Quickly Mahone sent in Major General Bryan Grimes' North Carolinians to retake the guns.

As more and more of Lee's troops arrived on the field, Gordon's corps fell in on Poague's right, then Longstreet's left connected with Gordon's right. With Mahone holding the left flank of the entire line, his position was the most vulnerable. Some of Fitz Lee's cavalry moved to that area to provide protection.

After his initial stab at the Confederate line along the Jamestown Road, Miles moved his division further west and

131

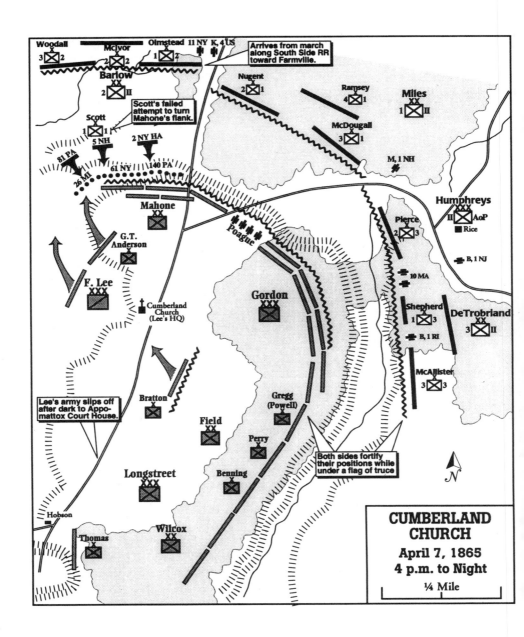

Woodall
3 ⊠ 2

McIvor
2 ⊠ 2

Olmstead
1 ⊠ 2

11 NY K, 4 US

Arrives from march
along South Side RR
toward Farmville.

Barlow
XX
2 ⊠ II

Nugent
2 ⊠ 1

Ramsey
4 ⊠ 1

Miles
XX
1 ⊠ II

Scott's failed
attempt to turn
Mahone's flank.

Scott
1 ⊠ 1

McDougall
3 ⊠ 1

5 NH

2 NY HA

M, 1 NH

81 PA

26 MI

61 NY

140 PA

Mahone
XX

Humphreys
XXX
II ⊠ AoP

Rice

Pogue

Pierce
2 ⊠ 3

G.T.
Anderson
⊠

B, 1 NJ

10 MA

F. Lee
XXX

Gordon
XXX
⊠

Shepherd
1 ⊠ 3

DeTrobriand
XX
3 ⊠ II

Cumberland
Church
(Lee's HQ)

B, 1 RI

Lee's army slips off
after dark to Appo-
mattox Court House.

Bratton
⊠

McAllister
3 ⊠ 3

Field
XX
⊠

Gregg
(Powell)
⊠

Perry
⊠

Both sides fortify
their positions while
under a flag of truce

Longstreet
XXX
⊠

Benning
⊠

N

Hobson

Thomas
⊠

Wilcox
XX
⊠

CUMBERLAND
CHURCH
April 7, 1865
4 p.m. to Night

¼ Mile

north of the Southern defenses. Scott's brigade then held his extreme right and was ordered to make an attempt to turn Mahone's flank. This attack was to coincide with one which General Wright was supposed to order from the south at the same time. Unaware that the bridges had been destroyed at Farmville, General Humphreys was under the impression that the *VI Corps* had crossed the river and would assail Lee's rear while he did the same on their front. When firing was heard in that direction, the bugle order was given: "Forward—double quick—charge!"

Mahone's men were entrenched along the top of a slight ridge "covered by works breast-high," facing north, while in front of them was a series of rolling hills and valleys which the Federals had to pass over in their assault. This was described as "old pine land, washed out by gullies." The first brigade formed with the *26th Michigan, 61st New York* and *140th Pennsylvania* as skirmishers, while the *81st Pennsylvania, 5th New Hampshire* and *2nd New York Heavy Artillery* were placed in line of battle.

As Scott's men advanced with fixed bayonets around 4:15 p.m., the Confederates began to pour musketry and canister into the ranks. Some of the Union soldiers actually made it to the works—like the *5th New Hampshire* men—only to be captured with their battleflag. Others began to turn Mahone's flank and got in his rear but were thrown back by reinforcements sent by Longstreet in the form of Brigadier General George "Tige" Anderson's Georgians. General Bratton's brigade was also sent but arrived too late to be of help.

After Anderson's brief counterattack, Scott's men fell back to their lines. It appears that the gunfire heard earlier behind Mahone's position was not Wright's corps attacking, but rather Crook's cavalry. After fording the river and proceeding up the Buckingham Plank Road, at 4:00 p.m. General J. Irvin Gregg's brigade spied a Confederate wagon train passing through a road intersection southwest of Cumberland Church. This was about two and a half miles up the road from Farmville. With Colonel Samuel Young's *4th Pennsylvania Cavalry* leading the column, Gregg was supported by Davies' then Smith's brigades, along with Lieutenant James H. Lord's *2nd United States Artillery (Battery A)*.

As Gregg's troopers assaulted the line of wagons, Munford's cavalry, supported by Rosser on his right, attacked the Union cavalry. Munford, using Companies E and K of the 3rd Virginia Cavalry to strike the Federals on their right flank, broke them, and took General Gregg as prisoner.

Colonel Young then reformed the remnants of Gregg's scattered command on the left of the road, while Davies fell in on his right, with Lord's Battery in support. Smith's brigade was held in reserve. Moving ahead once more against the wagons, this time the Union battleline ran into both Confederate artillery and infantry, which proved to be from Brigadier General William Gaston Lewis's North Carolina brigade, supported by Lieutenant Colonel William M. Owen's guns. General Lewis led a counterattack and was severely wounded, eventually falling into the hands of Federal surgeons. General Lee personally witnessed this attack and attempted to lead the charge himself, only to have his men cry out, "No, no, but if you will retire we will do the work." The troops were successful this time in forcing back the Union cavalry and Crook retreated back across the river into Farmville.

That night Humphreys' surgeons established a field hospital about halfway between High Bridge and Cumberland Church at Brook's house, located along the Jamestown Road. The casualties were later taken to Burkeville Junction, where a major Federal hospital had been established. From that point, they rode the railroad back to the Depot Field Hospital in City Point for their final recuperation.

*   *   *

Back in Farmville, General Grant decided to open communications with General Lee about the possibility of surrender. At 5:00 p.m. he wrote:

General:

The results of the last week must convince you of the hopelessness of further resistance on the part of the Army of Northern Virginia in this struggle. I feel that it is so, and regard it as my duty to shift from myself the responsibility of any further effusion of blood, by asking of you the surrender of that portion of the C.S. Army known as the Army of Northern Virginia.

A Fatal Mistake:

Very respectfully,
your obediant servant,
U.S. Grant
Lieutenant-General,
Commanding Armies of the United States

This message was sent with General Seth Williams of Grant's staff by way of High Bridge and came in through General Mahone's lines. General Lee, who at the time was either at Cumberland Church or nearby Blanton's Shop, received the dispatch from Captain Herman H. Perry between 9:15-9:30 p.m. With him as he read the communication was General Longstreet. After silently studying it, he passed the document to his First Corps commander. Longstreet scanned it and returned the note to Lee. "Not yet," was his reply. General Lee then set about writing a response to Grant.

His reply simply stated that he disagreed with the Union general's assessment of the situation but, hoping "to avoid the useless effusion of blood," he asked Grant for the terms he would offer on condition of his army's surrender.

*   *   *

During the evening, Barlow's division returned to Humphreys at Cumberland Church. He held Miles' old position on the right flank, while Miles then moved to the center; De Trobriand secured the left. General Humphreys' headquarters was in the Rice house behind the third division's right flank.

Earlier in the day, at 3:00 p.m., Humphreys sent a message to General Meade concerning recent intelligence he had received. "From the prisoners I have it appears that Lee's army is moving from Farmville to Lynchburg." The Federals were beginning to receive information which would allow Grant to maneuver his army the next day.

Until a pontoon bridge could be erected at Farmville, Wright's infantry had to cross the river on either the wreckage of the burnt wagon bridge or ford as best as possible. As they marched up Main Street to the river crossing, bonfires were lit along the streets, and passing soldiers seized straw and pine knots, improvising them into torches. With bands playing, and colors waving, cheers rose from the ranks as the *VI Corps* men passed by General Grant's hotel headquarters in grand review.

It was their delay in supporting Humphreys' corps on this day that some Union officials felt was the cause of Lee escaping the area. One later wrote that the war could have ended at Cumberland Church, "forty miles by road and forty-six hours by time, short of the quiet surrender at Appomattox Court House; yes, ended in a blaze of glory for the Army of the Potomac, which deserved such a termination to their labors and sufferings."

By nightfall most of the *VI Corps* had reached the north bank of the river and gone into bivouac. Wright established his headquarters near Dr. Taliaferro's house. The artillery had also located a nearby ford and began crossing.

That evening, the *Army of the James*, which stayed south of the river and occupied Farmville, lent their pontoon bridge to the *VI Corps*. It was used throughout the next morning until the *50th New York Engineers* arrived at 9:30 a.m. and placed a ninety foot bridge.

While the *XXIV Corps* went into camp just west of the town, two of Birney's three *U.S.C.T.* brigades, the second and third, were put under Gibbon's command. Colonel Ulysses Doubleday's was assigned to Foster's division, and Colonel William W. Woodward's to Turner's division. The artillery, under Captain Loomis Langdon, was also placed with Turner. Colonel James Shaw, Jr.'s first brigade was marching well behind the rest of Ord's column and did not join the army until April 10th at Appomattox Court House. The reason for this change in command structure was that General Birney had been reassigned to the Petersburg area where he was placed in command of the Division of Fort Powhatan, City Point and Wilson's Wharf, all located along the James River.

Crook's division, upon returning to Farmville, rode west along the railroad to Prospect Station where they went into camp.

While most of Grant's men were involved in the heavy activity centering around Lee's army, Mackenzie's small force rode from Burkeville cross-country to Prince Edward Court House (present-day Worsham), reaching there at noon. Skirmishing slightly with some Confederate outposts, they captured thirty-eight prisoners. Since this village was located due south of Farmville along the direct road to Keysville and the Danville Railroad, Grant had to cover the area should Lee try to escape in this direction. Obviously, Grant was not aware that the Confederate commander already had changed his plans and was now attempting to pass his entire army to the north side of the Appomattox.

By 3:00 in the afternoon, lead elements of Sheridan's other two divisions, Custer's and Devin's, arrived at this county seat village. They had ridden that day from the Sailor's Creek battlefield via Rice's Depot, taking a bypass road to the east of Farmville. In doing so, they passed "Longwood," the home of Colonel Charles Scott Venable, a member of Lee's staff. (Confederate general Joseph Eggleston Johnston was born here in 1807.) After riding six miles, they reached their destination and stopped for a rest. One trooper described Prince Edward Court House as "a neat little town of one broad street [the Richmond-Prince Edward-Danville Pike], with two or more stores, and twenty or thirty houses, mostly snuggled in behind hedges of evergreen, and nestling under the shadow of heavy overhanging boughs."

After dining with a local resident, James P. Smith, Sheridan ordered the Federal cavalry to move in a westward direction. Eventually reaching the area of Buffalo Creek and Spring Creek, seven miles southwest of Farmville and four miles from Prospect Station, the horse soldiers went into bivouac.

At some point during the day, General Sheridan was given a message from Grant in Farmville. The commander had been receiving conflicting information about the way Lee's army was leaving the area. One was "that Lee is going to Maysville [Buckingham]; another, that he will strive south by roads farther up river." Sheridan was told to watch for the latter.

Following along behind Sheridan and Mackenzie was Griffin's *V Corps* which arrived at the Court House around 7:30 p.m. After leaving their camp near Ligontown in the morning, they too passed through Rice's and headed to the south of Farmville. Up to this point in the pursuit, the *V Corps* had seen very little action except for long, strenuous marches. This could have been because of their heavy struggle at Five Forks on the 1st, and that Griffin's new leadership role needed to be solidified since he was now commanding his former peers. Whenever there was a reorganization of a unit, particularly on a corps level, it would take time for things to get realigned.

Upon reaching the village, Griffin moved his men to the western outskirts and on the grounds of Hampden-Sydney College. Established in 1776, the college was used as headquarters and campgrounds for the *V Corps*. Depending on their position in the column, the men had marched between twenty and twenty-eight miles during the day.

*   *   *

That evening, General Lee realized that to escape Grant's clutches he must once again make another night march. He therefore issued orders for Mahone and the troops holding the lines at Cumberland Church to withdraw from their position at 11:00 p.m. Lee's tentative plan for his army was to reach Appomattox Station, issue supplies and rations, then head west to Campbell Court House (now Rustburg) where he could move southward into Pittsylvania County and Danville. If this point could be safely reached, there possibly was still hope for a juncture with Johnston's forces in North Carolina.

Once again the Southerners fell in under the cover of darkness as they began their third night march in a row. Some of the men had already been on their feet between eighteen and forty hours. Since the Army of Northern Virginia now consisted only of Longstreet's and Gordon's corps, the two left the area north of Farmville by two separate routes. Longstreet's corps moved to the Piedmont Coal Mine (also known as the Buckingham Plank) Road, headed north for five miles, and then turned west toward the village of Curdsville. This was the same route General Walker's column had taken earlier in the day. General Lee rode with Longstreet.

Gordon's corps followed on a parallel route known as the Lynchburg Wagon Road for a couple of miles before reaching the Richmond-Lynchburg Stage Road. Here his column turned west and headed for New Store. Fitz Lee's cavalry followed Gordon as the rearguard.

The History of the South Side Railroad and High Bridge

The South Side actually saw its beginnings in 1836, when the City Point Railroad was chartered. This nine-mile long line was completed in 1838 and carried goods from Petersburg to the deep water port at City Point, now Hopewell. In 1847 the railroad was purchased by the town of Petersburg and renamed the Appomattox Railroad.

In 1846 the South Side Railroad was chartered, and the line between Petersburg and Lynchburg completed by 1854. It was at this time that the Appomattox Railroad was purchased and became an extension of the South Side. William Pannill was the first president of the railroad, and S.O. Sanford chief engineer.

The railroad was constructed of "U" rail purchased from Carrn Kelyn Iron Works in Wales and built with a 5-foot gauge. The first two locomotives were constructed by Uriah Well's foundry in Petersburg and eventually the line consisted of passenger, mail, baggage, box, flat, cattle, and dump cars. The locomotives carried such names as the *Virginia*, *Tennessee*, *Nottoway*, *Amherst*, *Campbell*, *Petersburg*, *Farmville*, and the *Sam Patch*.

Because of grades in the area, the line was charted to pass south of Farmville. However, Farmville residents raised $100,000 to bring the railroad through the town. The funds were used to build High Bridge which routed the railroad away from the steep grades beyond Rice's Station.

Eventually the South Side traversed the 123 miles from Petersburg to Lynchburg, ending at Percival's Island in the latter town. An express train could cover the distance in five hours, including one hour for stopovers.

Apparently there was some concern among passengers about the ride over High Bridge, but it was reported in 1855 "the Board is pleased to say that the apprehension of the public in regard to the safety of the High Bridge has subsided and they feel very confident that there is not a more secure half mile on any railroad in the United States."

Once the war began, the railroad complained that the Confederate authorities paid only 25% of the passenger fare for troops and 50% for freight. Although later rectified, the problem remained that the railroad was privatized rather than taken over completely by the military. Therefore the directors were more interested in profitable business than working with the government.

Because of the extreme military importance of the line to Petersburg and Richmond during the final year of the war, it was the target of at least three Federal cavalry raids. Consequently the "Southside Railroad Guards" was formed, Captain H.D. Bird's Company, Hood's Battalion Virginia Reserves.

After the war's end in 1865, President Lemuel Peebles remarked that only $675,000 cash was on hand, with $3,000 actually in Federal greenbacks. Seven passenger cars, two baggage, and seventy-five freight cars were destroyed. The depots at Ford's, Wilson's, Wellville, Blacks & Whites, Burkeville, Appomattox and Concord also had to be rebuilt. In Petersburg, the bridge over the Appomattox River to the railroad shops on the north side was burned during the evacuation, along with two locomotives and all the cars in the area.

The Federal Government returned the line to the South Side Company on July 24, 1865. Of course the biggest problem facing the railroad was in the Farmville area where the two bridges had been burned by Lee's retreating army. Once traffic began to use the line again after the surrender, trains had to be unloaded at High Bridge. A boat was used to cross the Appomattox River, then a horse drawn ambulance took passengers the mile and a half to a waiting train.

By September 22, 1865, the 450-foot burned section of High Bridge was replaced (83,000 feet of lumber). The other railroad bridge at Farmville, which lost 2 1/3 spans (260 feet), was also soon repaired. The costs to the railroad were

$15,750 for High Bridge; $1,490 for the other.

After the war, former Confederate General William Mahone consolidated the Norfolk & Petersburg, the South Side, and the Virginia & Tennessee railroads. By 1870 they were known as the Atlantic, Mississippi and Ohio Railroad, and Mahone was president. This line evolved into the Norfolk and Western Railroad in 1881. Recently it has become the Norfolk-Southern line.

The final affront to the South Side Railroad was not until over a century after the war. The original 1854 depot in Petersburg, with its passenger and freight sections, sat for many years abandoned. Recently it was restored to its former grandeur as the oldest railroad station existing in Virginia. After surviving Grant's artillery during the siege and the elements of time, nature was its downfall. In August 1993, a tornado whipped through the historic district of Petersburg, literally flattening one wing, and heavily damaging the rest of the structure. Fortunately, the owners have been able to restore what remains, a memorial to the role of the railroads during the Civil War.

Generals Thomas Smyth and James Dearing: The Last Union and Confederate Generals to Die in the War

Thomas Smyth was born on Christmas Day 1832, at Ballyhooley, a parish in the barony of Fermoy, County of Cork. This Irish born immigrant came to Philadelphia in 1854 and eventually settled in 1858 in Wilmington as a coach maker.

When the war arrived he offered the services of a company of infantry, but since Delaware was not forming any regiments, his men joined up with the all-Irish *24th Pennsylvania*, a three-month regiment. Upon its disbanding, he was appointed major of the *1st Delaware Infantry*, a three-year unit. He quickly moved up the chain of command to Lieutenant Colonel on December 24, 1862, and Colonel in February of 1863.

His regiment saw service at Suffolk, Antietam, Fredericksburg, Chancellorsville, and Gettysburg, where it was part of Major General Winfield S. Hancock's *II Corps* with Smyth commanding a brigade in Brigadier General Alexander Hay's third division. They were instrumental in helping repel Pickett's Charge on July 3rd.

In the Battle of the Wilderness, Colonel Smyth commanded the *Irish Brigade*. Later he returned to the 3rd brigade in the 2nd division, leading it in the battles of Spotsylvania and Cold Harbor. After serving meritoriously in the Overland and Petersburg Campaigns, he was promoted to Brigadier General of Volunteers on October 1, 1864. He continued to see action at Deep Bottom, Boydton Plank Road, and Hatcher's Run.

General Smyth was active with his brigade during the Appomattox Campaign, until his fateful mortal wounding north of Farmville on April 7. The general kept a diary, and on the day before his last entry read "April 6th, the orders to march at 5 a.m. and at 6 o'clock to assault the enemy."

After being paralyzed, he was put on a stretcher and moved to the Brook's farm house, *II Corps* hospital. The next morning Smyth was placed in an ambulance bound for Burkeville Station, about twelve miles away. Near the home and tavern of Colonel Samuel Dabney Burke, for whom the nearby settlement was named, the general began to fail. He asked to be taken into the residence. When he inquired of physicians about his chances for recovery, he remarked: Don't hesitate, Doctor, but speak candidly, for I am no coward and not afraid to die!" Colonel Burke and his family showed the general "the greatest of kindness and care," for which Smyth thanked them before he succumbed.

At 4 a.m. on the morning of April 9th, General Thomas Smyth died, unaware that Lee and his army would surrender that afternoon. He was posthumously promoted to Major General by brevet from the date of his wounding, April 7. Union General Thomas Smyth was buried in the Wilmington & Brandywine Cemetery, Wilmington, Delaware.

* * *

The Virginian **James Dearing** was born at "Otterburne" in Campbell County, on April 25, 1840. He attended school and graduated from Hanover Academy, and in July 1858 was appointed to West Point Academy, from which he resigned on April 22, 1861.

Returning to the South, he enlisted as a lieutenant in the Washington Artillery of New Orleans. He later became second captain in Company D, 38th Battalion Virginia Artillery, known as "Latham's Battery," or the Lynchburg Artillery.

Serving under General George E. Pickett's command during the Peninsula Campaign of 1862, General James Longstreet remarked: "I desire also to mention the conspicuous courage and energy of Captain James Dearing, of the Lynchburg Artillery, and his officers and men. His pieces were served under the severest fire as his serious loss will attest...."

His battery saw action at Fredericksburg and Chancellorsville, after which he was promoted to major and given a battalion of eighteen guns in Longstreet's Reserve Artillery, known as "Dearing's Battalion" in honor of their commander.

At Gettysburg in 1863, assigned to Pickett's division, they participated in the famous Confederate artillery bombardment on July 3. When General Lee saw Dearing riding forward to reconnoiter the enemy's position, he chastised him, saying: "Major Dearing, I do not approve of young officers needlessly exposing themselves; your place is with your batteries."

In the winter of 1863-4, General Pickett asked to have Major Dearing assigned head of his cavalry in the District of North Carolina, headquartered in Petersburg. He was given the rank of colonel and commissioned lieutenant colonel.

On April 5, 1864, he was assigned to command horse artillery known as "Dearing's Confederate Artillery." They were involved in the New Berne, North Carolina, expedition under Pickett, and at Plymouth on April 19, Dearing ordered the first charge of artillery known in the annals of war. In command of cav-

alry, he was charging a fort and when he recognized his old artillery battalion, he ordered it to charge with the cavalry. Plymouth was captured and Dearing was promoted to Brigadier General on April 29, just after turning 24 years old.

General Dearing returned to Petersburg where his cavalry command consisted of the 7th Confederate, 8th Georgia, 4th and 6th North Carolina, along with two companies of the 24th Virginia. During the Battle of Drewry's Bluff on May 16, he was stationed near Swift Creek with Major General William H.C. Whiting's two infantry brigades and one artillery battalion.

On June 9, when Petersburg was threatened by a Federal attack, the local "old men and young boys" militia were forced to respond to the emergency. Initially they were successful in holding off the Union cavalry, but soon were forced to fall back into the city. Fortunately they held out against the enemy long enough for regular troops to be called to the scene. General G.T. Beauregard ordered General Dearing and Captain Edward Graham's Company Horse Artillery, also known as the Petersburg Artillery, forward to the battlefield. They arrived in time to stop the Federal cavalry from entering Petersburg.

During the siege which followed, Dearing was given a brigade in General William Henry Fitzhugh Lee's division, which was shortly thereafter involved in the Wilson-Kautz Raid, then Weldon Railroad, Wade Hampton's Cattle Raid, and Burgess' Mill during 1864.

In March 1865, "Jimmy Dearing," Lee's boy general, was given command of the old "Laurel Brigade" under General Thomas Rosser. Rosser's division then consisted of Dearing's brigade and one under General John McCausland. It was said of Dearing in his new position: "He was a man of soldierly appearance, and being a courageous and dashing soldier, and withal a man of winning disposition, during his short but eventful career as commander of the brigade, he became greatly endeared to the officers and men."

During the retreat on April 5, his troopers fought General Henry Davies' cavalry at Amelia Springs after they returned from the Painesville wagon train raid.

It was during the first battle for High Bridge that James Dearing received his untimely mortal wounding. In the melee between Colonel Francis Washburn's *4th Massachu-setts Cavalry* and the Confederate cavalry, it is thought Dearing was hit in the act of discharging his pistol at Union General Theodore Read, who fell dead from the shot. Others reported that Dearing was accidentally shot by his own men. He was eventually taken to a nearby house, and finally to Lynchburg to the Ladies Relief Hospital, where he died three weeks later on April 23. Dearing had in his possession a letter from General Lee stating papers for his promotion to Major General were in the hands of the Secretary of War, "a promotion too long delayed by reason of my inability to fill your present command of the Laurel Brigade."

James Dearing, the last Confederate general to die of wounds received in action, was buried in Lynchburg's Spring Hill Cemetery.

The Capture of Union General J. Irvin Gregg near Farmville

Brevet Brigadier General John Irvin Gregg holds the inglorious honor of being the last Union general captured by Lee's army. It was while charging a Confederate wagon train north of Farmville that Gregg was taken and held prisoner until the Army of Northern Virginia surrendered.

J. Irvin Gregg was born on July 19, 1826, in Bellefonte, Pennsylvania. He began his military career in the Mexican War, and became captain of the *5th Pennsylvania Reserves* when the Civil War broke out. He later served as captain of the *3rd* and *6th United States Cavalry*, until assuming the position as Colonel of the *16th Pennsylvania Cavalry*.

On August 1, 1864, he was promoted Bvt. Brig. Gen., USV, for gallantry and distinguished services in the engagement at the defenses of Richmond, on the Brook Turnpike, and Trevilian Station. He was breveted brigadier general, USA, on March 13, 1865, for gallant and meritorious services in the field. On the same day, he was made Bvt. Maj. Gen., USV, for the same.

During the final campaign, Gregg's cavalry participated in the battles of Dinwiddie Court House and Little Sailor's Creek before reaching Farmville on April 7. After fording the Appomattox River near the town, the troopers rode up the Buckingham Plank Road toward Lee's army entrenched around Cumberland Church. The "road wound through cultivated farms and fine timber, and was lined with sturdy fences" as it passed the Jackson and Armstead farms. Upon nearing a road intersection at the Piedmont Coal Mines, they saw the Confederate wagon train heading westward. With Colonel Samuel Young's *4th Pennsylvania Cavalry* in the lead, Gregg and his men charged before the rest of the brigade could deploy.

Using the cover of nearby hills, the Confederate cavalry countercharged and enclosed Gregg's column on the narrow road. General Gregg, a heavy man riding a small horse, was fence-cornered and taken along with about thirty of his men. The Union cavalry began to retreat, prompting one man to write "extra horses, beasts of burden, lazy mules, and frightened contrabands united, suddenly, in the glorious charge, invincible—but, to the rear."

Apparently, had Gregg been successful with his assault, not only might his men have captured some wagons, but possibly General Lee himself. Lieutenant Colonel Elijah White, now commanding Dearing's Brigade, wrote in later years that when Gregg's cavalry were charging, they were not over 100 yards from the Confederate commander.

He was off his horse and leaning against a tree looking over a map. White said he "drove them [Gregg's men] back, doubling them up on the main column. I had them going too fast to rally around Gregg, who tried frantically to stop them. We captured Gregg."

Early the next morning after his capture, General Gregg was standing around a fire with his full uniform and hat adorned with a black ostrich feather. A Confederate soldier, passing by, grabbed the general's hat and replaced it with a butter-nut Scotch cap. Gregg, not happy with the exchange, threw his new hat in the mud.

On the morning of April 9, as Confederate General Tom Rosser was preparing to ride his troopers away from Appomattox, he gathered all his prisoners from the fight near Farmville and told them he was turning them loose. Before his men left, however, his horse soldiers began exchanging their boots for those of the prisoners. General Gregg protested but was finally grabbed from the back while another took off his boots from the front—the general kicking all the time.

Apparently, unlike the other Union prisoners with Lee's army at the time of the surrender, General Gregg did not have to go to Camp Parole, Maryland, to be exchanged. General Sheridan was told by General Grant on April 14 that when he got to Richmond, he would have Gregg immediately exchanged. He was then placed in command of the

District of Lynchburg on May 25, 1865.

Gregg continued on with his military service after the war, retiring as a colonel in the Regular Army. He died on January 6, 1892, and was buried at Arlington National Cemetery.

CHAPTER VII

The Final Days' March and the Battle of Appomattox Station

April 8

*S*aturday the 8th was one of relative quiet for the two armies. The Confederates continued their movement unmolested as they trudged along the routes of escape. The Federal *II* and *VI Corps*, finding that Lee had abandoned his position around Cumberland Church, followed in pursuit at early dawn. Wright's corps fell in behind Longstreet and trailed his column through Curdsville. Humphreys did likewise after Gordon.

As lead elements of the Confederate line of march proceeded westward, they caught their first glimpses of the Blue Ridge Mountains, forty miles distant. At Curdsville in Buckingham County, Lee's men found a small community of three hundred persons, a Masonic Temple, tobacco warehouse, several mechanic shops, and a small tavern and mill. Three miles north rose the geographic prominence known as Willis Mountain, towering at least 1,159 feet in elevation. After passing through the village, Longstreet bore to the south from the Plank Road and took a byway to New Store.

Since Gordon's route to New Store was somewhat shorter, he reached that destination before Longstreet. Continuing their march, the Second Corps was then in the van, and the combined

First and Third Corps in the rear of the infantry column, joining it at New Store Presbyterian Church.

New Store, a stage stop along the Richmond-Lynchburg Road, consisted of Louis D. Jones' home, "Keswick," a store, cobbler's shop, and three offices. It was near this area that in the afternoon General Lee decided to relieve from duty Generals Richard Anderson, George Pickett and Bushrod Johnson. One possibility for this action was because their commands were still disorganized from the Battle of Sailor's Creek. Certainly the generals' conduct on that field was in question. Evidently the latter two were never informed of their dismissals, or decided to ignore them since they were still with the army at Appomattox.

Anderson did leave the army with orders to proceed home and then report to Secretary of War Breckinridge. Pickett's men remained with Mahone's division, while Johnson's were placed with General Byran Grimes's division.

It was about this time that sheer exhaustion and the lack of proper food was taking a major toll on the condition of the Southern troops. Men who had stood by their colors from the beginning of the war were now losing hope and falling by the wayside. When they came to a road that headed in the direction of their homes, many simply left. Mentally they were numb, as the quick succession of events over the last week was more than they could handle. Still there were some who pressed forward along the muddy road.

About 9:00 a.m., one of the four messages sent by Grant to General Lee arrived at the rear of the Confederate column. It was passed along by members of Rosser's cavalry and eventually carried by General Seth Williams. Although it came through the lines early in the day, it did not reach the Confederate commander until sometime in the afternoon.

In this letter, the Federal commander supplied an answer to Lee's previous request for a statement of Grant's terms. Simply stated, General Grant insisted that the men surrendering not bear arms until properly exchanged. He went on to make an offer to Lee for a meeting to arrange the conditions for the surrender of the Army of Northern Virginia.

General Lee set about writing a response. In it he told Grant that he did not intend to propose the surrender of his army, but only to ask the terms which might be given. He informed the Union commander, "To be frank, I do not think the emergency has risen to call for the surrender of this Army," although he was interested in "the restoration of peace." Lee called for a meeting between his rearguard and Humphreys' line at 10:00 a.m. on the 9th.

Later in the day at 4:00 p.m., somewhere in the New Store area, the Federal *II Corps* caught up with the Confederates. They, like Gordon, were following a shorter route and so reached New Store before Wright's men. Marching approximately two miles behind the Confederate cavalry, at 6:30 p.m. Humphreys halted his column just past New Store and allowed the men to rest.

*   *   *

South of the Appomattox River, Confederate General E.P. Alexander's prophesy was coming true. The other wing of Grant's army was moving into place for the final race to cut off Lee's route of retreat. With Sheridan's cavalry in the van, Ord followed by Griffin took the shorter road to Appomattox Station, just as Lee's artillery commander suspected. Walker's artillery train had a lead on the rest of the Confederate army, but the question was whether it would reach the station before the Federals did. It fell upon those who gave the orders and carried out the movements to determine who would be successful this day.

After a ride of eight miles from Farmville, General Crook's cavalry went into bivouac at Prospect Station on the South Side. One of his men commented: "We found neither station nor prospect." Four miles southeast at Spring and Buffalo Creeks were Devin, Custer, and Mackenzie. Early in the morning Crook received word from Sheridan to pull out and follow the road alongside the railroad. Shortly thereafter, Mackenzie was ordered to reduce his division to a brigade and attach itself to Crook's command.

Before leaving his headquarters near "Buffalo River" (Creek), General Sheridan reported to Grant that "... the enemy must have taken the fine road north of the Appomattox River. I will move on Appomattox Court House...." This was in response to a note received from Merritt shortly after noon. "I sent a force toward Appomattox Court House. ...The officer in command reports a thin line of the enemy."

The lieutenant general, at some point during the day, also communicated with his cavalry general from Farmville. "I think Lee will surrender to-day. I addressed him on the subject last evening and received a reply this morning asking the terms I wanted. We will push him until terms are agreed upon."

Custer's division was the first which rode into Prospect Station from Merritt's command, after waiting until most of Crook's men had left. Finally, with Devin's appearance, the two divisions moved along behind Crook for about three miles. At this point, the *Army of the Shenandoah* cavalry turned off and headed in a northwest direction toward Walker's Presbyterian Church (present-day Hixburg). General Crook continued beside the railroad, eventually reaching Pamplin's Depot.

As his men entered the station area, they found the Confederate ration and supply trains sent the day before from Farmville. After quickly capturing them, they gleaned three engines and the accompanying rolling stock, along with boxes of new Springfield muskets.

Soon after the day's march had begun, General Sheridan received news at Prospect that eight trains had been located some miles west of Appomattox Station. This later turned out to be erroneous information as only four trains were actually sighted. The cavalry commander knew they should be there since he was aware that trains had been dispatched from Lynchburg. Sheridan's scouts earlier intercepted the message Lee sent requesting rations to be transmitted down the tracks from Danville and Lynchburg. Since the scouts were wearing Confederate uniforms, they went ahead and delivered these orders to the proper authorities in an effort to capture the trains.

All three cavalry division commanders were informed of this new information and told to press forward with haste. After a seven-mile ride, Sheridan, with Merritt's column, reached Walker's Church and sent a communication to Crook. He told him that the rest of the cavalry would rejoin him at Appomattox Station, and if he got there first to strike the enemy trains. After crossing Sawney's Creek, Sheridan continued along for another twelve miles before reaching the vicinity of the station.

Maj. Gen. E.O.C. Ord commanded XXIV Corps *in 1865.*

Turner's division led the *Army of the James* on this day, in front of Foster. Following the railroad out of Farmville in the morning, they reached Prospect after most the cavalry had left. Around noon, the head of Griffin's corps arrived from Hampden-Sydney College at this South Side Railroad depot after a ten-mile march. Griffin was once again under Sheridan's immediate command, although his corps was separated from him by Ord's army.

Leaving the road open for the artillery, wagons and ambulances, the infantry marched on both sides. Ord moved in behind Merritt's cavalry and followed them through Walker's Church, while the *V Corps* brought up the rear.

With the immediacy of the situation at Appomattox Station and the possibility of cutting Lee off, General Ord rallied his troops at various points along the march: "Legs will win this battle, men." "It rests with us to head them off." "This march will save all others." "Whichever army marches best wins."

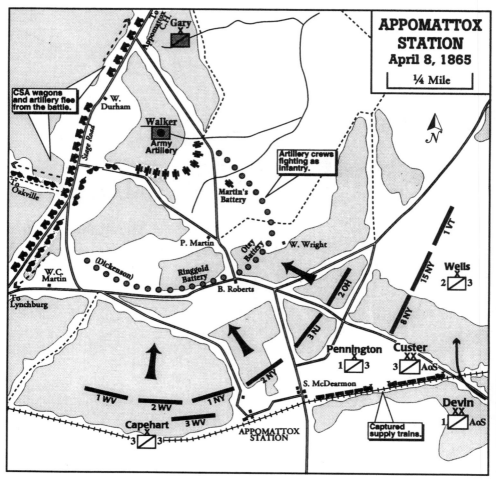

Gary

CSA wagons and artillery flee from the battle.

W. Durham

Walker
Army Artillery

Artillery crews fighting as infantry.

To Oakville

Martin's Battery

P. Martin

Otey Battery

W. Wright

(Dickenson)

W.C. Martin

Ringgold Battery

B. Roberts

To Lynchburg

1 VT

15 NY

Wells
2 X 3

8 NY

2 OH

3 NJ

Pennington
X
1 X 3

Custer
XX
3 X AoS

S. McDearmon

3 NY

1 WV

2 WV

1 NY

Capehart
X
3 X 3

3 WV

APPOMATTOX STATION

Captured supply trains.

Devin
XX
1 X AoS

"The campaign is in your legs, men." "Good marching will carry it." "They can't escape, if you will keep up to it." "One good steady march, and the campaign is ended." Around 8:00 p.m. Griffin's corps passed through Walker's Church after a slow and tedious journey.

In the van of Grant's column moving south of the river was Colonel Pennington's brigade of Custer's cavalry. With the *2nd New York Harris Light Cavalry* in the lead, they reached the South Side Railroad near Evergreen Station before continuing along to Appomattox Station (the present-day town of Appomattox), six miles to the west. On approaching the depot, they found only two or three houses there since the county seat village was located just three miles away. Waiting for them was what Sheridan's scouts reported earlier in the day: the ration and

Holding up Lee's supply trains, by the **2nd New York Cavalry** *at Appomattox Station on the evening of April 8, 1865.*

supply trains from Lynchburg. Two of the trains were drawn by locomotives, the third was pushed by one. The locomotive and crew of the fourth train sighted earlier had been able to get away before the Federals arrived on the scene.

The trains themselves were actually captured by just a few men of *Company K, 2nd New York,* who rode up to the engineers and ordered them to surrender. Without so much as a fight, the supplies, intended for Lee's army, were handed over to Custer's men. It appeared that the only troops nearby were some of Colonel T.M.R. Talcott's engineers. They offered little resistance since most were probably weaponless.

As the troopers opened the boxcars, what they found were 300,000 rations and various quartermaster stores. These included shoes, shirts, gray drawers and jackets, underclothing, English blankets, camp equipage, ordnance stores and medical supplies. One cavalryman recalled seeing fifty-one cars of supplies, three of which had nothing but bacon in them.

*   *   *

In advance of Lee's army on the 8th was Walker's artillery and wagon train. Leaving their camp at New Store at 1:00 in the morning, they had reached Appomattox Court House by 10:00 a.m. Continuing another two miles in the direction of Appomattox Station, they went into park between 2-3 o'clock. Not realizing Federals might be in the area, the artillerymen placed no pickets. The only support they had with them was Gary's 500-man cavalry brigade.

Behind them in the line of march was Gordon's corps. He began halting his men at 3:00 p.m. about a mile from Appomattox Court House. The rest of the army continued to come up and spread out to the northeast along the Stage Road for ten miles. Since it appeared that the enemy was not in the vicinity, orders were given to the men for the preparation of rations. For the first time in days, they were able to camp unmolested and receive rations from the wagon trains. Flour and bacon were the basic ingredients of the meal, probably one of the only meals not eaten on the run in days. By morning the two corps concentrated into a four mile area, fortifying their rear at New Hope Baptist Church with breastworks.

Back in Walker's camp the cry rang out "Yankees! Sheridan!" "The cavalry are coming, they are at the station and coming up the hill!" Commands were given as the men readied themselves for the impending attack. It was then about 4 p.m. Walker placed Gary's dismounted cavalry on either flank while setting his guns along a slight ridge in a hollow circle facing the station, a mile away. Many of his artillerymen were armed with muskets and acting as skirmishers in front of the approximately 100 cannons at his disposal. The field of the pending battle was densely overgrown with timber and brush and intersected by small dirt wagon roads, suitable for neither artillery nor cavalry fighting.

When Custer's *First Brigade*, led by Colonel Pennington, arrived on the field, they made uncoordinated and haphazard attacks against the Confederate artillery. Firing canister at close range, the Southerners quickly threw back these probes. Colonel Henry Capehart's *"West Virginia"* or *Third Brigade* followed, and they too were ineffective against Walker's cannoneers. Finally, between 8 and 9 p.m., under a full moon, Custer ordered all his brigades (Colonel William Wells, *Second Brigade*) up for a final push. Moving through a hail of canister, Custer led his men forward into the wooded landscape until they reached the artillery camp, this time scattering and capturing all who had not already withdrawn. That night Custer's division claimed as its spoils between 24 and 30 cannon, 150 to 200 wagons, five battle flags, and close to 1,000 prisoners. Also taken was Confederate General Young Moody, who had been riding in the wagons, ill. More important, the Federal cavalry was then in front of Lee's army and two more of Sheridan's divisions would shortly be on the scene.

The remaining guns belonging to Walker would either escape the field and head west toward Lynchburg, north to Oakville and the vicinity of Red Oak Church, or fall back into Appomattox Court House. The latter would be supported by Gary's cavalry.

Custer, wishing to ascertain the location of the main body of Lee's army, sent a probe forward toward Appomattox. This was in the form of the *15th New York Cavalry*, led by Lieutenant Colonel Augustus I. Root. As the troopers reached the village, they rode down the main street until they confronted Confederate pickets at the eastern edge of town. Traveling ahead of his squad was Colonel Root, who was shot down and killed, along with a few others.

It was then certain to Lee's men that at least some Union cavalry were in the area. Although they had heard the sound of gun fire earlier to the west (at Appomattox Station), it was unlikely they knew what it actually meant. The high command on the other hand did. The Federals were once again in their front, as at Jetersville, and were continuing to keep up pressure in the rear.

Lee's headquarters were set up about one mile from the village. Discussing the situation in a council of war with Generals James Longstreet, John Gordon and Fitzhugh Lee, Lee decided that if it was only Sheridan's cavalry in their front, he would attempt a breakthrough the next morning in the direction of Lynchburg. If the Federal infantry somehow managed to close in behind the troopers, that would be another matter. Lee might not have believed that Union foot soldiers could march from Farmville in time to get in front of his army.

For the next days' movement, he chose Generals Gordon and Fitz Lee to lead the way. They were to form their battleline along the western edge of the village and attempt to open the Stage Road by brushing away the enemy cavalry they knew were somewhere in front. With the Federal roadblock eliminated, the infantry would form to protect the road and allow the wagons to continue on. They were directed to inform Lee immediately if Union infantry did manage to cut them off, "... in order that a flag of truce should be sent to accede to the only alternative left us."

*　　*　　*

Since Custer's division did all the work on the night of the 8th, Sheridan sent one of Crook's brigades, under General Charles H. Smith, to move forward to a commanding ridge west of and overlooking the village. Composed of just four cavalry regiments, the *1st Maine*, *2nd New York Mounted Rifles*, *6th* and *13th Ohio*, along with two pieces of Lord's *2nd U.S. Artillery*, Smith straddled the Stage Road just west of the Oakville Road with his small battleline. This was the extent of troops emplaced to hold back the Southern army until the following Union infantry could come up. The other two cavalry divisions, Devin's and Custer's, were held in support near Appomattox Station.

Throughout the 8th, Ord pushed his men, as did Griffin, so that many had marched nearly thirty-some miles from their starting point by nightfall. They traveled until midnight, took a few hours break, then resumed the movement towards Appomattox Station early in the morning. They knew that if Sheridan could hold on long enough, they might arrive in time to finish the job. The men raced for the front with vigor.

The night before, General Meade spent the evening at Rice's Station while Grant quartered in Farmville. On the 8th, the two commanders joined together after crossing the Appomattox, and then followed in the wake of the *II Corps*. Upon reaching Sheppards, on the Richmond-Lynchburg Stage road, they stopped for the night at "Clifton," home of Joseph Crute. While Meade camped a few hundred yards from the house, Grant used one of its bedrooms.

It was here at midnight that a courier arrived with Lee's second letter to Grant, who was apparently suffering from a migraine headache. The courier was accompanied to Grant's room by chief of staff Brigadier General John A. Rawlins. Rawlins, who read the note out loud, stated that it was "a positive insult; and an attempt to change the whole terms of the correspondence."

Grant took it another way. Remarking that "Lee was only trying to be let down easily," he agreed to meet with him as requested. Rawlins reminded the commander that he had no authority to meet with Lee to discuss the subject of peace, but could only receive the surrender of his army.

It would not be until the morning of the 9th that Grant replied. He informed Lee that "I have no authority to treat on the subject of peace. ..." but went on to say that "The terms upon which peace can be had are well understood. By the South laying down their arms they will hasten that most desirable event, save thousands of human lives, and hundreds of millions of property not yet destroyed. Sincerely hoping that all our difficulties may be settled without the loss of another life. ..."

The Federal officers returned to their quarters and tried to get some rest for what could be the last day of the war in Virginia.

CHAPTER VIII

Last Bloodshed: Battle of Appomattox Court House

April 9

For his early morning operation against Smith's cavalry, General Lee had already chosen Gordon's Second Corps, supported by Fitzhugh Lee's cavalry. They formed their battlelines along the western edge of the village and attempted to open the Stage Road by pushing aside the Federal cavalry in their front. Gordon later stated he had only 2,000 infantry to accomplish this task (although he paroled 7,000 men), while Fitz Lee said he had 2,400 troopers. Smith's dismounted cavalry estimated they were opposed by between 8,000-10,000 Southern troops.

On Gordon's left flank was Clement Evan's division of Georgians, Virginians, and Louisianians. Next to Evan's right were James Walker's Virginians and North Carolinians; then Bryan Grimes' Alabamians, Georgians and North Carolinians. Cox's Brigade of Grimes' division held Gordon's right flank.

Supporting Grimes' line of battle were remnants of Bushrod Johnson's division, commanded by General William Wallace, although still under Grimes' orders, in line as follows: Wise's Virginians, Ransom's North Carolinians, Stansel's (Moody's) Alabamians, and Wallace's South Carolinians.

William Henry Fitzhugh Lee's North Carolinians and Virginians held his uncle's left connecting with the infantry's right. In between Munford and "Rooney" Lee were Rosser's Virginians.

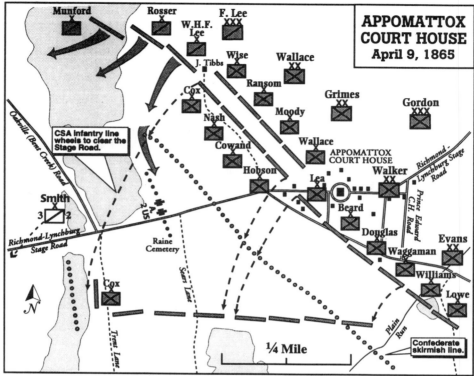

Munford held the extreme right of the Confederate line with his Virginians.

Leading the Confederate infantry that morning was General Grimes. Earlier, Generals Gordon and Fitz Lee had been arguing as to whether the cavalry or infantry should lead off. Becoming impatient, Grimes offered to begin the battle if given the command of the others.

At some point in the morning, General Lee asked Colonel Charles S. Venable to find General Gordon and inquire of him if he thought they could break through the enemy line. The Second Corps commander replied: "Tell General Lee I have fought my corps to a frazzle, and I fear I can do nothing unless I am heavily supported by Longstreet's corps."

At daybreak, the Confederate battleline moved forward en echelon with a final "Rebel Yell," Fitz Lee's horsemen riding ahead of the infantry. Consequently, it was they who actually came in contact with Smith's brigade and threatened their position.

The Union cavalry general had placed his pickets forward on a slight ridge beyond and east of his battle line behind the Oakville Road. The pickets were supported at their position by Lord's two guns. Both of Robert's North Carolina Cavalry regiments (the 4th and 7th) swept down upon the ordnance, quickly capturing them. The rest of W.H.F. Lee's cavalry then continued to press the rest of Smith's troopers.

Smith tried to deceive the Confederates into thinking that there was more than just a brigade of cavalry in their front. His men fired seven-shot Spencer repeating carbines, and a few sixteen shot Henry repeaters, as fast as possible. While the ploy held for awhile, eventually the men began to give ground. But they had gained time for the infantry to move up.

Meanwhile, General Crook had sent Mackenzie's brigade-size division and Young's brigade forward to support Smith, who had now completely fallen back from his position. Mackenzie arrived on the battlefield first and deployed his men in line along the high ground behind Smith's former post.

Fitz Lee sent some of "Rooney" Lee's cavalry regiments to continue the pursuit of Smith, while withdrawing most of his other two divisions, Munford's and Rosser's. They were directed to ride around the Federal troops and try to come up in their rear.

As Smith fell back toward Appomattox Station, along the next ridge the pursuing Confederate troopers again ran into Federal cavalry. This time it was Mackenzie's troopers. Mackenzie too was scattered by the Southerners before he could join up with Smith, and his four regiments also fell back. As they did so, Young approached from the west and ran into advance elements of W.H.F. Lee's cavalry, which proved to be the 9th and 14th Virginia. As the two forces clashed in the woods and along a wagon road, the Confederates captured another gun, this one belonging to Lieutenant Egbert W. Olcott's *Battery M, 1st U.S. Artillery*. In the foray the colorbearer of the 14th was shot down and a member of the *4th Pennsylvania Cavalry* retrieved the standard. It was the last battle flag taken in the combat.

Finally, lead elements of Ord's *XXIV Corps* broke through the woods and came onto the scene. Led by the capable General John Gibbon, they arrived just in the nick of time.

To the south of this action, Custer and Devin were reaching the battlefield. Colonel Charles Fitzhugh's brigade of Devin's command, moved in on the right of Smith's withdrawing line. Soon they were pushed back by the advancing Confederate skirmish line. Colonel Peter Stagg's Michigan cavalry brigade arrived and joined them as the two defended the crest along which the LeGrand Road ran. Alfred Gibb's brigade rode up and dismounted. Not only was Devin to provide a diversion for Crook's men fighting along the Stage Road, but also hold this ridge.

He soon found out why. With the Confederates still in fighting distance, the cavalry general turned around from his men. Behind them the hillside was covered with Union infantry. Devin's troopers then pulled out and rode down the LeGrand Road, following Custer who had already ridden past his rear.

As Fitz Lee's men took care of Crook's cavalry on the western front, the Confederate infantry line swung in an arc, eventually facing south and covering the Stage Road. Word was sent back to General Lee that the escape route was successfully opened, and the Federal cavalry had been thrown back. Gordon was so confident about this that most of his troops were told to lie down and rest, keeping their weapons handy. In fact, only one brigade, that of Brigadier General William R. Cox, was guarding his right flank and facing west along the ridge Smith originally held. He was the only one looking in the direction that Ord's men would be coming from.

As General Robert Foster's lead brigade, that of Colonel Thomas O. Osborn, moved onto the battlefield, they hurriedly prepared for an attack on Cox's position. With the *62nd Ohio* on the left, followed by the *199th Pennsylvania* and *39th Illinois*, the men rushed forward only to be thrown back. As they sought cover in a nearby ravine, they were joined by reinforcements from Colonel George B. Dandy's brigade, the *67th Ohio*, *10th Connecticut*, and *11th Maine*. One unit in particular from this group, the *11th*, was cut off from the rest and ran into both Confederate cavalry and artillery fire while trying to rejoin the

Brig. Gen. William Birney led the division of U.S. Colored Troops *in the Appomattox campaign.*

brigade, losing heavily in killed, wounded and captured. Finally, Foster's remaining brigade, under Colonel Harrison S. Fairchild, maneuvered up with Osborn and Dandy into the ravine to await the arrival of Turner's force. Turner's division came on the scene and began deploying into a line of battle along a ridge about a half mile behind Foster's men. Mixed in with the *Independent Division* were Woodward's and Doubleday's two brigades of *United States Colored Troops*, formerly under Birney of the *XXV Corps*. Some of Cox's North Carolinians, upon seeing Turner's men, noted that they looked like a blue checkerboard in the distance, with the white and black soldiers lined up together. They then knew the path of escape to Campbell Court House was cut off.

By this time, most of Fitz Lee's troopers were aware of the inevitable and began their ride around the Federal left flank in hopes of going on to Lynchburg. While it was possible Lee might have to surrender his infantry, the horse soldiers were not about to be part of it. Since some of the troopers were actually from the Appomattox area, it was not difficult for them to go cross-country to a position along the Richmond-Lynchburg Stage Road in the Federal rear. Some actually exchanged parting shots with Crook's men at their destination, before riding off unmolested.

Meanwhile, the rest of Gordon's battleline began skirmishing with the Union infantry. Griffin's *V Corps*, having followed Ord, was moving onto the LeGrand Road ridge south of the village and pressing from that front. Since Gordon realized that the Union army was now blocking the road to Campbell Court House, he began withdrawing his troops. They passed through the village and down into the Appomattox River valley, eventually reaching the high ground beyond. There, a second battleline was formed by General E.P. Alexander. The rallying position was made up of Field's, Mahone's and Wilcox's divisions.

Griffin, seeing this retrograde movement, ordered a skirmish line forward to contest the Southern infantry. General Chamberlain commanded a portion of it with the *185th New York, 198th Pennsylvania* and *155th Pennsylvania*. On their left were the *190th, 191st,* and *157th Pennsylvania* regiments led by Colonel Joseph B. Pattee. In conjunction with Griffin's movement, Sheridan sent Custer's and Devin's divisions of cavalry around to Griffin's right to help in that sector of the battlefield.

With Foster's division pinned down below the Confederates in the ravine, Turner moved his brigades forward and connected on Foster's right. Supported by Lieutenant Charles Muhlenberg's *Battery A, 5th U.S.*, and Captain Samuel Elder's *Battery B, 1st U.S. Artillery*, Gibbon's men advanced in line of battle perpendicular to the Richmond-Lynchburg Stage Road. Elder's 3-inch ordnance rifles were unhitched along the road and fired what is believed to be the last shot sent at the Confederates from this area of the field.

*   *   *

Lee's troubles were not only in his front but also in his rear. By early morning on the 9th, Longstreet's entrenched rearguard had stationed itself near New Hope Church, four miles away. Advancing quickly on them were skirmishers from Colonel George Scott's brigade of the *II Corps*. Following directly behind was the rest of Miles', then Barlow's and De Trobriand's divisions. Coming up quickly in support was Wright's *VI Corps*. Lee, in examining his situation, observed in his front and to the west

Ord's *Army of the James*, on his southeastern flank Griffin's *V Corps* and Sheridan's cavalry, while in his rear to the northeast the *II* and *VI Corps*. The only avenue of escape was to the northwest, an area devoid of major roadways and in the opposite direction from where he wanted to go. Lee was left with no alternative: He had to meet with Grant and discuss terms of surrender.

At various points along the lines, Confederate couriers equipped with white truce flags were sent out to stop the fighting. Between 10 and 11:00 a.m. the ceasefiring began, but not before additional casualties. As the *V Corps* skirmish line advanced on the village, eighteen-year-old Private William Montgomery of the *155th Pennsylvania* was mortally wounded by an exploding artillery round. When he died on April 28 in the hospital at Farmville, he was considered to be possibly the last Union enlisted man to die in this final Virginia battle.

A Confederate artillery piece near the village fired on Chamberlain's line and an officer was seen to go down. Lieutenant Hiram Clark, *185th New York*, was the last Federal officer to be killed at Appomattox.

As the truce flags passed through the Union lines and the battle was suspended, Federal officers rode out from the lines to the courthouse. Among them were Generals Ord, Sheridan, Gibbon, Griffin and others. They met a group of Confederate officers, including Generals Longstreet, Gordon, Heth and Wilcox.

While the white flags appeared on Ord's and Griffin's fronts, Sheridan's two divisions on the LeGrand Road confronted Martin Gary's cavalry near the intersection with the Prince Edward Court House Road. The Southerners were not aware of what had transpired with the rest of Lee's army. Supported by a battery of artillery, Talcott's Engineers, and some infantry, they saw Custer's cavalry forming in their front. But they too would soon cease firing.

When one of the flag of truce couriers came through the Federal lines, he was referred to General Custer. The young cavalry officer told the bearer, "We will listen to no terms but that of unconditional surrender. We are behind your army now

The Richmond Howitzers firing its last gun from the yard of George Peer's house in the village of Appomattox.

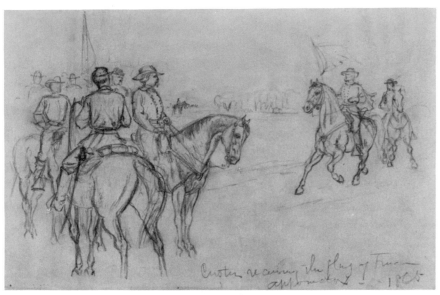

Custer receiving the flag of truce, Appomattox, 1865.

The flag of truce. (Edwin Forbes)

and it is at our mercy." The Southern officer then left with the message, going first to Gordon and then to Longstreet.

Shortly afterwards, Custer, with an orderly, rode into the Confederate lines. He ran into General Longstreet and the two conferred. Again Custer demanded unconditional surrender and told Longstreet if he did not agree he would be responsible for further bloodshed. Longstreet replied to Custer with a firm refusal that he could "go ahead and have all the bloodshed he wanted." The Northern general then learned that Lee and Grant were meeting so he rode off.

Some of Longstreet's forces were still entrenched in the rear of the army at New Hope Church. It was to this point at 8:30 a.m. that General Lee, Colonel Walter Taylor, Colonel Charles Marshall and Sergeant George W. Tucker rode. Expecting General Grant to arrive from this direction, Sergeant Tucker was sent out with a white flag toward General Humphreys' skirmish line. The group of Southern officers was met by Lieutenant Colonel Charles A. Whittier, of Humphreys' staff, instead. He had with him a letter from Grant to Lee and delivered it to the Confederate commander. It was the one in which Grant proposed terms for the restoration of peace: that the Southern forces must lay down their weapons and surrender.

General Lee told Colonel Marshall: "Well, write a letter to General Grant and ask him to meet me to deal with the question of the surrender of my army, in reply to the letter he wrote me at Farmville." In response, Marshall penned to the general:

> I received your note of this morning on the picket-line, whither I had come to meet you and ascertain definitely what terms were embraced in your proposal of yesterday with reference to the surrender of this army. I now request an interview in accordance with the offer contained in your letter of yesterday for that purpose.
>
> Very respectfully, your obedient servant,
> R.E. Lee
> General

The message was sent through Humphreys' front and received in General Meade's hands around 10:00 a.m. Lt. Col. Whittier had brought the note to the ailing commander. With it was a query from Lee for a suspension of hostilities, which Meade granted for one hour.

At Meade's suggestion, Lee also sent another letter to Grant by way of Sheridan's front, hoping one or the other would reach the Union commander quickly. Explaining first why he was sending a duplicate note to Grant, he then went on to say: "I therefore request an interview, at such time and place as you may designate, to discuss the terms of surrender of this army in accordance with your offer to have such an interview...."

The commander of the Army of Northern Virginia then returned in the direction of Appomattox Court House. Before reaching the Stage Road ford across the narrow tributary of the Appomattox River, the general dismounted in Sweeny's apple orchard to await news of Grant's arrival.

*   *   *

After leaving "Clifton" that morning, Grant and Meade had headed westward along the muddy Richmond-Lynchburg Stage Road. Grant was still suffering from his headache. Passing the road junction where the *VI Corps* had closed in behind the *II*, then New Store, the two generals decided to separate. Grant realized that if he continued forward, he would have to pass his two corps, then go through Lee's army to reach Appomattox Court House. Meade, still riding in an ambulance, headed for Humphreys' front. Grant and his staff turned off this road and rode south to Cutbank ford. After wading across the Appomattox River, they continued their ride to Walker's Presbyterian Church, where they turned to the west again and headed for Sheridan's front.

A little before noon, Lieutenant Charles E. Pease of Meade's staff overtook Grant's entourage about four miles west of Walker's Church. He handed Lee's third note to the commander. Pease also informed him about Meade's call for a short truce.

The Union commander wrote later: "When the officer reached me I was still suffering from the sick-headache; but the instant I saw the contents of the note [from Lee] I was cured."

Grant gave the letter to General Rawlins who read the message aloud. After the staff members had heard it, there was a period of silence. Then someone proposed three cheers. The shouts were rather subdued and soon changed to tears. At long last, it appeared that the war was about to be over.

The Federal lieutenant general dismounted and sat by the roadside, penning his reply. Telling Lee he had just received his dispatch at 11:50 a.m., Grant explained that he had changed his route to the Farmville and Lynchburg Road "and will push forward to the front for the purpose of meeting you. Notice sent to me on this road where you wish the interview to take place will meet you." This was given to Colonel Orville E. Babcock of his staff to deliver to General Lee.

As the group rode on in the direction of Appomattox Court House, Colonel Frederic C. Newhall, Sheridan's adjutant general, came up with Lee's other message and handed it over. After reading it, Grant and the other Union officers then continued their ride to Sheridan's lines.

Front view of Mr. W. McLean's house, at Appomattox Court House, Virginia, in which General Lee signed the terms of surrender, April 9, 1865.

Moving ahead of the rest to Appomattox, General Babcock found the Confederate commander sitting upon an embankment, his feet in the road below and his back resting against an apple tree. It was about 1:00 p.m. when he handed the letter to Lee.

Initially General Lee asked Colonels Marshall and Taylor to accompany him to the surrender conference with Grant, but Taylor declined. Consequently with Lee were Marshall, their orderly Private Joshua O. Johns, Babcock and his orderly, Captain William M. Dunn.

Upon reaching the outskirts of the village, Colonel Marshall and Private Johns rode ahead to find a suitable place for the meeting. The first white civilian they came across was Wilmer McLean whose assistance they asked. First showing the men an unfurnished and run-down house, McLean was informed it would not suit. He then offered his home, a nice brick structure on the western edge of the settlement.

Agreeing that it would do, Marshall sent Johns to retrieve the others in the group. Generals Lee and Babcock entered and sat down in Wilmer McLean's parlor to await Grant's arrival.

Numerous participants in this final drama remembered the county seat village of Appomattox Court House. One noted it "consisted of a courthouse, jail, post office and a few scattered houses," although he went on to say it "was not an interesting spot of the earth." Another remembered that it included "about a dozen houses of rather ordinary architecture and appearance. A store, court-house, jail, hotel, and a few dwellings, are all it can boast."

It was almost 1:30 p.m. when Grant and his officers rode from the west into the village. By this time Generals Sheridan and Ord had joined them along with other staff members. After the group dismounted in McLean's fenced-in yard, they walked up the front steps, across the porch, through the door and into the center hallway. As they turned left to enter the parlor, they saw General Lee standing.

General Grant extended his hand and offered a greeting, after which both sat down. General Lee sat by a marble-top parlor table, while Grant was beside an oval spool spindle table of pine. Grant borrowed his caster-wheel chair from the corner secretary; Lee used a simple chair with caned back and seat.

To all those present, there was an obvious clash in the personal appearance of two generals.

Since 1:00 a.m., General Lee had been dressed in a new uniform with a fine buff sash and presentation sword. When questioned by one of his men about his attire, he had replied, "I have probably to be General Grant's prisoner, and I must make my best appearance."

General Grant had been eighteen miles away on the morning of the 9th at "Clifton." When he received the important message from Lee saying that he wanted to meet, Grant chose to ride on, rather than wait for his headquarters wagon. He therefore had not changed from his field uniform. He was without a sword, and wore a simple fatigue blouse with his three star shoulder straps. After the muddy ride along the trail of the *II Corps*, fording the river, then continuing the long journey to Appomattox Court House, Grant was dirty. Lee, having ridden only two miles from his headquarters, was relatively clean in appearance.

As the Union officers attending Grant assembled in the McLean parlor, they saw that only Colonel Marshall had accompanied General Lee. With Grant were: Brig. General John A. Rawlins, Maj. General Seth Williams, Maj. General Rufus Ingalls, Lt. Colonel Horace Porter, Colonel O.E. Babcock, Maj.

General Grant entering the McLean house to receive the surrender of General Lee's army.

General P. H. Sheridan, M.R. Morgan, Colonel E.S. Parker, Colonel Theodore S. Bowers, Captain Robert T. Lincoln, Lt. Colonel Adam Badeau, and Maj. General E.O.C. Ord. They were introduced to General Lee. Notably absent were Generals Meade, Humphreys and Wright, who were four miles away in Lee's rear.

Grant and Lee initially began the conference with small talk about their earlier military careers in the Mexican War. It was Lee who eventually cut the conversation short and brought up the subject of surrender. He said: "General, I have come to meet you in accordance with my letter to you this morning, to treat about the surrender of my army, and I think the best way would be for you to put your terms in writing."

The Lieutenant General then set about writing down his terms of surrender in a manifold order-book which provided three copies. After he was finished, and Ely S. Parker, his secretary, had looked over the document, it was passed over to General Lee. The Southern commander read:

Headquarters, Armies of the United States,
Appomattox Court House, Va., April 9, 1865
General R.E. LEE,
Commanding C.S. Army

GENERAL:

In accordance with the substance of my letter to you ... I propose
to receive the surrender of the Army of Northern Virginia on the
following terms, to wit: Rolls of all the officers and men to be
made in duplicate ...; the officers to give their individual paroles
not to take up arms against the Government of the United States
until properly exchanged.... The arms, artillery, and public
property are to be parked and stacked, and turned over to the
officers appointed by me to receive them. This will not embrace
the side-arms of the officers, nor their private horses or baggage.
This done, officers and men will be allowed to return to their
homes, and not be disturbed by United States authority so long
as they observe their paroles and the laws in force where they
may reside.

Very respectfully,
U.S. GRANT,
Lieutenant-General

Since it was specifically mentioned that side arms were
allowed to be retained by the officers, it meant the men would
not have to suffer the humiliation of turning over their swords.
This also relieved Lee from tendering his sword to Grant which
was customary in a situation like this.

Even though the Army of Northern Virginia was the largest
and most powerful left in the Confederacy, when it surrendered
there were still other active Southern forces in existence. Should
they continue to carry on the struggle, the Confederate States of
America would have to exchange an equal number of Union
prisoners for the number of Lee's men who surrendered at
Appomattox. Then, conceivably, the Southerners could return to
duty as those who surrendered at Vicksburg did earlier in the
war.

One item that was left out of the terms was the disposition of
the cavalrymen and artillerymen who owned their own horses.
These men brought their own horses into service and received a

stipend from the government for their use. General Lee brought this situation to Grant's attention.

Realizing that the vast number of Lee's army were probably simple farmers and would need the animals for the spring planting, Grant decided to make a concession. While not wanting to rewrite the document, he promised to instruct his officers to allow the Confederates to keep their mounts upon leaving the area.

General Lee asked Colonel Marshall to draft a reply to General Grant's letter. It said:

> Headquarters, Army of Northern Virginia
> April 9, 1865

> Lieut-Gen. U.S. Grant,
> Commanding Armies of the United States.

> General: I have received your letter of this date containing the terms of surrender of the Army of Northern Virginia as proposed by you. As they are substantially the same as those expressed in your letter of the 8th instant, they are accepted. I will proceed to designate the proper officers to carry the stipulations into effect.

> Very respectfully, your obedient servant,
> R.E. LEE
> General

Both generals signed their respective documents which were handed to each other. The fighting was finally over on this solemn Palm Sunday.

Eventually the subject of rations came up. General Grant asked Lee how many were still in his army. "Indeed, I am not able to say," was his reply. "My losses in killed and wounded have been exceedingly heavy, and, besides, there have been many stragglers and some deserters. All my reports and public papers, and indeed some of my own private letters, had to be destroyed. ... I have not seen any returns for several days, so I have no means of ascertaining our present strength."

General Grant offered 25,000 rations which the Southern commander felt would be sufficient for his men. Much of this

Union soldiers sharing their rations with the Confederates. From a sketch made at the time.

was provided from the captured trains at Appomattox Station or by the Union soldiers, who shared what was in their haversacks.

The Federal army was actually low on subsistence itself. Not until April 10 would the U.S. Military Railroad have the line open as far as Burkeville Junction, 48 miles away from Appomattox Station. When Grant left Petersburg he ordered twelve days rations to be carried by his men. This was the twelfth and last day of the campaign.

The topic of appearance was brought up by the Lieutenant General who explained why he did not have his sword. Telling Lee that he did not wish to detain him, and rather than send back to his wagons, he decided not to wait for his sword.

Sometime after 3:00 in the afternoon, General Lee and Colonel Marshall began their exit from the parlor in the direction of the front door of the house. As they walked down the porch steps, Private Johns brought up their horses. The two commanders, one Northern, one Southern, respectfully saluted each other before Lee rode off to his army to deliver the sorrowful news.

As Lee, Marshall and Johns rode downhill from the village into the river bottom, they found the head of the army positioned along the Stage Road. The soldiers stood uncovered as Lee and his entourage rode down between them. As he ap-

General Lee's return to his lines after the surrender. From a war-time sketch.

proached each group of men, the Southerners gave a wild cheer, and gathered around their commander. When Lee addressed his troops, he said he did all he could for them, and told them to go quickly and quietly to their homes, resume peaceful advocations, and be as good citizens as they were soldiers.

After stopping at the apple tree site for awhile, the Confederate commander rode a mile further to his lines and went into bivouac next to the Stage Road. Once again he was thronged by men as he passed through their campsites; many veterans were in tears.

Grant remained behind at the McLean house as various orders for his army were being prepared by Colonel Parker. He also had to appoint three Union commissioners to be "designated to carry into effect the stipulations" agreed upon concerning the surrender. For this Generals Gibbon, Griffin and Merritt represented Grant; Longstreet, Gordon and Pendleton were later appointed by Lee. On the following day they provided the commanders with a document detailing the formal terms of surrender.

When Grant and his staff eventually left the village, they rode off to his headquarters, about a mile to the west. Along the way, the Federal commander dismounted and sent a message at 4:30 p.m. to Secretary of War Stanton in Washington. It said: "General Lee surrendered the army of Northern Virginia this afternoon on terms proposed by myself. The accompanying additional correspondence will show the conditions fully." Stanton received the news at about 9:00 p.m.

*   *   *

The batteries which had escaped from General Walker's debacle at Appomattox Station the night before either went on to Lynchburg or Red Oak Church. The general was with the contingent at the church and, after returning from a meeting with Lee, ordered the artillery units to disband. The guns were spiked, dismounted and buried, while the carriages were destroyed. Those which made it to Lynchburg did likewise at the Fair Grounds.

Eventually the Federals were sent to retrieve the ordnance destroyed at the church. They returned with the remnants of 54 iron and bronze guns, 36 carriages and caissons, and one battleflag.

Back in the Confederate bivouac, now compacted along the Stage Road between the Appomattox River and Rocky Run, the news of the surrender was received by 5:00 p.m. The same was true along the Federal lines which then encircled the Southern army in the shape of a "C." Although orders had been issued for no fraternization between the former enemies, the soldiers slipped back and forth between the pickets to share rations and trade souvenirs. One item in popular demand was a piece of the apple tree under which Lee sat while meeting with Colonel Babcock. It seemed that witnesses to this conference thought Babcock was Grant and that the surrender meeting actually took place under the tree. When word got out about this incident, every soldier wanted a piece.

Upon hearing of the surrender, the men in the Union ranks had immediately set about celebrating. Cheers were heard throughout the army as bands struck up patriotic tunes. The artillery followed with salutes in honor of the victory. General

Grant, hearing these, sent word to have them stopped. "The Confederates are now our prisoners, and we do not want to exult over their downfall."

That evening General Meade received an order from Grant concerning the disposition of the various corps for the next few days. The *V* and *XXIV Corps* were to remain at Appomattox to carry out the stipulations of the surrender, while the rest returned to Burkeville. All captured ordnance also was to be sent to the railroad junction.

As Grant's designated officials issued the promised rations to Lee's men, the Southerners were able to eat their hardtack and meat in peace. From sheer exhaustion many of them physically collapsed before the evening arrived. It was their first night back in the Union.

*   *   *

It is obvious that the Appomattox Campaign was a successful one for the Union army, instrumental in bringing about Lee's decision to surrender. Ever since the spring of 1864, when Grant moved to fight in the east, the objective of his army had been the destruction of Lee's forces. It took almost a year and three campaigns, the Overland, Petersburg and Appomattox, to accomplish this goal. Along the way, thousands of Northerners and Southerners lost their lives in the process. By the time the Southern commander reached Appomattox after the six-day march, he could muster only about 30,000 men to be paroled. Grant had within a ten mile-range about 63,000 men; his casualties for the last week had been about 8,600 soldiers.

As evident in the various correspondences issued between the Northern commanders in the campaign, they never were quite sure which route Lee was taking in his retreat from day to day. On the other hand, they did realize he was trying to reach Johnston's army in North Carolina. It was Grant's intention throughout the movement to prevent Lee from accomplishing this objective. Daily marching orders for each of the corps demonstrate that this was the Northern general-in-chief's plan.

The final day of the campaign proved to be the most critical. Grant had divided his army into two separate wings, with one pushing Lee, the other hoping to confront him. By way of a shorter road network and a quick pursuit by the Federal cavalry and infantry, this was accomplished. What evolved, although it was probably not recognized at the time, was a classic envelopment situation: an attack on the enemy's flank and toward his rear, accompanied by an assault on his front. Grant was able to place his forces in Lee's front with Ord's army on his left flank with Griffin and Sheridan, and in the rear with Humphreys supported by Wright. Lee was virtually surrounded at Appomattox after the final battle movements on the 9th. Lee did not come to Appomattox Court House to surrender; he did so only when forced into this predicament.

Why did Lee allow this last engagement to take place? The answer probably lies in two attributes which exemplified his life: *duty* and *honor*. After hearing Lee's message to Jeff Davis on the 7th concerning his thoughts about the situation, John Wise remarked: "It revealed him as a man who had sacrificed everything to perform a conscientious duty against his judgement … at the call of his State he had laid his life and fame and fortune at her feet, and served her faithfully to the last." The commander wanted to demonstrate to his men that he had made every possible effort to continue the struggle before considering surrender, even though he sensed little chance for success. When he realized that his army was virtually surrounded, he knew the time had come.

The quick succession of events which followed Lee's surrender overshadowed the fact that many lives were lost in those final hours of combat in Virginia. Union soldiers who died there were later buried in Poplar Grove National Cemetery near Petersburg, transported from the field of Appomattox in 1867. The Confederate dead, other than those eighteen who are now in the cemetery near the village, were probably all reclaimed and taken home.

Lee's Retreat: Was It Actually One?

Although officially this final military movement was called the "Appomattox Campaign," to most students of the war the sobriquet "Lee's Retreat" leaves no misunderstanding about which event is being referred to. Other than his retreat from Gettysburg back to Virginia, it is the only one written about in any length. The question that then arises is was it a military retreat or merely a change of operations.

For a better understanding it is necessary to refer to *Farrow's Military Encyclopedia* (1885) and H.L. Scott's *Military Dictionary* for the meaning of the word "retreat" in the 19th century. Farrow's describes a military retreat as a "retrograde movement of a force [the Army of Northern Virginia withdrawing from the Petersburg and Richmond front] with the intention of avoiding an encounter with a hostile body in the front [which would eventually happen at Appomattox]. ... When the enemy pursue, if the retreat is not to degenerate into a rout, the retreating army must be covered by a powerful rear-guard [an entire Confederate corps did so from Amelia Springs to Appomattox], which from time to time must hold the pursuers at bay, while the artillery-train and baggage pass defiles, cross streams, and over come other special obstacles [this would prove to be the eventual cause of the Battles of Sailor's Creek]." On the other hand Scott's merely says a "retreat" is a "retrograde movement before an enemy [Grant's pursuing army]."

From period sources we learn that the word "retreat" in connec-

tion with Lee's final campaign was used quite freely. A letter by a resident of Petersburg describing Lee's evacuation from the city stated, "The second day of April will ever be remembered as the saddest day of my life. ... there were many rumors but we all... still hoped they were not on a retreat—after breakfast ... went to the city, returned and confirmed the report that Lee was retreating. ..."

In a diary entry for April 13, 1865, written by Sergeant R.A. Boyd of the 2nd Engineer Regiment, he noted: "On the retreat from Petersburg to Appomattox C. House, I suffered extremely as did also the whole Army from rapid marching."

General Robert E. Lee himself, while writing to President Jefferson Davis on April 12, 1865, said "... with the advance of the army, on its retreat from the lines in front of Richmond and Petersburg ...."

In *The Lost Cause; A New Southern History of the War of the Confederates* (1867), by Virginian Edward A. Pollard and heralded as "drawn from official sources and approved by the most distinguished Confederate leaders," Chapter XLII has a subtitled section called "Retreat and final surrender of Lee's Army." In this narrative alone such phrases as: "The retreating army ..."; "So far the retreat ..."; "he took up this line of retreat"; "Its final retreat"; "Confederate line of retreat," are used throughout the text.

As the history of the war was looked at by the next generation of writers, none was more distinguished than Douglas Southall Freeman. Writer of the classics *R.E. Lee* (1935) and *Lee's Lieutenants* (1946), Freeman variously referred to the final campaign in his works as "a retreat to Amelia"; "proposed lines of retreat of the Army of Northern Virginia"; "when Grant found the direction of the army's retreat and set out after Lee"; "Lee's line of retreat." Freeman's father, a Confederate soldier who followed Lee to Appomattox with the 34th Virginia, also referred to the march from Petersburg to Appomattox as "the retreat" in his memoirs.

In the late 1920s the Virginia State Commission on Conservation and Development began a program of placing highway historical markers at points of significance in the Commonwealth. One subject matter addressed was "Lee's Retreat." By the latest count, some thirty-one signs were placed under this category dealing with various historical episodes. Of those, ten are simply labeled: "Lee's Retreat."

In 1956, the Virginia Department of Highways developed a twenty-stop tour called "Lee's Retreat Route from Petersburg to Appomattox." It was researched by Wilmer R. Turner of Blackstone and his "work was carefully studied by the Historical Division of the State Library and authenticated prior to submission of the idea to the Appropriations Committee" of the General Assembly. Two thousand dollars was allocated for small black and white signs which carried a crossed saber and rifle logo encircled with: "Route of Lee's Retreat." (See "Lee's Retreat Today" on page 209.)

"Those last days of the war in Virginia demonstrate, better than any other episode, the unbounded limits men will strive for and the suffering they will tolerate when properly led and motivated. For them it was a triumph of personal endurance and leadership and a testament to the tenacity of the human spirit. For many, it was a period that foreshadowed the downfall of their way of life, but through it all, they would survive, as man has always done in the many crises that confront him." It is a story that should never be forgotten by our country.

Black Troops of the Union and Confederate Armies in the Last Campaign

While most of the *United States Colored Troops* in the Federal army were involved with the occupation of Richmond on the morning of April 3rd, 1865, some did enter Petersburg when it fell on the same day. With Brigadier General William Birney's second division operating south of the Appomattox, they were among the first units to come into the city from the west. It was noted that the 7th regiment, recruited in Maryland, and the 8th, from Philadelphia, were on the skirmish line that morning and with those who marched into the evacuated railroad center. The 7th's commander, Lieutenant Colonel Oscar E. Pratt, wrote, "I entered the city of Petersburg at 6 a.m., amidst the joyous acclamations of its sable citizens. Marched from the city at 9 a.m...."

A soldier in the *29th* regiment remembered that "We were among the first troops to enter Petersburg, and the orderly, well-behaved disposition of our command elicited the praise of our officers, and the universal commendations of the people, sobriety and decorum being the order of the day....Colored men, you know, can be, are, and will be gentlemen as well as soldiers."

There were seven Black units (about 2,000 men) which made the journey all the way to Appomattox Court House with Ord's *Army of the James* and arrived in time to be involved in the final fighting. On their way they passed through the settlements of Blacks & Whites (Blackstone), Nottoway Court House, Burkeville Junction, Rice's Station and Farmville. From the latter point they stayed south of the Appomattox River and travelled via Walker's Church (present day Hixburg) to Appomattox. These regiments were of Colonel William W. Woodward's third brigade, the *29th* and *31st U.S.C.T.*, along with the *116th U.S.C.T.*, assigned to them from the first brigade. Colonel Ulysses Doubleday's *8th, 41st, 45th,* and *127th U.S.C.T.*, were also present. The first brigade, under Colonel James Shaw, Jr., would not arrive until the day after the surrender, having marched ninety-six miles in four days. His brigade was detached from the others and sent back to Sutherland Station for a period of time, causing their delay.

Colonel Shaw reported that his two regiments, the *7th* and *109th U.S.C.T.*, stopped in Farmville on the 8th for a rest as they advanced to reach the others. "Farmsville [sic] is a pretty place of about 1,500 inhabitants. It is well built, and we saw many respectable-looking people as we passed through....A lady came to her door, where I was resting for a moment as the brigade passed, and invited me in. Speaking of the troops that had passed through, she said, 'You have armies enough to conquer the world.' 'This is only one of them,' I replied, as I bowed my adieu."

Earlier, while at Farmville on the night of the 7th, Birney's two brigades were divided: one was assigned to Brevet Major General John W. Turner's *Independent Division*, the other to Brigadier General Robert S. *Foster's First Division*, both of the *XXIV Corps*. General Birney was sent back to Petersburg to command the Division of Fort Powhatan (James River), City Point and Wilson's Wharf.

On the morning of the 9th at Appomattox Court House, the Black units were sent forward to support Foster's division in the closing phase of the battle. Consequently, only Woodward's brigade participated in the final advance on the Confederate line. Some of Doubleday's skirmishers did proceed forward, and the only casualty for the *XXV Corps* was Captain John W. Falconer of *Company A, 41st U.S.C.T.*, a white officer. He was mortally wounded and died on April 23rd.

According to Surgeon-in-Chief Charles P. Heichhold, during the entire campaign, the *Second Division* lost 4 men killed, 1 officer (mortally) and 30 men wounded, a total of 35 casualties.

On the 10th of April, the division was put under the command of Brevet Brigadier General Richard Henry Jackson and then ordered back to Petersburg. Upon returning to the latter place, they went into camp near Warren's Station on the Petersburg & Weldon Railroad.

Sergeant Major William McCeslin of the *29th U.S.C.T.* recalled after the last campaign, "We, the colored soldiers, have fairly won our rights by loyalty and bravery — shall we obtain them? If they are refused now, we shall *demand them.*"

* * *

With General Robert E. Lee's manpower reserves quickly draining, on March 23, 1865, General Orders #14 was issued which allowed for the enlistment of Blacks into the Confederate service. Shortly thereafter, a notice was posted in Petersburg's *The Daily Express*, "The commanding General deems the prompt organization of as large a force of negroes as can be spared, a measure of the utmost importance, and the support and co-operation of the citizens of Petersburg and the surrounding counties is requested by him for the prosecution to success of a scheme which he believes promises so great benefit to our cause.... To the slaves is offered freedom and undisturbed residence at their old homes in the Confederacy after the war. Not the freedom of sufferance, but honorable and self won by the gallantry and devotion which grateful coun-

trymen will never cease to remember and reward."

This recruitment effort did bear fruit in Richmond where Majors James W. Pegram and Thomas P. Turner put together a "Negro brigade" of Confederate States Colored Troops. The *Richmond Daily Examiner* noted of the unit "the knowledge of the military art they already exhibit was something remarkable. They moved with evident pride and satisfaction to themselves."

As the Confederate army abandoned Richmond on April 3rd, apparently these Black Confederate soldiers went along with Major General G.W. Custis Lee's wagon train on its journey. They moved unmolested until they reached the area of Painesville on April 5. Here they were attacked by General Henry E. Davies' troopers. A Southern soldier remembered that "I saw a wagon train guarded by Confederate negro soldiers....When within about one hundred yards of and in the rear of the wagon train, I observed some Union cavalry a short distance away on elevated ground forming to charge and the negro soldiers forming to meet the attack, which was met successfully....The cavalry charged again, and the negro soldiers surrendered."

A Confederate officer, who rode upon this situation as it was transpiring, recalled: "Several engineer officers were superintending the construction of a line of rude breastworks....Ten or twelve negroes were engaged in the task of pulling down a rail fence; as many more occupied in carrying the rails, one at a time, to the desired spot; and several were busily throwing up the dirt....The darkeys thus employed all wore good gray uniforms and I was informed that they belonged to the only company of colored troops in the Confederate service, having been enlisted by Major Turner in Richmond. Their muskets were stacked, and it was evident that they regarded their present employment in no very favorable light."

Although Davies made no mention of these Black Confederate soldiers in his captures for the day, he does state that he took 310 "teamsters" at Painesville. Presumably he was not aware that they were considered formal Southern infantry.

A *New York Times* correspondent reported on the 5th from nearby Jetersville that after the engagement "several hundred negroes were brought in." At least some were happy with their new found dilemma as he noted: "the negroes...were highly delighted, and frequently in their rejoicing shouted, "De day of Jubilee hab come at last."

On April 10th, as Confederate prisoners were being marched from Sailor's Creek and elsewhere to City Point and eventually off to Northern prison camps, a Union chaplain observed the column. "The first instalment [sic] of Rebel prisoners, numbering seventeen hundred and seventy, have just passed, under a strong guard....In the squad were many negroes recently armed by Jef. Davis."

This incident along the retreat to Painesville, seems to be the only documented episode of official Black troops serving the Confederacy in Virginia as a unit under fire.

Also along the retreat, a squad of twelve Afro-Confederate soldiers throwing up earthworks along the road to Farmville was seen. They were armed with rifles and commanded by white officers who identified them as "the only company of colored troops in the Confederate service."

African-Americans also accompanied the Confederate army on the retreat with the First Regiment Engineer Troops and provided yeoman service. One member of this unit remembered that they mounded roads, repaired bridges and cut new parallel roads to old ones when they became impassable. When this was not possible, an engineer officer would post a group near the trouble spot to extricate wagons and artillery pieces.

When Lee surrendered his army at Appomattox, thirty-six African-Americans were listed on the Confederate paroles. Most were either servants, free Blacks, musicians, cooks, teamsters or blacksmiths.

CHAPTER IX

Epilogue
The Final Bivouac

April 10 - 12

*T*he men of both armies woke up to a chilly drizzling rain as the distribution of rations among the Confederates continued on the 10th. Northern and Southern soldiers persisted in visiting with each other in the camps, even though orders had been issued to the contrary.

At some point after the surrender meeting with Grant, General Lee directed Colonel Marshall to write a farewell letter to the army. Interrupted constantly, Marshall finally retired to the general's ambulance on the morning of the 10th. After a slight bit of editing, the Southern commander then issued,

GENERAL ORDER, NO. 9
Headquarters, Army of Northern Virginia
April 10, 1865

After four years of arduous service, marked by unsurpassed courage and fortitude, the Army of Northern Virginia has been compelled to yield to overwhelming numbers and resources.

I need not tell the brave survivors of so many hard fought battles, who have remained steadfast to the last, that I have consented to this result with no distrust of them.

But feeling that valor and devotion could accomplish nothing that would compensate for the loss that must have attended the continuance of the contest, I determined to avoid the useless sacrifice of those whose past services have endeared them to their countrymen.

By the terms of the agreement officers and men can return to their homes and remain until exchanged. You will take with you the satisfaction that proceeds from the consciousness of duty faithfully performed, and I earnestly pray that a Merciful God will extend to you His blessing and protection.

With an increasing admiration of your constancy and devotion to your country, and a grateful remembrance of your kind and generous considerations for myself, I bid you all an affectionate farewell.

R.E. Lee
General

This order was copied by many of the officers and then read to their troops.

At 10:00 a.m. the two commanders met on the eastern edge of the village along a little rise. After discussing the events of the last few days, Grant tried to convince Lee, who was general-in-chief, to use his influence to get the other Confederate armies to surrender. His reply was that he must first confer with Jefferson Davis before he could do anything.

What eventually came out of the horseback conference were three points of understanding: Each Confederate soldier would be given a printed pass, signed by his officers, to prove he was a "paroled prisoner." All cavalrymen, artillerymen and couriers would be able to retain their horses. Confederate soldiers who must pass through Federal occupied territory to get home were allowed free transportation on government railroads and vessels.

After the two generals departed, the three Union and three Confederate commissioners joined together and rode into Appomattox Court House for their meeting. They first used the Clover Hill Tavern to discuss the formal terms of surrender, then decided to move over to McLean's house. Their agreement stipulated five points:

"The [Confederate] troops shall march by brigades and detachments to a designated point, stack their arms, depot their flags, sabers, pistols, etc. ... and from thence march to their homes under charge of their officers..." was the first.

The others included that all public horses and property be turned over to Federal officials and that transportation necessary for private baggage could be used by the Southern officers. At the end of their trip, their conveyances were to be turned over to the United States quartermasters in the area.

Finally, and in writing this time, it was stated that mounted men could keep their horses if they were originally their private property. Most importantly though, the bounds of those included in the surrender were designated. All forces with the Confederate army on the 8th, except for Fitzhugh Lee's cavalry which escaped to Lynchburg, and all artillery more than twenty miles from Appomattox Court House at the time of the surrender, were included in the terms.

The six officers made this agreement official by signing the document on General Gibbon's old pine camp table.

Designated Union soldiers then began preparing for the printing of 30,000 parole passes. Portable army printing presses were set up in the tavern and certificates churned out, then taken to the Confederate campsite and distributed among the various commands. Southern officers filled out and signed each one, keeping duplicate rolls of the men issued them.

To help remedy the desperate need for forage for horses, it was decided that the cavalry troops would turn in their accoutrements on the 10th, the artillery would follow on the 11th, and the infantry finally on the 12th.

General Ranald Mackenzie's troopers received the equipments from the remnant of Fitz Lee's Corps. Colonel Alexander Cheves Haskell of the 7th South Carolina was designated to lead the Confederate horse column to Mackenzie. A total of 1,559 cavalry turned their weapons in on the 10th.

At 8:00 a.m in the morning, General Sheridan's cavalry mounted and began their ride back to Nottoway Court House. Later in the afternoon, Grant and his staff left for the railroad at Burkeville Junction. They, like the cavalry, reached Prospect Station the first day out and went into camp.

Before he left Appomattox, General Grant appointed General Joshua L. Chamberlain to receive the formal surrender of the Confederate foot soldiers. Chamberlain was told that night at

Brig. Gen. Joshua L. Chamberlain received Confederate infantry in surrender parade at Appomattox.

division headquarters about his role and was given instructions for carrying it out.

Humphreys' and Wright's corps also began a retrograde movement to Farmville, then on to Burkeville. Both corps left Appomattox with officers and men getting no closer than four miles from the village and Lee's army.

On the 11th the rain continued as the surrender ceremony for Lee's remaining artillery battalions began. General Turner's *Independent Division* initially was assigned to receive the ordnance, with General Joseph Bartlett's *V Corps 1st Division* relieving them at noon. A total of 2,576 artillerymen surrendered, along with 60-65 cannons turned in during this ceremony. When all the captured, extricated, and abandoned guns were brought in, Lee surrendered about 180 pieces of artillery at Appomattox.

At about 2:00 p.m. Grant and his party reached Burkeville Junction, from which the rail line was open to City Point. After leaving at 4:00, he had spent twelve hours traveling the sixty-one miles to his former headquarters site at the confluence of the Appomattox and James Rivers. After sitting out the war at the mouth of the Appomattox for ten months of siege warfare, he had pursued Lee's army along its entire length, only to end the fighting at its headwaters in Appomattox County.

General Grant on the way to City Point after the surrender of Lee.
(Edwin Forbes)

On the afternoon of the 12th, Grant left by boat from City Point for Washington, D.C.

Since Mackenzie and Turner took care of receiving the Confederate cavalry and artillery, General Chamberlain began preparing to superintend the infantry ceremony. He had been instructed by both Generals Grant and Griffin that they "wished the ceremony to be as simple as possible, and that nothing should be done to humiliate the manhood of the Southern soldiers."

General Chamberlain had assumed the role of *1st Division* commander in place of General Bartlett for the formal surrender ceremony on the early morning of the 12th. Chamberlain's *3rd* brigade, Pearson's *1st*, and Gregory's *2nd* brigade were marched from the *V Corps* camp by the general and into the village, aligning themselves along its main street, the Richmond-Lynchburg Stage Road. The *3rd* was on one side of the byway, the *2nd* facing them; the *1st* behind the *3rd*. The troops extended from one end to the other of the settlement, with General Chamberlain, mounted and posted on the right of the line.

Looking to the north, Chamberlain saw the valley through which flowed the north branch of the Appomattox River, a mere stream at this point. Beyond this the Stage Road meandered over the next crest, passing through numerous Confederate camp-sites. With the Federal troops drawn up in line and waiting, the Confederates could be seen forming in column along the road. At their head rode thirty-three-year-old General John B. Gordon of Georgia. General Lee had chosen to remain behind in his headquarters tent during the ceremony.

As the Southerners tramped from their final bivouac, they forded the river, then followed the Stage Road up the hill toward the village. Near the top of the grade, and close to where Grant and Lee had met on the 10th, Gordon spied Chamberlain and his staff.

The young Maine general had previously instructed his men as to how they were to receive Lee's troops. When the head of Gordon's column reached the Federal troops, the Southerners heard a bugle sound orders, followed by the clattering of weapons as the Northern troops went to the marching salute of "carry arms." It was out of respect and admiration that the conquerors offered this for the vanquished. General Gordon, seeing this, responded by returning the salutation to Chamberlain with his sword. He then ordered his men to follow suit and return the salute to the rest of the Union troops.

Surrender parade at Appomattox, April 12, 1865.

Stacking arms. (Edwin Forbes)

As the Confederate infantry filed between the two lines of Union soldiers, they reached the area of the McLean house and stopped—the Stage Road holding about a division at a time. Chamberlain's men then went from "carry" to "order arms" and "parade rest." On receiving orders from their officers, the Southerners turned and faced their former enemy. By command, they stacked rifles and accoutrements, then sadly placed their battleflags across the stacks. Many times only a staff would be rendered, the men having ripped apart the flag itself as a memento of four years of service to the Confederacy.

The ceremony which started at about 6:00 a.m. was not complete until 4:00 p.m. Although sources vary, it appears that General Clement Evan's division of Gordon's corps led the column that morning, with the rest of the Second Corps following. Longstreet's men came next, with A.P. Hill's corps last. After each group of Confederates stacked their weapons and marched away, the Federals loaded them into wagons and dumped the ammunition from the cartridge boxes in the road.

Of the occasion, a Confederate remembered that "We suffered no insult in any way from any of our enemies. No other army in the world would have been so considerate of a foe that it had taken so long, so much privation, so much sacrifice of human life, to overwhelm." Another said, "And they, the Yankees, acted with so much consideration, and like good soldiers, and good Americans can only act, did not show that exultation they must have felt. While they seemed to feel proud, of course, at the result, yet we had their sympathy and good will."

As the last Confederate unit passed between the Federal soldiers, a Southern officer recalled that "someone in the blue line broke the silence and called for three cheers for the last brigade to surrender … but for us this soldierly generosity was more than we could bear. Many of the grizzled veterans wept like women, and my own eyes were as blind as my voice was dumb."

The parole lists show that 23,512 infantry surrendered that day, 1,747 of those being recorded as headquarters and miscellaneous troops.

With the stacking of arms ceremony complete, the former Confederate soldiers, once more civilians, were free to begin

General Lee's army after the surrender. (Edwin Forbes)

their journeys home. After packing up their few belongings, the Southerners left in small groups by the numerous byways heading in the direction of their eventual destinations. Parole passes permitted Lee's men to travel unmolested through areas where there were still Union troops. Many arrived at their homeplaces in time to put in early crops.

A ride through the final Confederate encampment evoked this comment by a Northern soldier: "[I] … kept on through the sad remnants of an army that has its place in history. It would have looked a mighty host, if the ghosts of all its soldiers that now sleep between Gettysburg and Lynchburg could have stood there in the lines, beside the living."

As the two armies departed Appomattox Court House following the ceremony on the 12th, they left with the feeling of having set the tone for the country's reunification after such a costly four-year war. In reaching this small Virginia county-seat village, over 618,000 Americans had given their lives. Now, the

On the way home. (Edwin Forbes)

survivors just wanted to end the war honorably, go home, and begin their lives anew. Unfortunately, their efforts toward peaceful reunification went unnoticed at the home front. Two days after the ceremony, President Abraham Lincoln was assassinated and died the next day. This news overshadowed what had happened at Appomattox Court House.

Soldiers of the *Army of the Potomac* and the *James* remained on active duty for another month or so, performing picket duty along the Southern railroad systems or acting as provost guards. These civilian soldiers were responsible for keeping the peace in the areas so recently fought over and supplying rations to those who had been the enemy. They also had to deal with the beginning of a social issue of primary importance in the country: the immediate emancipation of the slaves. Assimilation into society of this large population would take more than a century.

On May 23, the *Army of the Potomac* marched down Pennsylvania Avenue from the Capitol to the White House in the "Grand Review." Shortly thereafter, they were mustered out of service and returned to their home states and families.

Epilogue

The story of the final days of the war in Virginia can best be described in the words of a historian who wrote: "We cannot blame the officers and men who participated in the drama of Appomattox for the social and cultural wreckage that followed the surrender. The human spirit rose to great heights on that memorable occasion and the memory of it still towers over the materialism that precipitated and followed it. The humanity of Lincoln was present, and so, too, the chivalry and gentleness of Grant and Lee and Chamberlain and Gordon. ..." This is the legacy of our Civil War which is left to us today.

Lt. Col. Briscoe G. Baldwin's Report to Lee on the Ordnance Department State of Affairs, April 14, 1865

Richmond, Va.
April 14, 1865

Genl. R.E. Lee,
Commanding Army of Northern Virginia

General,

I have the honor to report that on the 2d Inst., in obedience to your order, I moved all the Reserve Ordnance Trains in the direction of Chesterfield C.H.

Upon evacuation of Petersburg, with the efficient aid of my assistants I succeeded in destroying all the arms, ammunition and ordnance there in the depots in Petersburg and vicinity—I have reason to believe that nothing of value was left to the enemy.

Between Chesterfield C.H. and Amelia C.H. I found 12 Ordnance wagons their contents, and 22 caissons filled with ammunition, abandoned, the animals being broken down—These I destroyed with the aid of my couriers.

Upon my arrival at Amelia C.H. I found 96 caissons, filled with ammunition, 164 boxes of artillery harness and 200 boxes of artillery ammunition—These had been sent to that point from Richmond about two months previous in obedience to my order under your advice. It being impossible to obtain transportation for these stores, the deficiencies of the army

were supplied and the balance necessarily destroyed.

On the march from Amelia C.H. to Farmville the Reserve Ordnance Train and Field Park of the Army, the Reserve Ordnance Trains of the 1st and 3d Corps were attacked and destroyed by the enemy, and also a great portion of the Division Ordnance Wagons of the Army.

At 12 o'clock P.M. of the 8th Inst. near Appomattox C.H. from the most accurate reports I could obtain from the Ordnance officers of the army there were 63 pieces of field artillery, 13 caissons, and an average of 93 rounds of ammunition for each gun, and 7892 armed men, with an average of 75 rounds of ammunition per man—

At Farmville I had telegraphed to Lynchburg for information in regard to the amount of reserve Ordnance stores in the depot at that place and had also made efforts to communicate with Danville on the same subject, but was unable to obtain any response from either place. From my knowledge of the resources of the Ordnance Department I was convinced that the supplies actually on hand with the army as above reported were our sole dependence in the State of Virginia.

I regret, General, not to be able to make a more accurate and detailed report at present— I deemed it prudent at Farmville to deposit the most important records of my office in safe hands until I could have opportunity of regaining them—

I have the honor to be General,
With the highest respect,
Your Obedient Servant:
Briscoe G. Baldwin
Lt. Col. Ord.

A.N.V.

The importance of this document is that General Lee apparently used Baldwin's April 8th reports to provide President Jefferson Davis with information about the condition of his army at the time of the surrender. On April 12, Lee wrote to Davis, "On the morning of the 9th, according to the reports of the ordnance officers, there were 7,892 organized infantry with arms, with an average ..." Repeating the statistics which Baldwin gave him, he added, "I have no accurate report of the cavalry, but believe it did not exceed 2,100 effective men. The enemy were more than five times our numbers."

It is interesting to speculate exactly how Lieutenant Colonel Baldwin could have collected such accurate information about the army, considering its condition during those final days. The men had to make four night marches, three of them in a row. It was scattered at Sailor's Creek, held up at Cumberland Church, sent on two different routes during the 8th, along with having both corps change positions in their line of march. Possibly this

is why Baldwin, when giving his figures, vaguely says in his letter to Lee that "from the most accurate reports I could obtain."

When the formal surrender ceremony was completed on April 12, the tally for the arms and artillery eventually turned in at Appomattox amounted to 180 cannon and between 15,000 to 27,000 weapons. The higher figure would probably include those rifles left behind in the camps and not stacked during the ceremony.

Another statement that Baldwin was mistaken about is ordnance located elsewhere in Virginia. When General John W. Turner's division marched into Lynchburg on April 12, they found the following pieces of weaponry: 30 pieces of "old" artillery, 7 10 pdr. Parrott guns, nine howitzers, two 20 pdr. Blakely guns, three 100 pdr. Parrott Guns, two 200 pdr. Columbiads, and forty-one 4.5 inch and 8 inch Coehorn mortars. These also included 12,000 stands of small arms, six carloads of fixed artillery ammunition, and one carload of cannon powder.

Further to the south in Danville, an arsenal was located where small arms and cannon were produced. On April 11, before Federal troops could occupy the city, there was a tremendous explosion at the arsenal, killing at least fourteen individuals. How much ordnance was destroyed is unknown although when General Horatio Wright's VI Corps came into Danville, they did find some items. Two cannon, 3,000 shell, and the ironwork for 10,000 stands of arms along with their manufacturing machinery were among the spoils.

Finally, exactly how many men did Lee have with his army at the surrender? Looking closely at those officially paroled at Appomattox the number is 29,394. Add 1,700 from the field of Appomattox who were paroled at Farmville, along with 2,000 more at Lynchburg, and General Lee probably had close to 33,000 with the Army of Northern Virginia in its final days.

The Danville Expedition, April 23 - 27, 1865

With the surrender and disbanding of Lee's army at Appomattox, many of Grant's soldiers thought their military service was about to end. The men in the Union army soon found out that this was not exactly true. Except for those left behind at Appomattox to police the area for abandoned Confederate ordnance, the others were ordered to reconcentrate at Burkeville Junction.

Sheridan's cavalry had left the field and were on their way to Nottoway Court House, where they rested and foraged for a few days. On April 17 they continued their journey to the western edge of Petersburg where they again went into bivouac.

Shortly after reaching the railroad junction, General Horatio Wright and his *VI Corps* received a directive to be ready to march. On April 22 General Henry W. Halleck sent a message to General Sheridan, ordering his cavalry to move "immediately to Greensborough, N.C." He was also informed that General Meade would supply him with an infantry corps from Burkeville as support.

It should be remembered that Generals Sherman and Johnston were still negotiating the surrender of the Army of Tennessee at the Bennett place between Durham and Greensboro. Should this have failed and fighting reconvened between the armies, it was thought that Sherman might need reinforcements from Grant's army.

Sheridan moved his column out of Petersburg on the morning of the 24th, with instructions for Wright to meet him at "some point on the railroad north of Danville." The troopers were to follow the Boydton Plank Road as they headed toward North Carolina.

The *VI Corps* more-or-less followed the Richmond & Danville Railroad as they departed Burkeville on the 23rd. They made it to Keysville Station on the first day out, a march of twenty-two miles.

The cavalry passed through Dinwiddie Court House, then had to cross Stony Creek, the Nottoway and Meherrin rivers. Eventually they reached Boydton, county seat village of Mecklenburg County, where they went into camp near Randolph-Macon College. The next morning they encountered the Staunton River where they were forced to construct a 600 foot bridge of ferry boats to get across. This was above Clarksville near Abbyville.

Once over, Sheridan's men continued along to Scottsburg on the Richmond & Danville Railroad, a march of about twenty-five miles from Danville. Crossing the Bannister River on the 28th, they eventually rode for South Boston in Halifax County. Here they received the news that Sherman and Johnston had agreed to the terms of surrender on April 26. Since the cavalry would no longer be needed, Sheridan began his return ride back to Petersburg. They did not make their rendezvous with the *VI Corps*.

After leaving Keysville, the Union infantry also had to cross the Staunton River on a pontoon bridge before entering Halifax Court House. The men went into camp around the town that evening. The march the next day brought them to a small community called Brooklyn. Here General Wright issued orders for the corps to prepare for a march into Danville the next day to take possession of that place.

At 9:45 a.m. on April 27, Mayor James M. Walker met Wright at the eastern outskirts of Danville next to Fall Creek Bridge and formally surrendered the city. The *VI Corps* commander then marched his troops through Danville to its southern limits, where, two miles out, they went into camp. He placed pickets across the Yanceyville Road just over the state line in Caswell County, North Carolina. Wright at this time issued his General Orders No. 9, which congratulated his corps on their movement from Burkeville, where "in four days and four hours not less than 100 miles have been trav-

ersed—a march almost unprecedented in this or any other war, even under the most favorable auspices."

General Wright located his headquarters on Main Street at the southwestern edge of town. The site he chose for his tent was directly across from the mansion of Major William T. Sutherlin. It was here that a few weeks earlier Confederate President Jefferson Davis remained while awaiting the results of Lee's movements. At the news of the surrender, Davis began his flight from Danville, considered to be the "Last Capital of the Confederacy."

Danville was an important Southside cotton and tobacco center during the war, with a population of about 5,000. It was the terminus of the Richmond & Danville Railroad, and the Piedmont, which carried supplies from Danville to Greensboro. An arsenal for producing small arms and cannon for the Confederacy was located here, as well as a general hospital. Established about 1862, it treated not only diseased and wounded Southerners, but also Union soldiers, presumably from the prisons in the town.

While occupying the city, many of the *VI Corps* members had time to look around. They saw six tobacco warehouses used by the Confederate government for prisons. They also visited the nearby cemetery, built for comrades who died while being incarcerated.

Others rented the "Danville Register," and printed their own newspaper, calling it "The Sixth Corps." Seventeen issues of this 11x16 tabloid were published at 25 cents a copy. Such phrases as "We have the

Wright men in the Wright place" were sprinkled throughout the text. In the vein of fun, faked Northern dispatches were printed right next to original poetry.

Once all items were accounted for in Danville, the Union army claimed they found "500 prisoners, 4 locomotives, 67 box and platform cars, 2 cannon, dismounted and mostly disabled; 3,000 shell, the iron-work for 10,000 stand of arms, and the machinery for manufacturing muskets, & c., taken from Harper's Ferry and subsequently from Richmond." One hundred thirty-two invalid soldiers were found in the hospital.

On May 1, members of the *VI Corps* began their journey back to Burkeville. A local Danvillian said, "I will do the Yankees the justice to say that they generally were well behaved, and conducted themselves properly. ... I neither heard of, nor saw, any disorderly conduct on their part nor any indulgence in excess of any kind, which was certainly most remarkable and creditable." It was not until the 16th that all the Federal forces were completely gone from the city. Eventually the entire corps was placed on picket duty along the Richmond & Danville and South Side Railroads.

Since the *VI Corps* did not participate at the "Grand Review" in Washington D.C. with Meade's and Sherman's armies, they had their own review by Generals Halleck, Ord and others in Richmond on May 24. On June 8, they received their official Washington review in front of President Johnson and his cabinet, accompanied by Generals Grant and Meade. Soon after, the war for the veterans of Sedgwick's and Wright's *VI Corps*, those who fought under the "Greek Cross," was over.

Numbers and Losses in the Appomattox Campaign: March 29 - April 9, 1865

CONFEDERATE STRENGTH

Captured March 31 - April 9	19,132
Surrendered at Appomattox	
Infantry	22,349
Cavalry	1,559
Artillery	2,576
Misc. Troops	1,747
Cavalry which escaped Appomattox	2,400
Cavalry which left ranks (estimated)	1,000
Desertions (estimated at 100 per day)	800
Paroled at Burkeville Junction by the IX Corps from April 14-17	(1,614)
Killed and wounded	6,266
Total (approximately)	**57, 829**

FEDERAL STRENGTH

:	Beginning	Losses	At Appomattox
Army of the Potomac			
II Corps	18,381	2,024	16,327
V Corps	14,788	2,465	12,323
VI Corps	16,734	1,542	15,192
IX Corps			
(Farmville)	4,200		
Army of the James			
XXIV Corps	7,500	946	6,554
XXV Corps	2,000	90	1,910
Cavalry			
Mackenzie	2,328	71	2,257
Sheridan	10,212	1,490	8,722
Totals:	76,143	8,628	63,285

CASUALTIES IN THE APPOMATTOX CAMPAIGN

NOTE: Confederate casualty lists are almost non-existent for this period of the war. Approximations are used when available.

K - killed   W - wounded   M - missing (prisoners)

March 29, LEWIS FARM (QUAKER ROAD)
U.S.   V Corps: 53 K, 306 W, 22 M.   Aggregate: 381
C.S.   Johnson: 371, of which about 200 were captured and 130 killed.

March 30, WHITE OAK ROAD
U.S.   Sheridan: 1 K, 7 W, 15 M.   Aggregate: 23

March 31, WHITE OAK ROAD (GRAVELLY OR HATCHER'S RUN)
U.S.   V Corps: 126 K, 811 W, 470 M.   Aggregate: 1,407
       II Corps: 51 K, 323 W, 87 M.   Aggregate: 461
C.S.   Johnson: about 800 K,W,M.

March 31, DINWIDDIE COURT HOUSE
U.S.   Sheridan: 40 K, 254 W, 60 M.   Aggregate: 354
C.S.   Pickett: 400 K,W,M.   Aggregate: 760
       Fitz Lee: 360 K,W,M.

April 1, FIVE FORKS
U.S.   V Corps: 75 K, 506 W, 53 M.
       Sheridan: 28 K, 164 W, 4 M.   Aggregate: 830
C.S.   Pickett: 545 K & W, 2,000 - 2,400 M.
       Fitz Lee: (combined)   Aggregate: 2,945

April 2, FORT GREGG
U.S.   XIIV Corps: 122 K, 592 W,   Aggregate: 714
C.S.   Harris: 57 K, 120 W, 30 M.   Aggregate: 207

April 2, VI CORPS ASSAULT
U.S.   VI Corps: 123 K, 899 W, 59 M.   Aggregate: 1,081
C.S.   Heth - Wilcox 3,000 M   Aggregate: 3,000

April 2, IX CORPS ASSAULT

U.S.   IX Corps: 266 K, 1,377 W, 66M.   Aggregate: 1,706
C.S.   Gordon's Corps: 1,045 M.

April 2, SUTHERLAND STATION
U.S.   II Corps (Miles): 33 K, 236 W, 97 M. Aggregate: 366
C.S.   Heth (Cooke): 600 M.

April 2, WHITE OAK ROAD
U.S.   Sheridan: 2 K, 25 W.   Aggregate: 27

April 3, NAMOZINE CHURCH
U.S.   Sheridan: 4 K, 15 W.
C.S.   Barringer: 350 M.

April 3, NAMOZINE AND SWEATHOUSE CREEKS
U.S.   Sheridan: 11 K, 65 W, 5 M.   Aggregate: 70

April 4, PAINESVILLE
U.S.   Sheridan: 1 K, 6 W, 2 M.   Aggregate: 9

April 5, JETERSVILLE
U.S.   Sheridan: 1 K, 6 W, 1 M.   Aggregate: 7

April 5, AMELIA SPRINGS
U.S.   Sheridan: 9 K, 58 W, 59 M.   Aggregate: 136

April 5, PAINESVILLE
U.S.   Sheridan: 3 K, 17 W, 12 M.   Aggregate: 32
C.S.   Wagon train: 630 M.

April 6, SAILOR'S CREEK
U.S.   VI Corps: 84 K, 358 W.   Aggregate: 442
C.S.   Ewell: (5,200 effectives)
        150 K & W, 3,250 M.   Aggregate: 3,400
U.S.   II Corps: Aggregate: 536
C.S.   Gordon's Second Corps: 1,700 M.
U.S.   Sheridan (Merritt): 30 K, 128 W, 14 M. Aggregate: 172
C.S.   Anderson: (6,300 effectives) 2,600 M.

April 6, HIGH BRIDGE
U.S.   Read: 42 K & W, 800+ M.
C.S.   Fitz Lee: 100 (approximate)

April 7, FARMVILLE
U.S.   Crook: 11 K, 33 W, 30 M.   Aggregate: 74

April 7, CUMBERLAND CHURCH
U.S.   II Corps: 40 K, 210 W, 321 M.   Aggregate: 571
C.S.   Mahone: ?

April 8, APPOMATTOX STATION
U.S.   Sheridan: 5 K, 40 W, 3 M.   Aggregate: 58
C.S.   Walker: 1,000 M.

April 9, APPOMATTOX COURT HOUSE
U.S.   Sheridan: 6 K, 52 W, 13 M.   Aggregate: 61
U.S.   Army of Potomac & Army of James:
        14 K, 76 W, 68 M.   Aggregate: 164
C.S.   Approximate: 500

Appomattox Campaign Medal of Honor Recipients in the Federal Army

NAME	REGIMENT	DATE	REASON
Pearson, Alfred L.	155 Pa.	3/29	Gallantry
Higby, Charles	F, 1 Pa. Cav.		Capture of flag
Sova, Joseph E.	H, 8 N.Y. Cav.		Capture of flag
Tobie, Edward P.	1st Me. Cav.	4/6-7	Twice wounded
Boehm, Peter M.	K, 15 N.Y. Cav.	3/31	Gallantry
Hooper, William B.	L, 1 N.J.Cav.	3/31	Gallantry
King, Horatio C.	Quartermaster	3/31	Gallantry
Lutes, Franklin	D, 111 N.Y.	3/31	Capture of flag
O'Connor, Albert	A, 7 Wisc.	3/31-4/1	Gallantry; Capture of flag
Sickles, William H.	B, 7 Wisc.	3/31	Gallantry
Wilson, John	L 1 N.J. Cav.	3/31	Gallantry
Benyaurd, William H.H.	Engineers	4/1	Gallantry
Blackmar, Wilmon W.	H, 1 W.Va. Cav.	4/1	Gallantry
Bonebrake, Henry G.	G, 17 Pa. Cav.	4/1	Capture of flag
De Lavie, Hiram H.	I, 11 Pa.	4/1	Capture of flag
Edwards, Davaid	H, 146 N.Y.	4/1	Capture of flag
Everson, Adelbert	D, 185 N.Y.	4/1	Capture of flag
Fernald, Albert E.	F, 20 Me.	4/1	Capture of flag
Gardner, Charles N.	E, 32 Mass.	4/1	Capture of flag
Grindlay, James G.	146 N.Y.	4/1	Capture of flags
Kauss, August	H, 15 N.Y.H.A.	4/1	Capture of flag
Koogle, Jacob	G, 7 Md.	4/1	Capture of flag
Murphy, Thomas J.	G, 146 N.Y.	4/1	Capture of flag
Scott, John Wallace	D, 157 Pa.	4/1	Capture of flag
Shipley, Robert F.	A, 140 N.Y.	4/1	Capture of flag
Shopp, George	E, 191 Pa.	4/1	Capture of flag
Stewart, Joseph	G, 1 Md.	4/1	Capture of flag
Thompson, Allen	I, 4 N.Y.H.A.	4/1	Gallantry
Thompson, James	K, 4 N.Y.H.A.	4/1	Gallantry
Tucker, Jacob	G, 4 Md.	4/1	Gallantry
Winegar, William W.	B, 1 N.Y. Cav.	4/1	Capture of flag
Allen, Abner P.	K, 39 Ill.	4/2	Gallantry
Apple, Andrew O.	I, 12 W. Va.	4/2	Gallantry
Babcock, William J.	E, 2 R.I.	4/2	Gallantry
Barber, James A.	G. 1 R.I.Lt.Art.	4/2	Gallantry
Blackwood, William R.	D. 48 Pa.	4/2	Gallantry
Boutwell, John W.	B, 18 N.H.	4/2	Gallantry
Buffington, John E.	C, 6 Md.	4/2	Gallantry
Camp, Carlton N.	B, 18 N.H.	4/2	Gallantry
Corcoran, John	G, 1 R.I.Lt.Art.	4/2	Gallantry

Corliss, Stephen P.	F, 4 N.Y.H.A.	4/2	Gallantry
Curtis, Josiah M.	I, 12 W. Va.	4/2	Gallantry
Dolloff, Charles W.	K, 1 Vt.	4/2	Capture of flag
Ennis, Charles D.	G, 1 R.I.Lt.Art.	4/2	Gallantry
Evans, Ira H.	B, 116 U.S.C.T.	4/2	Gallantry
Ewing, John C.	E, 211 Pa.	4/2	Capture of flag
Fesq, Frank	A, 40 N.J	4/2	Capture of flag
Fisher, Joseph	C, 61 Pa.	4/2	Gallantry
Fox, William R.	A, 95 Pa.	4/2	Capture of flag
Gardner, Robert J.	K, 34 Mass.	4/2	Gallantry
Gibbs, Wesley	B, 2 Conn.H.A.	4/2	Capture of flag
Gould, Charles G.	H, 5 Vt.	4/2	Gallantry
Hack, Lester	F, 5 Vt.	4/2	Capture of flag
Harmon, Amzi D.	K, 211 Pa.	4/2	Capture of flag
Havron, John H.	G, 1 R.I.Lt.Art.	4/2	Gallantry
Hawkins, Gardner C.	E, 3 Vt.	4/2	Gallantry
Highland, Patrick	D, 23 Ill.	4/2	Gallantry
Hoffman, Thomas W.	A, 208 Pa.	4/2	Gallantry
Howard, James	K, 158 N.Y.	4/2	Gallantry
Hunter, Charles A.	E, 34 Mass.	4/2	Gallantry
Ilgenfritz, Charles H.	E, 207 Pa.	4/2	Gallantry
James, Isaac	H, 110 Ohio	4/2	Capture of flag
Kane, John	K, 100 N.Y.	4/2	Gallantry
Lewis, Samuel E.	G, 1 R.I.Lt.Art.	4/2	Gallantry
Lilley, John	F, 205 Pa.	4/2	Capture of flag
Loyd, George	A, 122 Ohio	4/2	Capture of flag
Mangam, Richard C.	H, 148 N.Y.	4/2	Capture of flag
Marquette, Charles	F, 93 Pa.	4/2	Capture of flag
Matthews, John C.	A, 61 Pa.	4/2	Gallantry
Matthews, Milton	C, 61 Pa.	4/2	Capture of flag
McCauslin, Joseph	D, 12 W. Va.	4/2	Gallantry
McGraw, Thomas	B, 23 Ill.	4/2	Gallantry
McKee, George	D, 89 N.Y.	4/2	Gallantry
McMillen, Francis M.	C, 110 Ohio	4/2	Capture of flag
Merrill, Augustus	B, 1 Me.	4/2	Gallantry
Mitchell, Theodore	C, 61 Pa.	4/2	Capture of flag
Molbone, Archibald	G, 1 R.I.Lt.Art.	4/2	Gallantry
Orr, Robert L.	61 Pa.	4/2	Gallantry
Parker, Thomas	B, 2 R.I.	4/2-4/6	Gallantry
Phillips, Josiah	E, 148 Pa.	4/2	Capture of flag
Plimley, William	F, 120 N.Y.	4/2	Gallantry
Potter, George W.	G, 1 R.I.Lt.Art.	4/2	Gallantry
Reeder, Charles A.	G, 12 W.Va.	4/2	Capture of flag
Sargent, Jackson	D, 5 Vt.	4/2	Gallantry
Shubert, Frank	E, 43 N.Y.	4/2	Capture two
Sperry, William J.	6 Vt.	4/2	Gallantry

Thompson, Freeman C.	F, 116 Ohio	4/2	Gallantry
Tucker, Allen	F, 10 Conn.	4/2	Gallantry
Van Matre, Joseph	G, 116 Ohio	4/2	Gallantry
Welch, Richard	E, 37 Mass	4/2	Capture of flag
White, Adam	G, 11 W. Va.	4/2	Capture of flag
Wilson, Francis A.	B, 95 Pa.	4/2	Gallantry
Blickensderfer, Milton	E, 126 Ohio	4/2	Capture of flag
Brant, William	B, 1 N.J.	4/3	Capture of flag
Briggs, Elijah A.	B, 2 Conn. H.A.	4/3	Capture of flag
Brewer, WIlliam J.	C, 2 N.Y. Cav.	4/4	Capture of flag
Chandler, Stephen E.	A, 24 N.Y. Cav.	4/5	Gallantry
Thomas, Hampton S.	1 Pa. Cav.	4/5	Gallantry
Tompkins, Aaron B.	G, 1 N.J. Cav.	4/5	Capture of flag
Davidsizer, John A.	A, 1 Pa. Cav.	4/5	Capture of flag
Elliott, Alexander	A, 1 Pa. Cav.	4/5	Capture of flag
Landis, James P.	1 Pa. Cav.	4/5	Capture of flag
Locke, Lewis	A, 1 N.J. Cav.	4/5	Capture of flag
Peirsol, James K.	F, 13 Ohio Cav.	4/5	Capture of flag
Schmal, George W.	M, 24 N.Y. Cav.	4/5	Capture of flag
Stewart, George W.	E, 1 N.J. Cav.	4/5	Capture of flag
Streile, Christain	I, 1 N.J. Cav.	4/5	Capture of flag
Warfel, Henry C.	A, 1 Pa. Cav.	4/5	Capture of flag
Young, Andrew J.	F, 1 N.J. Cav.	4/5	Capture of flag
Benjamin, John F.	M, 2 N.Y. Cav.	4/6	Capture of flag
Bennett, Orren	D, 141 Pa.	4/6	Capture of flag
Boon, Hugh P.	B, 1 W. Va. Cav.	4/6	Capture of flag
Brest, Lewis F.	D, 57 Pa.	4/6	Capture of flag
Bringle, Andrew	F, 10 N.Y. Cav.	4/6	Gallantry
Calkin, Ivers S.	M, 2 N.Y. Cav.	4/6	Capture of flag
Chapman, John	B, 1 Me. H.A.	4/6	Capture of flag
Clapp, Albert A.	G, 2 Ohio Cav.	4/6	Capture of flag
Connell, Trustrim	I, 138 Pa.	4/6	Capture of flag
Cunningham, Francis M.	H, 1 W. Va. Cav.	4/6	Capture of flag
Davis, Thomas	C, 2 N.Y. H.A.	4/6	Capture of flag
Dockum, Warren C.	H, 121 N.Y.	4/6	Capture of flag
Eddy, Samuel E.	D, 37 Mass.	4/6	Gallantry
Evans, Coron D.	A, 3 Ind. Cav.	4/6	Capture of flag
Ford, George W.	E, 88 N.Y.	4/6	Capture of flag
Gifford, Benjamin	H, 121 N.Y.	4/6	Capture of flag
Gribben, James H.	C, 2 N.Y. Cav.	4/6	Capture of flag
Hagerty, Asel	A, 61 N.Y.	4/6	Capture of flag
Hawthorn, Harris S.	F, 121 N.Y.	4/6	Capture of flag
Hoffman, Henry	M, 2 Ohio Cav.	4/6	Capture of flag
Holmes, William T.	A, 3 Ind. Cav.	4/6	Capture of flag
Houlton, William	1 W. Va. Cav.	4/6	Capture of flag
Hughey, John	L, 2 Ohio Cav.	4/6	Capture of flag

Jordon, Absolom	A, 3 Ind. Cav.	4/6	Capture of flag
Kenyon, Samuel P.	B, 24 N.Y. Cav.	4/6	Capture of flag
Keough, John	E, 67 Pa.	4/6	Capture of flag
Kimball, Joseph	B, 2 W. Va. Cav.	4/6	Capture of flag
Kline, Harry	E, 40th N.Y.	4/6	Capture of flag
Lanfare, Aaron S.	B, 1 Conn. Cav.	4/6	Capture of flag
Larimer, Smith	G, 2 Ohio Cav.	4/6	Capture of flag
Mattocks, Charles P.	17 Me.	4/6	Gallantry
McElhinny, Samuel O.	A, 2 W. Va. Cav.	4/6	Capture of flag
McWhorter, Walter F.	E, 3 W. Va. Cav.	4/6	Capture of flag
Menter, John W.	D, 5 Mich.	4/6	Capture of flag
Miller, Frank	M, 2 N.Y. Cav.	4/6	Capture of flag
Morris, William	C, 1 N.Y. Cav.	4/6	Capture of flag
Mundell, Walter L.	E, 5 Mich.	4/6	Capture of flag
Neville, Edwin M.	C, 1 Conn. Cav.	4/6	Capture of flag
Norton, Elliott M.	H, 6 Mich. Cav.	4/6	Capture two flags
Norton, John R.	M, 1 N.Y. Cav.	4/6	Capture of flag
Norton, Llewellyn P.	L, 10 N.Y. Cav.	4/6	Gallantry
Payne, Irvin C.	M, 2 N.Y. Cav.	4/6	Capture of flag
Pitman, George J.	C, 1 N.Y. Cav.	4/6	Capture of flag
Porter, William	H, 1 N.J. Cav.	4/6	Gallantry
Richardson, William R.	A, 2 Ohio Cav.	4/6	Gallantry
Riddell, Rudolph	I, 61 N.Y.	4/6	Capture of flag
Savacool, Edwin F.	K, 1 W.Va. Cav.	4/6	Capture of flag
Shahan, Emisire	A, 1 W.Va. Cav.	4/6	Capture of flag
Shepherd, William	A, 3 Ind. Cav.	4/6	Capture of flag
Simmons, John	D, 2 N.Y.H.A.	4/6	Capture of flag
Southard, David	C, 1 N.J. Cav.	4/6	Capture of flag
Taggart, Charles A.	B, 37 Mass.	4/6	Capture of flag
Titus, Chalres	H, 1 N.J. Cav.	4/6	Gallantry
Wilson, Charles E.	A, 1 N.J. Cav.	4/6	Gallantry
Woods, Daniel A.	K, 1 W.Va. Cav.	4/6	Capture of flag
Lane, Morgan D.	Signal Corps	4/6	Capture of flag
Newman, William H.	B, 86 N.Y.	4/6	Capture of flag
Galloway, John	8 Pa. Cav.	4/7	Gallantry
Ludgate, William	G, 59 N.Y.	4/7	Gallantry
Anderson, Thomas	I, 1 W.Va. Cav.	4/8	Capture of flag
Read, Morton A.	D, 8 N.Y. Cav.	4/8	Capture of flag
Schorn, Charles	M, 1 W.Va. Cav.	4/8	Capture of flag
Shields, Bernard	E, 2 W.Va. Cav.	4/8	Capture of flag
Carey, James L.	G, 10 N.Y. Cav.	4/9	Gallantry
Donaldson, John	L, 4 Pa. Cav.	4/9	Capture of flag
Funk, West	121 Pa.	4/9	Capture of flag
Myers, William H.	A, 1 Md. Cav.	4/9	Gallantry

For full citations see: *The Medal of Honor of the United States Army*, Government Printing Office, Washington, 1948; or pp. 1257-261, *Official Records*, Series I, Volume XLVI, Part I, (1894).

Arms and Artillery Used in the Appomattox Campaign

By 1865, the equipment the two armies were using in the field was pretty much standardized, although there were some exceptions. Primary sources and archaeological documentation give evidence of what was used in the final campaign.

In the last year of the war, the average Union infantry man had either a .58 caliber 1861 or 1863 Springfield rifle musket, or possibly a .577 caliber British pattern '53 Enfield rifle musket.

Scattered throughout the infantry corps were skirmish regiments equipped with seven-shot .52 caliber Spencer repeating rifles. Some of these units included: the *10th Connecticut, 100th New York, 49th, 119th, 148th, 190-191st Pennsylvania*, and the *37th Massachusetts*. The latter unit used their Spencers effectively at Little Sailor's Creek.

It is also known that at least some men in the *151st New York* had .52 caliber Sharps rifles. They too were with the *VI Corps* at Sailor's Creek.

Ammunition issued to the Federal soldiers was for the most part the standard .58 caliber three-ring, William's regulation, and William's cleaner type III bullets.

The Confederate army seemed to rely on their own manufactured muskets, like the Richmond and Fayetteville, and the imports. A Union soldier, in looking over the surrendered rifles of Lee's army at Appomattox, remarked: "Their infantry muskets were mainly the English Enfield, though I saw numbers of old Harper's Ferry percussion muskets which had been rifled. I was informed that these had been used by the battalions of reserves which had gone with Lee's main army when Richmond was evacuated; but the standard weapon of the regular Confederate infantry appeared to be the Enfield, which was a trifle longer and heavier than our Springfield, and carried a trifle larger [actually smaller] ball. I believe that it was generally conceded by ordnance experts that the Enfield rifle of that day was considerable more effective than our Springfield, though not quite so handy."

Confederate arms ammunition was obviously more varied. The majority issued were .58 caliber three-ring nose cast bullets. These replaced the earlier standard issue Gardner insert rounds which the government discontinued after complaints about durability.

Other styles of manufactured ammunition were given to the troops, but it appears the .577 caliber English Enfield rounds actually made up a small number compared to the standard .58 caliber bullet. Occasionally a .69 caliber French, Belgium, or Austrian round is found, particularly around the Sailor's Creek area, but presumably these are from the Harper's Ferry muskets of General G.W.C. Lee's command.

Working among Lee's men were hand-picked sharpshooters, armed with .45 caliber British Whitworth rifles. These weapons, firing a cylindrical round through a hexagonal bore, had a range of up to 1500 yards. Several of these weapons were with the army.

The Southern horseman was armed with either of two weapons: the .52 caliber S.C. Robinson Richmond Sharps, or the .577 caliber Enfield carbine (or Confederate copy thereof). C.S. Richmond musketoons were also used. Many carried captured Federal weapons, most likely a .52 caliber Sharps carbine. In the case of Spencers and Henrys, obtaining the proper rimfire ammunition was a problem. The .44 caliber Henry rifles, scarce even in the Federal army, were taken at Reams Station in August, or during Wade Hampton's cattle raid in September 1864.

Numerous men in the Federal cavalry were armed with .52 caliber Sharps carbines. Many also had the seven-shot .52 caliber Spencer repeating carbine. At least one regiment, the *20th Pennsylvania*, had .54 Burnside carbines. Some members of the *1st District of Columbia* and *1st Maine* were both armed with the sixteen-shot Henry rifles.

Revolvers varied, .44 and .36 calibers being the most popular. Colts, Remingtons, Confederate manufac-

ture, and foreign styles were widely used.

The cavalry of both sides retained sabers, and used them with deadly force, as can be attested to in the cavalry fighting at Amelia Springs, Sailor's Creek and High Bridge.

*   *   *

The same individual who observed the surrendered Confederate weapons at Appomattox, said of the ordnance: "Their guns were a miscellaneous lot, embracing Parrott rifles (of which they made a very good imitation in their Tredegar Iron Works), light twelves, together with a 12-pound iron howitzer of their own make, which was modeled much like the 12-pounder Napoleon."

An examination of the twenty Confederate cannon captured April 2, 1865, by the *VI Corps* shows: light twelve-pounders, brass [bronze], Tredegar maker; 24 pounder howitzers, U.S.; light 12-pounders, brass [bronze], U.S.; 12-pounder iron guns, Tredegar maker; 3-inch rifled guns, U.S.; 3-inch Blakely, and a 10 pounder Parrott, Tredegar maker.

Even late in the war, Confederate artillery ammunition was still being perfected. In April 1864, William LeRoy Broun, commander of the Richmond Arsenal, modified the 3-inch rifled projectile by shortening it, rounding the nose, and providing a new style of sawn sabot. What has become known as the "Read-Broun pattern shell," along with Confederate manufactured Parrott shells, were widely used in the last year of the war for the 3-inch rifled guns.

Confederate ordnance used for the smooth-bore cannon included: 12 lb. field case shot, polygonal case shot, solid shot, and canister.

A survey of the Federal artillery used in the Appomattox Campaign shows mainly bronze 12 pounder Napoleon smooth-bore guns, or 3-inch ordnance rifles. The former generally utilized the Bormann fused 12 lb. balls, while the latter fired either 3-inch Hotchkiss or Schenkl shells, both using percussion or paper fuses.

While the Federal army had its supply base at City Point, along with the U.S. Military Railroad, to provide ordnance as needed, the South did not have such a complete operation. None the less, William Broun said, "I must add this, that never was an order received from General Lee's army for ammunition that it was not immediately supplied, even to the last order to send a train-load of ammunition to Petersburg after the order was received for the evacuation of Richmond ...."

Lee's Retreat Today

In April, 1995, during the 130th Anniversary of the Appomattox Campaign, a new "LEE'S RETREAT" twenty stop driving tour was instituted along this historic route. Using modern technology, visitors can arrive at the various points of interest and tune their radios to 1610 AM, receiving a narrative about what happened at each site. For further information and a driving tour map, simply call: 1-800-6-RETREAT. The following are brief vignettes of the locations which can be seen.

1. SUTHERLAND STATION, April 2, 1865. Confederate troops were placed here in battleline along Cox Road to protect the South Side Railroad. Federal troops would make three attacks on the Southerners, eventually overwhelming their position. This engagement enabled Grant's forces to sever Lee's last supply line and caused his army to abandon Petersburg that night.

2. NAMOZINE CHURCH, April 3. Early in the morning, as Lee's men continued their march toward Amelia Court House, a skirmish took place around this church between Union and Confederate cavalry. Eventually forced to withdraw from this position, the armies would continue a running battle that ended that evening near Deep Creek. The church also served as a hospital for the wounded of both armies.

3. AMELIA COURT HOUSE, April 4-5. At this village, located on the Richmond & Danville Railroad, General Lee ordered all columns of his army from the Richmond and Petersburg trenches to rendezvous. Here he hoped to obtain rations before continuing the march into North Carolina where he would join General Joseph E. Johnston's army.

4. JETERSVILLE, April 5. Moving toward North Carolina, Lee found

Union cavalry and infantry across his line of retreat at this station on the Richmond & Danville Railroad. Rather than attacking the entrenched Federals, he decided to change the direction of his movement and began making a night march toward Farmville where rations would await the army.

5. AMELIA SPRINGS, April 6. In the morning, a portion of the Union army came in contact with Lee's rearguard as the Southerners completed their night march around Grant's troops at Jetersville. This was also the scene of an engagement on April 5 as Union cavalry returned from the destruction of a Confederate wagon train at nearby Painesville.

6. DEATONVILLE, April 6. During this day, the entire Confederate line of march would move west on the Rice-Deatonville Road toward Farmville. Constantly pressing Lee's rearguard, Union troops would continuously fight brief actions at every high ground or road intersection. These delays would eventually lead to the Battles of Sailor's Creek.

7. HOLT'S CORNER, April 6. While passing through this intersection, the Confederate column was attacked by Union cavalry. Consequently, part of Lee's army, along with the main wagon train, turned north on to the Jamestown Road. The main portion would continue straight ahead to Rice's Depot on the South Side Railroad after crossing Little Sailor's Creek.

8. HILLSMAN HOUSE, April 6. Union forces formed their battleline along this ridge while the Confeder-

ate forces prepared for a fight on the opposite slope across Little Sailor's Creek. After passing over the creek, a fierce battle took place between the two forces, resulting in the surrender of a large number of Southern troops. The house served as a hospital for casualties of both armies.

9. MARSHALL'S CROSSROADS, April 6. At this intersection, Union cavalry found Confederate infantry posted along the road to Rice's Depot. Simultaneous with the fight going on along Little Sailor's Creek at Hillsman's farm, the horse soldiers attacked this portion of Lee's army which eventually withdrew from the field or were captured.

10. LOCKETT HOUSE, April 6. While Confederate troops were attempting to cross Sailor's Creek on the bridges below, the fighting between the two forces began here and continued into the bottomlands. After the battle, James Lockett's bullet ridden house was then pressed into usage as a field hospital.

11. DOUBLE BRIDGES, April 6. In this low ground, the Confederate column and wagon train which turned off at Holt's Corner became bogged down in crossing Sailor's Creek. The Union forces, which pursued this portion of Lee's army, then assailed the defenders and captured a large number of prisoners and wagons before darkness put an end to the fighting.

12. RICE'S DEPOT, April 6. Confederate troops, reaching here early in the morning, began entrenching on the high ground across the road from Burkeville Junction. Later that

afternoon, upon the approach of the Union army from that direction, the two armies skirmished briefly but darkness closed any further fighting. General Lee's headquarters were here for a time before he left on his night march to Farmville.

13. CAVALRY BATTLE AT HIGH BRIDGE, April 6. About 900 Union infantry and cavalry were sent from Burkeville on a mission to burn this South Side Railroad structure over the Appomattox River. Pursued by Confederate cavalry, in the engagement which followed near here, most were captured and their mission to destroy the bridge ended in failure.

14. FARMVILLE, April 7. This tobacco town of 1,500 inhabitants saw the Confederate army march through, followed by the Union army which occupied it. Lee, hoping to have rations issued to his men here before turning south, was unsuccessful and decided to then cross over to the north side of the Appomattox River. General Grant sent his first dispatch to Lee concerning surrender from here.

15. CUMBERLAND CHURCH, April 7. Union troops, successfully crossing the Appomattox River at High Bridge, advanced to this area and found Lee's army entrenched around the church. After a series of attacks on the Confederate position by Grant's men, Lee was forced to delay his movement until darkness when he began another night march. His destination was Appomattox Station on the South Side Railroad.

16. HIGH BRIDGE, April 7. Early in the morning, as Federal troops arrived from the Sailor's Creek battlefield, Confederate forces burned four spans of High Bridge but failed to destroy the lower wagon bridge. Consequently, the Union forces were able to cross to the north side of the Appomattox River and continue their pursuit of Lee's army now near Cumberland Church.

17. LEE'S REARGUARD, April 8. Confederate General James Longstreet built breastworks here at New Hope Church to protect the rear of Lee's army, most of which was four miles south at Appomattox Court House. On the morning of April 9, General Lee passed through these lines hoping to meet with General Grant, but determined he was approaching by another route. He then rode back toward the village.

18. BATTLE OF APPOMATTOX STATION, April 8. Union cavalry arrived at the station early in the evening and captured three of the four trains of supplies intended for Lee's army. They then advanced toward Appomattox Court House and ran into the surplus Confederate wagon and artillery train sent ahead of the main army. After a brief engagement, this command was scattered and numerous wagons and cannon were captured.

19. BATTLE OF NOTTOWAY, June 23, 1864. This was the first of a series of engagements fought on a cavalry expedition led by Union Generals James H. Wilson and August Kautz from Petersburg. The purpose of the raid was to destroy portions of the South Side and Richmond & Danville Railroads and cur-

tail the use of these important supply lines by Lee's army.

20. NOTTOWAY COURT HOUSE, April 5. Portions of the Union army, following the South Side Railroad, passed through this county seat village in their pursuit of Lee's army. They would continue through Burkeville and come in contact with the Confederate forces at Rice's Depot. General Grant spent part of the evening here before riding cross-country to confer with his generals at Jetersville.

Order of Battle

Abbreviations: Standard state abbreviations have been used. Unless otherwise noted a unit is always understood to be a regiment of infantry. Where capital letters are used companies or batteries are indicated; infantry regiments of both sides, and Confederate cavalry regiments, normally had companies A through K, omitting "J"; Union cavalry regiments normally had A-M, omitting "J"; but some regiments of both types had higher designated companies than the norm. Other abbreviations used are: Art., artillery; Btty., battery; Bn., battalion; Co., company; Hvy., Hvy.; Lt., light.

ARMIES OF THE U.S.
Lt. Gen. Ulysses S. Grant

Escort
  5th U.S. Cav., Cos. B, F and K

Headquarters Guard
  4th U.S.

Army of the Potomac
Maj. Gen. George G. Meade

Provost Guard, Brig. Gen. George N. Macy
  1st Ind. Cav.
  1st Mass. Cav., Cos. C and D
  3d Pa. Cav.
  11th U.S., 1st Bn.
  14th U.S., 2d Bn.

Headquarters Guard
  3d U.S.

Quartermaster's Guard
  Independent Co. Oneida (N.Y.) Cav.

Engineer Brigade, Brig. Gen. Henry W. Benham
  15th N.Y. (9 cos.)
  50th N.Y.

Independent Brigade, Brig. Gen. Charles H. T. Collis
  1st Mass. Cav. (8 cos.)
  61st Mass.
  80th N.Y. (20th Militia)
  68th Pa.
  114th Pa.

Battalion U.S. Engineers, Maj. Franklin Harwood

Artillery, Brig. Gen. Henry J. Hunt

Siege Train, Brig. Gen. Henry W. Abbot
1st Connecticut Hvy. Art.
Connecticut Lt., 3d Btty.

Artillery Reserve, Brig. Gen. William Hays (in command from 6 April)
Maine Lt., 2d Btty. (B)
Maine Lt., 3d Btty. (C)
Maine Lt., 4th Btty. (D)
Maine Lt., 6th Btty. (F)
N.Y. Lt., 12th Btty.
1st Oh. Lt., Co. H
1st Pa. Lt., Co. F
1st R.I. Lt., Co. E
Vermont Lt., 3d Btty.

II *Army Corps*, Maj. Gen. Andrew A. Humphreys

1st *Division*, Brig. Gen. Nelson A. Miles

1st Brigade, Col. George W. Scott
26th Michigan
5th N.H. (bn.)
2d N.Y. Hvy. Art.
61st N.Y.
81st Pa.
140th Pa.

2d Brigade, Col. Robert Nugent
28th Mass. (5 cos.)
63d N.Y. (6 cos.)
69th N.Y.
88th N.Y. (5 cos.)
4th N.Y. Hvy. Art.

3d Brigade, Brig. Gen. Henry J. Madill (wounded 2 April)
Brig. Gen. Clinton D. MacDougall
7th N.Y.
39th N.Y.
52d N.Y.
111th N.Y.
125th N.Y.
126th N.Y. (bn.)

4th Brigade, Brig. Gen. John Ramsey
64th N.Y.
66th N.Y.
53d Pa.

116th Pa.
145th Pa.
148th Pa.
183d Pa.

2d *Division*, Brig. Gen. William Hays (assigned to Artillery Reserve 6 April)
Brig. Gen. Thomas Smythe (temporary command)
Brig. Gen. Francis C. Barlow (assigned 7 April)

1st Brigade, Col. William A. Olmsted
19th Maine
19th Mass.
20th Mass.
7th Mich.
1st Minnesota (2 cos.)
59th N.Y. (bn.)
82d N.Y. (bn.)/detachment 4 cos. 2d N.Y. attached.
152d N.Y.
184th Pa.
36th Wisconsin

2d Brigade, Col. James P. McIvor
8th N.Y. Hvy. Art.
155th N.Y.
164th N.Y.
170th N.Y.
182d N.Y. (69th N.Y. National Guard Art.)

3d Brigade, Brig. Gen. Thomas A. Smyth (mortally wounded 7 April)
Col. Danielle Woodall
14th Conn.
1st Delaware
12th N.J.
10th N.Y. (bn.)
108th N.Y.
4th Oh. (4 cos.)
69th Pa.
106th Pa. (3 cos.)
7th W.V. (4 cos.)

Unattached
2d Company Minnesota Sharpshooters

3d *Division*, Maj. Gen. Gershom Mott (wounded 6 April)

Brig. Gen. Regis de Trobriand (1st Brigade)

1st Brigade, Brig. Gen. Regis de Trobriand
  Col. Russell B. Shepherd
  20th Ind.
  1st Me. Hvy. Art.
  40th N.Y.
  73d N.Y.
  86th N.Y.
  124th N.Y.
  99th Pa.
  110th Pa.

2d Brigade, Brig. Gen. Byron R. Pierce
  17th Me.
  1st Mass. Hvy. Art.
  5th Mich.
  93d N.Y.
  57th Pa.
  105th Pa.
  141st Pa.

3d Brigade, Brig. Gen. Robert McAllister
  11th Mass.
  7th N.J.
  8th N.J.
  11th N.J.
  120th N.Y.

Artillery Brigade, Lt. Col. John G. Hazard
  Mass. Lt., 10th Btty.
  1st N.H., Co. M
  1st N.J. Lt., Co. B
  N.Y. Lt., 11th Btty.
  4th N.Y. Hvy., Co. C
  4th N.Y. Hvy., Co. L
  1st R.I. Lt., Co. B
  4th U.S., Co. K

V Army Corps, Maj. Gen. Gouverneur K. Warren (relieved of command 1 April)
Maj. Gen. Charles Griffin (in command from 1 April)
  Escort
    4th Pa. Cav., Co. C
  Provost Guard
    104th N.Y.

1st Division, Maj. Gen. Charles Griffin,

Maj. Gen. Joseph J. Bartlett (command of 1st Division)

1st Brigade, Brig. Gen. Joshua L. Chamberlain
  85th N.Y.
  98th Pa.

2d Brigade, Brig. Gen. Edgar M. Gregory
  187th N.Y.
  188th N.Y.
  189th N.Y.

3d Brigade, Maj. Gen. Joseph J. Bartlett,
  Brig. Gen. Alfred L. Pearson
  1st Me. Sharpshooters
  20th Me.
  32d Mass.
  1st Mich.
  16th Mich./Brady's and Jardine's companies Mich. Sharpshooters attached.
  83d Pa.
  91st Pa.
  118th Pa.
  155th Pa.

2d Division, Maj. Gen. Romeyn B. Ayres

1st Brigade, Brig. Gen. Frederick Winthrop (mortally wounded 1 April)
  Col. James Grindlay
  Brig. Gen. Joseph Hayes (in command from 3 April)
  5th N.Y. (Veteran)
  15th N.Y. Hvy. Art.
  140th N.Y.
  146th N.Y.

2d Brigade, Brig. Gen. Andrew W. Denison (wounded 31 March)
  Col. Richard N. Bowerman (wounded 1 April)
  Col. David L. Stanton
  1st Md.
  4th Md.
  7th Md.
  8th Md.

3d Brigade, Brig. Gen. James
  Gwyn
  3d Delaware
  4th Delaware
  8th Delaware (3 cos.)
  157th Pa. (4 cos.)
  190th Pa.
  191st Pa.
  210th Pa.

3d *Division*, Maj. Gen. Samuel W.
  Crawford

1st Brigade, Col. John A.
  Kellogg
  91st N.Y.
  6th Wis.
  7th Wis.

2d Brigade, Brig. Gen. Henry
  Baxter
  16th Me.
  39th Mass.
  97th N.Y.
  11th Pa.
  107th Pa.

3d Brigade, Brig. Gen. Richard
  Coulter
  94th N.Y.
  95th N.Y.
  147th N.Y.
  56th Pa.
  88th Pa.
  121st Pa.
  142d Pa.

Unattached
  1st Bn. N.Y. Sharpshooters

Artillery Brigade, Brig. Gen.
  Charles S. Wainwright
  1st N.Y. Lt., Co. B
  1st N.Y. Lt., Co. D
  1st N.Y. Lt., Co. H
  15th N.Y. Hvy., Co. M
  4th U.S., Co. B
  5th U.S., Co. D and G

VI *Army Corps*, Maj. Gen. Horatio
  G. Wright

Escort
  21st Pa. Cav., Co. E

1st *Division*, Maj. Gen. Frank
  Wheaton

1st Brigade, Brig. Gen. William
  H. Penrose
  1st and *4th N.J.* (bn.)
  2d N.J. (2 cos.)
  3d N.J. (1 cos.)
  10th N.J.
  15th N.J.
  40th N.J.

2d Brigade, Brig. Gen. Joseph E.
  Hamblin
  2d Conn. Hvy. Art.
  65th N.Y.
  121st N.Y.
  95th Pa.

3d Brigade, Col. Oliver
  Edwards
  37th Mass.
  49th Pa.
  82d Pa.
  119th Pa.
  2d R.I.
  5th Wis.

2d *Division*, Maj. Gen. George W.
  Getty

1st Brigade, Col. James M.
  Warner
  62d N.Y.
  93d Pa.
  98th Pa.
  102d Pa.
  139th Pa.

2d Brigade, Maj. Gen. Lewis A.
  Grant (wounded 2 April)
  Lt. Col. Amasa S. Tracy
  Col. Charles Mundee (in
  command part of 2 April)
  Lt. Col. Amasa S. Tracy
  Maj. Gen. Lewis A. Grant
  2d Vt.
  3d Vt.
  4th Vt.
  5th Vt.
  6th Vt.
  1st Vt. Hvy. Art.

3d Brigade, Col. Thomas W.
  Hyde
  1st Me. (veteran)
  43d N.Y. (5 cos.)
  49th N.Y. (5 cos.)
  77th N.Y. (five cos.)
  122d N.Y.

61st Pa.

3d Division, Brig. Gen. Truman
Seymour

1st Brigade, Col. William S.
Truex
14th N.J.
106th N.Y.
151st N.Y. (5 cos.)
87th Pa.
10th Vt.

2d Brigade, Brig. Gen. J. Warren
Keifer
6th Md.
9th N.Y. Hvy. Art.
110th Oh.
122d Oh.
126th Oh.
67th Pa.
138th Pa.

Artillery Brigade, Maj. Andrew
Cowan
1st N.J. Lt., Co. A
N.Y. Lt., 1st Btty.
N.Y. Lt., 3d Btty.
9th N.Y. Hvy., Co. L
1st R.I. Lt., Co. G
1st R.I. Lt., Co. H
5th U.S., Co. E
1st Vt. Hvy., Co. D

IX Army Corps, Maj. Gen. John G.
Parke

Provost Guard
79th N.Y.

1st Division, Maj. Gen. Orlando
B. Willcox

1st Brigade, Col. Samuel
Harriman
8th Mich.
27th Mich.
109th N.Y.
51st Pa.
37th Wis.
38th Wis.

2d Brigade, Col. Ralph Ely
1st Mich. Sharpshooters
2d Mich.
20th Mich.
46th N.Y.
60th Oh.

50th Pa.

3d Brigade, Col. Gilbert P.
Robinson
Col. James Bintliff (in
command from 2 April)
3d Md. (4 cos.)
29th Mass.
57th Mass.
59th Mass.
18th N.H.
14th N.Y. Hvy. Art.
100th Pa.

Acting Engineers
17th Mich.

2d Division, Maj. Gen. Robert B.
Potter (wounded 2 April)
Brig. Gen. Simon G. Griffin

1st Brigade, Brig. Gen. John I.
Curtin
35th Mass.
36th Mass.
58th Mass.
39th N.J.
51st N.Y.
45th Pa.
48th Pa.
7th R.I.

2d Brigade, Brig. Gen. Simon G.
Griffin (assigned to
command 2nd Division)
Col. Walter Harriman
31st Me.
3d Md.
56th Mass.
6th N.H.
9th N.H.
11th N.H.
179th N.Y.
186th N.Y.
17th Vt.

3d Division, Maj. Gen. John F.
Hartranft

1st Brigade, Lt. Col. William H.
H. McCall
Col. Alfred B. McCalmont
(in command from 3 April)
200th Pa.
208th Pa.
209th Pa.

2d Brigade, Col. Joseph A.
Mathews
205th Pa.
207th Pa.
211th Pa.

Artillery Brigade, Brig. Gen.
John C. Tidball
Me. Lt., 7th Btty. (G)
Mass. Lt., 5th Btty. (E)
Mass. Lt., 9th Btty.
Mass. Lt., 11th Btty.
Mass. Lt., 14th Btty.
N.J. Lt., 3d Btty.

1st N.Y. Lt., Co. C
1st N.Y. Lt., Co. E
1st N.Y. Lt., Co. G
1st N.Y. Lt., Co. L
N.Y. Lt., 19th Btty.
N.Y. Lt., 27th Btty.
N.Y. Lt., 34th Btty.
1st Pa. Lt., Co. B
Pa. Lt., Co. D
5th U.S., Cos. C and I

Cavalry
2d Pa.

Army of the Shenandoah
Maj. Gen. Philip H. Sheridan

Cavalry Corps, Maj. Gen. Wesley
Merritt

1st Division, Brig. Gen. Thomas
C. Devin

1st Brigade, Col. Peter Stagg
1st Mich.
5th Mich.
6th Mich.
7th Mich.

2d Brigade, Col. Charles L.
Fitzhugh
6th N.Y.
9th N.Y.
19th N.Y.
17th Pa.
20th Pa.

3d (Reserve) Brigade, Brig. Gen.
Alfred Gibbs
2d Mass.
6th Pa.
1st U.S.
5th U.S.
6th U.S.

Artillery
4th U.S., Cos. C and E

2d Division (*Army of the
Potomac*), Maj. Gen. George
Crook

1st Brigade, Brig. Gen. Henry
E. Davies, Jr.
1st N.J.
10th N.Y.
24th N.Y.

1st Pa. (5 cos.)
2d U.S. Art., Co. A

2d Brigade, Brig. Gen. J. Irvin
Gregg (captured 7 April)
Col. Samuel B.M. Young
4th Pa.
8th Pa.
16th Pa.
21st Pa.
1st U.S. Art., Cos. H and I

3d Brigade, Brig. Gen. Charles
H. Smith
1st Me.
2d N.Y. Mounted Rifles
6th Oh.
13th Oh.

3d Division, Maj. Gen. George A.
Custer

1st Brigade, Col. Alexander C.
M. Pennington
1st Conn.
3d N.J.
2d N.Y.
2d Oh.

2d Brigade, Col. William Wells
8th N.Y.
15th N.Y.
1st Vt.
3d Ind. Cav. (Cos. A-F)

3d Brigade, Col. Henry
Capehart
1st N.Y. (Lincoln)
1st W.V.

218

2d W.V. (7 cos.)
3d W.V.
Cavalry Division (Army of the James) Brig. Gen. Ranald S. Mackenzie

1st Brigade, Col. Robert M. West
20th N.Y.

5th Pa.
2d Brigade, Col. Samuel P. Spear
1st District of Columbia (bn.)
1st Md.
11th Pa.

Artillery
Wis. Lt., 4th Btty.

Army of the James
Maj. Gen. Edward O.C. Ord

Headquarters Guard
3d Pa. Hvy. Art., Co. D
3d Pa. Hvy. Art., Co. I

Engineers
1st N.Y.

Pontoniers
3d Mass. Hvy. Art., Co. I

Unattached Cavalry
4th Mass., Cos. I, L, and M
5th Mass. (colored)
7th N.Y. (1st Mounted Rifles)

Defenses of Bermuda Hundred, Maj. Gen. George L. Hartsuff

Infantry Division, Maj. Gen. Edward Ferrero

1st Brigade, Brig. Gen. Gilbert H. McKibbin
41st N.Y.
103d N.Y.
2d Pa. Hvy. Art.
104th Pa.

2d Brigade, Col. George C. Kibbe
6th N.Y. Hvy. Art.
10th N.Y. Hvy. Art.

Artillery
N.Y. Lt., 33d Btty.

Artillery, Brig. Gen. Henry L. Abbot
13th N.Y. Hvy., Cos. A and H
N.Y. Lt., 7th Btty.
3d Pa. Hvy., Co. E
3d Pa. Hvy., Co. M

Separate Brigade, Brig. Gen. Joseph B. Carr

Fort Pocahontas, Va., Lt. Col. Ashbel W. Angel
38th N.J. (4 cos.)
20th N.Y. Cav., Co. D
16th N.Y. Hvy. Art., Cos. E and H
184th N.Y., Co. I

Harrison's Landing, Va., Col. Wardwell G. Robinson
184th N.Y.
1st U.S. Colored Cav., Co. I

Fort Powhatan, Va., Col. William J. Sewell
38th N.J. (6 cos.)
20th N.Y. Cav., Co. F
3d Pa. Hvy. Art. (detachment)
1st U.S. Colored Cav., Co. E

XXIV Army Corps, Maj. Gen. John Gibbon

Headquarters Guard, Capt. Charles E. Thomas
4th Mass. Cav., Co. F
4th Mass. Cav., Co. K

1st Division, Brig. Gen. Robert S. Foster

1st Brigade, Col. Thomas 0. Osborn
39th Ill.
62d Oh.
67th Oh.
85th Pa.
199th Pa.

3d Brigade, Col. George B. Dandy
10th Conn.
11th Me.
24th Mass.

100th N.Y.
206th Pa.

4th Brigade, Col. Harrison S.
  Fairchild
8th Me.
89th N.Y.
148th N.Y.
158th N.Y.
56th Pa.

3d Division, Brig. Gen. Charles
  Devens

1st Brigade, Col. Edward H.
  Ripley
11th Conn.
13th N.H.
81st N.Y.
98th N.Y.
130th N.Y.
19th Wis.

2d Brigade, Col. Michael T.
  Donahue
8th Conn.
5th Md.
10th N.H.
12th N.H.
96th N.Y.
118th N.Y.
9th Vt.

3d Brigade, Col. Samuel H.
  Roberts
21st Conn.
40th Mass.
2d N.H.
58th Pa.
188th Pa.

Independent Division, Maj. Gen.
  John W. Turner

1st Brigade, Lt. Col. Andrew
  Potter
34th Mass.
116th Oh.
123d Oh.

2d Brigade, Col. William B.
  Curtis
23d Ill.
54th Pa.
12th W.V.

3d Brigade, Brig. Gen. Thomas
  M. Harris
10th W.V.

11th W.V.
15th W.V.

Artillery, Maj. Charles C. Abell
3d N.Y. Lt., Co. B
3d New York Lt., Co. H
3d N.Y. Lt., Co. K
3d N.Y. Lt., Co. M
N.Y. Lt., 17th Btty.
1st Pa. Lt., Co. A
1st R.I. Lt., Co. F
1st U.S., Co. B
4th U.S., Co. L
5th U.S., Co. A
5th U.S., Co. F

XXV Army Corps, Maj. Gen.
  Godfrey Weitzel

Provost Guard
  4th Mass. Cav., Cos. E and H

1st Division, Maj. Gen. August V.
  Kautz

1st Brigade, Brig. Gen. Alonzo
  G. Draper
22d U.S. Colored Troops
36th U.S. Colored Troops
38th U.S. Colored Troops
118th U.S. Colored Troops

2d Brigade, Brig Gen. Edward
  A. Wild
29th Conn. (Colored)
9th U.S. Colored Troops
115th U.S. Colored Troops
117th U.S. Colored Troops

3d Brigade, Brig. Gen. Henry
  G. Thomas
19th U.S. Colored Troops
23d U.S. Colored Troops
43d U.S. Colored Troops
114th U.S. Colored Troops

Attached Brigade, Brig. Gen.
  Charles S. Russell
10th U.S. Colored Troops
28th U.S. Colored Troops

Cavalry
  2d U.S. Colored

2d Division, Brig. Gen. William
  Birney

1st Brigade, Col. James Shaw, Jr.
7th U.S. Colored Troops
109th U.S. Colored Troops

116th U.S. Colored Troops

2d Brigade, Col. Ulysses
 Doubleday
 8th U.S. Colored Troops
 41st U.S. Colored Troops
 45th U.S. Colored Troops
 127th U.S. Colored Troops

3d Brigade, Col. William W.
 Woodward
 29th U.S. Colored Troops
 31st U.S. Colored Troops

Artillery Brigade, Capt. Loomis
 L. Langdon
 Conn. Lt., 1st Btty.
 N.J. Lt., 4th Btty.
 N.J. Lt., 5th Btty.
 1st Pa. Lt., Co. E
 3d R.I., Co. C
 1st U.S., Co. D
 1st U.S., Co. M
 4th U.S., Co. D

CONFEDERATE FORCES

Army of Northern Virginia
Gen. Robert E. Lee

Provost Guard, Maj. D. B.
 Bridgford
 1st Va. Bn.
 44th Va. Bn. Cav., Co. B

Escort
 39th Va. Bn.

Engineers, Col. T. M. R. Talcott
 1st Confederate Engineers
 2d Confederate Engineers

First Army Corps, Lt. Gen. James
 Longstreet

Pickett's Division, Maj. Gen.
 George E. Pickett

Steuart's Brigade, Brig. Gen.
 George H. Steuart
 9th Va.
 14th Va.
 38th Va.
 53d Va.
 57th Va.

Corse's Brigade, Brig. Gen.
 Montgomery D. Corse
 (captured 6 April)
 Col. Arthur Herbert
 15th Va.
 17th Va.
 29th Va.
 30th Va.
 32d Va.

Hunton's Brigade, Brig. Gen.
 Eppa Hunton (captured 6
 April)
 Maj. Michael P. Spessard
 8th Va.
 18th Va.
 19th Va.
 28th Va.
 56th Va.

Terry's Brigade, Brig. Gen.
 William R. Terry (disabled
 31 March)
 Col. Joseph Mayo (in
 command 1 April)
 Maj. William W. Bentley
 1st Va.
 3d Va.
 7th Va.
 11th Va.
 24th Va.

Field's Division, Maj. Gen.
 Charles W. Field

Law's Brigade, Brig. Gen.
 William F. Perry
 4th Al.
 15th Al.
 44th Al.
 47th Al.
 48th Al.

Anderson's Brigade, Brig.
 Gen. George T. Anderson
 7th Ga.

8th Ga.
9th Ga.
11th Ga.
59th Ga.

Benning's Brigade, Brig. Gen.
  Henry L. Benning
2d Ga.
15th Ga.
17th Ga.
20th Ga.

Gregg's Brigade, Col. R. M.
  Powell
3d Ark.
1st Tx.
4th Tx.
5th Tx.

Bratton's Brigade, Brig. Gen.
  John Bratton
1st S.C.
5th S.C.
6th S.C.
2d S.C. Rifles
Palmetto Sharpshooters

Kershaw's Division, Maj. Gen.
  Joseph B. Kershaw

DuBose's Brigade, Brig. Gen.
  Dudley M. DuBose
  (captured 6 April)
  Capt. J.F. Espy
16th Ga.
18th Ga.
24th Ga.
3d Ga. Bn. Sharpshooters
Cobb's (Ga.) Legion
Phillips' (Ga.) Legion

Humphrey's Brigade, Brig.
  Gen. Benjamin G.
  Humphreys (captured 6
  April)
  Capt. Gwin R. Cherry
13th Miss.
17th Miss.
18th Miss.
21st Miss.

Simms' Brigade, Brig. Gen.
  James P. Simms (captured
  6 April)
  Capt. George W. Waldron
10th Ga.
50th Ga.

51st Ga.
53d Ga.

Second Army Corps, Lt. Gen. John
  B. Gordon

Grimes' Division, Maj. Gen.
  Bryan Grimes

Battle's Brigade, Col. Edwin L.
  Hobson
3d Al.
5th Al.
6th Al.
12th Al.
61st Al.

Grimes' Brigade, Col. D. G.
  Coward
32d N.C.
43d N.C.
45th N.C.
53d N.C.
2d N.C. Bn.

Cox's Brigade, Brig. Gen.
  William R. Cox
1st N.C.
2d N.C.
3d N.C.
4th N.C.
14th N.C.
30th N.C.

Cook's Brigade, Col. Edwin A.
  Nash
4th Ga.
12th Ga.
21st Ga.
44th Ga.

Archer's Bn., Lt. Col. Fletcher
  H. Archer
3 Bn. Va. Reserves
44th Va. Bn.
Patterson s (Ga.) Bat.

Early's Division, Brig. Gen.
  James A. Walker

Johnston's Brigade, Col. John
  W. Lea
5th N.C.
12th N.C.
20th N.C.
23d N.C.
1st N.C. Bn., Sharpshooters

Order of Battle

Lewis' Brigade, Capt. John
Beard
6th N.C.
21st N.C.
54th N.C.
57th N.C.

Walker's Brigade, Maj. Henry
Kyd Douglas
13th Va.
31st Va.
49th Va.
53d Va.
58th Va.

Gordon's Division, Brig. Gen.
Clement A. Evans

Evans' Brigade, Col. John H.
Lowe
13th Ga.
26th Ga.
31st Ga.
38th Ga.
60th Ga.
61st Ga.
9th Ga. Bn. Art.
12th Ga. Bn. Art.
18th Ga. Bn. Infantry

Terry's Brigade, Col. Titus V.
Williams
2d Va.
4th Va.
5th Va.
10th Va.
21st Va.
23d Va.
25th Va.
27th Va.
33d Va.
37th Va.
42d Va.
44th Va.
48th Va.

York's Brigade, Col. Eugene
Waggaman
1st La.
2d La.
5th La.
6th La.
7th La.
8th La.
9th La.
10th La.

14th La.
15th La.

Third Army Corps, Lt. Gen. A. P. Hill

Provost Guard
5th Al. Bn.

Mahone's Division, Maj. Gen.
William Mahone

Forney's Brigade, Brig. Gen.
William H. Forney
8th Al.
9th Al.
10th Al.
11th Al.
13th Al.
14th Al.

Weisiger's Brigade, Brig. Gen.
David A. Weisiger
6th Va.
12th Va.
16th Va.
41st Va.
61st Va.

Harris' Brigade, Brig. Gen.
Nathaniel H. Harris
12th Miss.
16th Miss.
19th Miss.
48th Miss.

Sorrel's Brigade, Col. George
E. Tayloe
3d Ga.
22d Ga.
48th Ga.
64th Ga.
2d Ga. Bn.
10th Ga. Bn.

Finegan's Brigade, Col. David
Lang
2d Fl.
5th Fl.
8th Fl.
9th Fl.
10th Fl.
11th Fl.

Heth's Division, Maj. Gen.
Henry Heth

Davis' Brigade, Brig. Gen.
Joseph R. Davis
1st Confederate Bn.

2d Miss.
11th Miss.
26th Miss.
42d Miss.

Cooke's Brigade, Brig. Gen.
John R. Cooke
15th N.C.
27th N.C.
46th N.C.
48th N.C.
55th N.C.

MacRae's Brigade, Brig. Gen.
William MacRae
11th N.C.
26th N.C.
44th N.C.
47th N.C.
52d N.C.

McComb's Brigade, Brig. Gen.
William McComb
2d Md. Bn.
1st Tn.
7th Tn.
14th Tn.
17th Tn.
23d Tn.
25th Tn.
44th Tn.
63d Tn.

Wilcox's Division, Maj. Gen.
Cadmus M. Wilcox

Thomas' Brigade, Brig. Gen.
Edward L. Thomas
14th Ga.
35th Ga.
45th Ga.
49th Ga.

Lane's Brigade, Brig. Gen.
James H. Lane
18th N.C.
28th N.C.
33d N.C.
37th N.C.

McGowan's Brigade, Brig.
Gen. Samuel McGowan
1st S.C. (P. A.)
12th S.C.
13th S.C.
14th S.C.
Orr's Rifles

Scales' Brigade, Col. Joseph H.
Hyman
13th N.C.
16th N.C.
22d N.C.
34th N.C.
38th N.C.

Anderson's Corps, Lt. Gen. Richard
H. Anderson (relieved of
command 8 April)

Johnson's Division, Maj. Gen.
Bushrod R. Johnson (relieved
of command 8 April)

Wallace's Brigade, Brig. Gen.
William H. Wallace (in
command 9 April)
17th S.C.
18th S.C.
22nd S.C.
23rd S.C.
26th S.C.
Holcombe Legion (S. C.
Infantry)

Moody's Brigade, Brig. Gen.
Young M. Moody (sick 31
March to 8 April when
captured)
Col. Martin L. Stansel (in
command)
41st Al.
43rd Al.
59th Al.
23rd Al. Bn.

Wise's Brigade, Brig. Gen.
Henry A. Wise
26th Va.
34th Va.
46th Va.
59th Va.

Ransom's Brigade, Brig. Gen.
Matthew W. Ransom
24th N.C.
25th N.C.
35th N.C.
49th N.C.
56th N.C.

Cavalry Corps, Maj. Gen. Fitzhugh
Lee

224

Order of Battle

Fitzhugh Lee's Division, Brig. Gen. Thomas L. Munford (promoted 6 April)

Munford's Brigade
1st Va.
2d Va.
3d Va.
4th Va.

Payne's Brigade, Brig. Gen. William H. Payne (wounded 6 April)
Col. Rueben B. Boston (killed 6 April)
5th Va.
6th Va.
15th Va.
36th Va. Bn.

Gary's Brigade, Brig. Gen. Martin W. Gary
7th Ga.
7th S.C.
Hampton (S.C.) Legion
24th Va.

W. H. F. Lee's Division, Maj. Gen. William H. F. Lee

Barringer's Brigade, Brig. Gen. Rufus Barringer (captured 3 April)
1st N.C.
2d N.C.
3d N.C.
5th N.C.

Beale's Brigade, Capt. Samuel H. Burt
9th Va.
10th Va.
13th Va.
14th Va.

Roberts' Brigade, Brig. Gen. William P. Roberts
4th N.C.
16th N.C. Bn.

Rosser's Division, Maj. Gen. Thomas L. Rosser

Dearing's Brigade, Brig. Gen. James Dearing (mortally wounded 6 April)
Col. Elijah V. White (in command)
7th Va.

11th Va.
12th Va.
35th Va. Bn.

McCausland's Brigade
16th Va.
17th Va.
21st Va.
22d Va.

Artillery, Brig. Gen. William N. Pendleton

First Corps, Brig. Gen. E. Porter Alexander

Cabell's Bn., Maj. S. P. Hamilton
Anderson's (Va.) Bat.
Callaway's (Ga.) Bat.
Carlton s (Ga.) Bat.
Manly's (N. C.) Bat.

Huger's Bn., Maj. Tyler C. Jordan
Fickling's (S. C.) Bat.
Moody's (La.)Bat.
Parker's Va.) Bat.
J. D. Smith s (Va.) Bat.
Taylor's (Va.) Bat.
Woolfolk's (Va.) Bat.

Hardaway's Bn., Lt. Col. Robert A. Hardaway
Powhatan (Va.) Art.
3d Company Richmond Howitzers
Rockbridge (Va.) Art.
Salem Flying Art.

Haskell's Bn., Maj. John C. Haskell
Flanner's (N. C.) Bat.
Garden's (S. C.) Bat.
Lamkin's (Va.) Bat.
Ramsay's (N. C.) Bat.

Stark's Bn., Lt. Col. Alexander W. Stark
La. Guard Art.
Mathews (Va.) Art.
McComas (Va.) Art.

Johnson's Bn., Maj. Marmaduke Johnson
Clutter's (Va.) Art.
Fredericksburg Art.

Second Corps, Brig. Gen.
  Armistead L. Long
  Nelson's Bn., Lt. Col. William
    Nelson
    Amherst Art.
    Milledge's (Ga.) Art.
    Fluvanna Art.
  Braxton's Bn., Lt. Col. Carter
    M. Braxton
    Alleghany Art.
    Lee Art.
    Stafford Art.
  Cutshaw's Bn., Maj. Wilfred E.
    Cutshaw
    Orange Art.
    Staunton Art.
    2d Richmond Howitzers
Third Corps, Col. R. Lindsay
  Walker
  McIntosh's Bn., Col. David G.
    McIntosh
    1st Md. Bat.
    4th Md. Bat.
    Danville Art.
    Hardaway Art.
    2d Rockbridge Art.
  Pegram's Bn., Col. William J.
    Pegram
    Ellett's Art.
    Letcher Art.
    Pee Dee Art.
    Purcell Art.
  Poague's Bn., Lt. Col. William
    T. Poague
    Madison Art.
    Albemarle Art.
    Brooks Art.
    Charlotte Art.
  Richardson's Bn., Lt. Col.
    Charles Richardson
    Lewis Art.
    Donaldsonville (La.) Art.
    Norfolk Light Art.
    Huger Art.
  Lane's Bn., Maj. John Lane
    Ross' Bat.
    Patterson's Bat.

  Irwin Art.
  Owen's Bn., Maj. William M.
    Owen
    Chamberlayne's Bat.
    Dickenson's Art.
    Walker's Bat.
  Washington Art., Lt. Col.
    Benjamin Eshleman
    1st Co.
    2d Co.
    3d Co.
    4th Co.
Anderson's Corps, Col. Hilary P.
  Jones
  Coit's Bn., Maj. James C. Coit
    Wright's (Va.) Bat.
    Pegram's (Va.) Bat.
    Bradford's (Miss.) Bat.
    Kelly's (S. C.) Bat.
  Blount's Bn., Maj. Joseph G.
    Blount
    Cumming's (N. C.) Bat.
    Lowry's Bat.
    Miller's (N. C.) Bat.
    Slaten's (Ga.) Bat.
  Stribling's Bn., Maj. Robert M.
    Stribling
    Marshall's (Va.) Bat.
    Macon's (Va.) Bat.
    Sullivan's (Va.) Bat.
    Dickerson's (Va.) Bat.
  Sturdivant's Bn., Capt. N. A.
    Sturdivant
    Martin's (Va.) Bat.
    Sturdivant's (Va.) Bat.

Horse Artillery, Lt. Col. R.
  Preston Chew
  Breathed's Bn., Maj. James
    Breathed
    Johnston's (Va.) Bat.
    Shoemaker's (Va.) Bat.
    Thomson's (Va.) Bat.
  Chew's Bn.
    Petersburg Art.
    2d Jeb Stuart (Va.) Horse
      Art.

Department of Richmond
Lt. Gen. Richard S. Ewell (captured 6 April)
Lt. Col. Thomas J. Spencer

G. W. C. Lee's Division, Maj. Gen. G. W. C. Lee (captured 6 April)

Barton's Brigade, Brig. Gen. Seth M. Barton (captured 6 April)
22d Va. Bn.
25th Va. Bn.
40th Va.
47th and 50th Va.

Moore's Brigade, Brig. Gen. Patrick T. Moore (apparently did not accompany his command on retreat)
3d Local Defense Troops
1st Va. Reserves
2d Va. Reserves
1st Va. Bn. Reserves
2d Va. Bn. Reserves

Artillery Brigade, Col. Stapleton Crutchfield (killed 6 April)
10th Va. Bn. Hvy. Art.
18th Va. Bn. Hvy. Art.
19th Va. Bn. Hvy. Art.
20th Va. Bn. Hvy. Art.

Chaffin's Bluff Garrison , Maj. Robert Stiles
18th Ga. Bn.

Drewry's Bluff (acting as infantry), Maj. F. W. Smith (accidentally killed 5 April)
Young's Howitzers
Johnston's (Epes) Hvy. Art.
Lunenburg Hvy. Art.
Pamunkey Hvy. Art.
Southside Hvy. Art.

Chaffin's Bluff, Lt. Col. J. M. Maury

Naval Brigade, Commodore John Randolph Tucker (captured 6 April)

Marines, Captain John D. Simms (captured 6 April)

Department of North Carolina and Southern Virginia

First Military District, Brig. Gen. Henry A. Wise

Petersburg, Maj. W. H. Ker
3d Bn. Va. Reserves
44th Va. Bn.

Hood's Bn. Operatives
Second-Class Militia
Independent Signal Corps

Bibliography

Agassiz, George R. *Meade's Headquarters 1863-1865,* Letters of Colonel Theodore Lyman from the Wilderness to Appomattox, Massachusetts Historical Society, 1922.

Bearss, Edwin & Christopher Calkins. *The Battle of Five Forks,* H.E. Howard, 1985. details the Battles of Lewis Farm, White Oak Road, Dinwiddie Court House and Five Forks.

Calkins, Christopher. *Thirty-Six Hours Before Appomattox, April 6-7, 1865,* Farmville Herald Pub. Co., 1980 (reprint 1989). Details the Battles of Sailor's Creek, High Bridge, Farmville and Cumberland Church.

Calkins, Christopher. *From Petersburg to Appomattox, April 2-9, 1865,* Farmville Herald Pub. Co., 1983 (reprint 1989). A tour guide for following all the routes of Lee's withdrawal and Grant's pursuit.

Calkins, Christopher. *The Battles of Appomattox,* H.E. Howard, Inc. 1987. Details the Battles of Appomattox Station and Appomattox Court House.

Calkins, Christopher. *The Final Bivouac,* H.E. Howard, Inc., 1988. Covers the Surrender Parade at Appomattox and the disbanding of the armies, April 10-May 20, 1865.

Calkins, Christopher. *Blue & Gray Magazine,* "The Battle of Five Forks: Final Push for the South Side," Vol. IX, Issue 4, April 1992. Quick synopsis of events which led up to the battle, along with a narrative of the Battle of Five Forks. A driving tour of the area is included.

Cauble, Frank P. *The Biography of Wilmer McLean, May 3, 1814-June 5, 1882*. H.E. Howard, Inc., 1989. It was in McLean's house that the surrender took place. He originally lived on the Manassas battlefield.

Cauble, Frank P. *The Proceedings Connected With the Surrender of the Army of Northern Virginia*. Originally published in 1962, reissued by H.E. Howard, Inc. Correspondence between lee and Grant concerning the surrender at Appomattox court House.

Chamberlain, Joshua Lawrence. *The Passing of the Armies*, (Morningside reprint), 1915. Covers Quaker Road, White Oak Road, Five Forks and Appomattox Campaign from hsi standpoint as brigade commander in V Corps.

Davis, Burke. *To Appomattox: Nine April Days*, Rinehart & Company, New York, 1959. Flowing narrative from April 1 to April 9 using first person accounts.

Hatcher, Edmund N. *The Last Four Weeks of the War*. The Co-operative Publishing Co., 1892. Newspaper type account of events taking place througout the country in the final weeks of the war.

Hoehling, A.A. and Mary. *The Day Richmond Died*. A.S. Barnes & Co., San Diego, 1981. Information on both the fall of Petersburg and Richmond.

Humphreys, Andrew A. *The Virginia Campaign of '64 and '65*. Charles Scribner's Sons, 1907. Best overall summary written by a Federal corps commander.

Korn, Jerry. *Pursuit to Appomattox*. Time-Life Books, 1987. Good narrative beginning in January 1865 to surrender.

McCarthy, Carlton. *Detailed Minutiae of Soldier Life in the Army of Northern Virginia, 1861-65*. B.F. Johnson Publishing Co., Richmond, 1899. Contains a chapter on the retreat to Appomattox.

Newhall, Col. F.C. *With General Sheridan in Lee's Last Campaign*, J.P. Lippencott & Co., Philadelphia, 1866. Details the movements of the Federal cavalry in the Appomattox Campaign.

Nine, William G. and Ronald G. Wilson. *The Appomattox Paroles*, H.E. Howard, Inc., 1989. Alphabetical listing of Confederate soldiers paroled at Appomattox.

Papers of the Military Historical Society of Massachusetts. *The Shenandoah Campaigns of 1862 and 1864 and the Appomattox Campaign 1865*, Vol. VI. A series of articles by contemporary sources.

Patrick, Rembert W. *The Fall of Richmond*, Louisiana State University Press, 1960. Events of April 2-4, 1865, in Richmond.

Porter, Horace. *Campaigning with Grant*, The Century Co., 1897. Covers from the Battle of the Wilderness to Appomattox. Porter was on Grant's staff.

Rodick, Burleigh. *Appomattox: The Last Campaign*. Philosophical Library, Inc., New York, 1965. Narrative using first person accounts.

Schaff, Morris. *The Sunset of the Confederacy*. John W. Tuce and Co., Boston, 1912. Narrative of the fnal campaign by a contemporary source, although he was not involved in it.

Stern, Philip Van Doren. *An End to Valor: The Last Days of the Civil War*. Houghton Mifflin Co, Boston , 1958. Follows the same style as Davis and Rodick.

Tremain, Henry Edwin. *Last Hours of Sheridan's Cavalry*, Bonnell, Silver & Bowers, New York, 1904. Details the movements of the Federal cavalry from March 31 to April 10, 1865.

Trudeau, Noah Andre. *The Last Citadel: Petersburg, Virginia, June 1864-April 1865*. Little, Brown and Company, 1991. Flowing narrative using many new first person accoutns.

Trudeau, Noah Andre. *Out of the Storm: The End of the Civil War, April-June 1865*. Little, Brown and Co., 1994. This contains a section on the Appomattox Campaign, also using new first person accounts.

Index